*Birds and Other Wildlife
of South Central Texas*

NUMBER TWENTY-FOUR
THE CORRIE HERRING HOOKS SERIES

Birds and Other Wildlife of South Central Texas

A Handbook
by Edward A. Kutac and S. Christopher Caran

University of Texas Press, Austin

Requests for permission to reproduce material
from this work should be sent to
Permissions, University of Texas Press,
Box 7819, Austin, TX 78713-7819.

∞ The paper used in this publication meets
the minimum requirements of American
National Standard for Information Sciences
—Permanence of Paper for Printed
Library Materials, ANSI Z39.48-1984.

Library of Congress Cataloging-in-Publication Data
Kutac, Edward A.
    Birds and other wildlife of south central Texas :
a handbook / Edward A. Kutac, S. Christopher
Caran. — 1st ed.
        p.   cm. — (The Corrie Herring Hooks
        series : no. 24)
    Includes bibliographical references (p.   ) and
index.
    ISBN 0-292-75550-3. — ISBN 0-292-74315-7
(pbk.)
    1. Bird watching—Texas—Guide-
books. 2. Wildlife watching—Texas—Guide-
books. 3. Wildlife viewing sites—Texas—
Guidebooks. 4. Natural history—Texas—
Guidebooks. 5. Birds—Texas. 6. Zoology—
Texas. I. Caran, S. Christopher. II. Title.
III. Series.
QL684.T4K877   1993
598'.07234764—dc20   93-15432

Contents

Introduction
and Acknowledgments

THE OBJECTIVE of this guide is to provide residents of and visitors to South Central Texas with a concise overview of the natural features and biological diversity of the area. It is intended that the information be up-to-date and technically accurate yet presented in a manner accessible to any interested reader. The text includes the scientific and English (common) names of all birds, mammals, reptiles, amphibians, fishes, land snails, and butterflies known or suspected to inhabit South Central Texas at present and /or in the historic past. Brief comments are provided regarding the current status, preferred habitat, and abundance of each species, along with other information where appropriate. Terms used to describe species characteristics are defined in the Appendix. Published sources of information concerning these species are cited in the Selected References. In the listing of birds, specific locations where certain species have been observed previously are included. In Chapter 2, selected public lands and campgrounds are listed with facilities offered, and special attention is given to bird-finding opportunities.

For purposes of this guide, South Central Texas has been somewhat arbitrarily defined to include the following counties: Bastrop, Bell, Bexar, Blanco, Burleson, Burnet, Caldwell, Comal, Fayette, Gillespie, Gonzales, Guadalupe, Hays, Kendall, Lee, Llano, Milam, Travis, and Williamson. These counties lie wholly or partly within a radius of 70 miles from Austin, Travis County, the state capital. This guide focuses on the natural history of these nineteen counties; however, the fauna, flora, geology, and habitats discussed are represented in counties outside this area as well.

In the pages that follow, South Central Texas will often be referred to as "the area." Included within these nineteen counties are fifteen sites administered by the Texas Parks and Wildlife Department: Bastrop State Park, Blanco State Park, Buescher State Park, Enchanted Rock State

Natural Area, Guadalupe River State Park, Inks Lake State Park, Lake Somerville State Park, Lockhart State Park, Longhorn Cavern State Park, Lyndon B. Johnson State Historical Park, McKinney Falls State Park, Monument Hill/Kreische Brewery State Historical Parks, Old Tunnel Wildlife Management Area, Palmetto State Park, and Pedernales Falls State Park. Also, the parks of many of the cities, towns, and counties, as well as those of the Lower Colorado River Authority, provide at least limited opportunities for observing nature. Many of these parks are significant natural areas.

The diversity of flora and fauna at any given site is, of course, determined by the available habitats. Within its *range*, or the geographic area that a species normally occupies, individuals will likely be found only in their preferred habitats. For example, a typically marsh-dwelling bird probably will be found in a marsh, but not elsewhere in its range. Each habitat, in turn, is defined by its geology, physiography, soils, climate, vegetation, wildlife, and land use.

The ecological diversity of South Central Texas will easily arouse the curiosity of the most avid naturalist. These nineteen counties encompass a wide variety of habitats. The Balcones Fault System, a network of fractures in the Earth's crust, runs generally northeast to southwest across the middle of the area. There are relict pine forests in Bastrop County; sphagnum peat bogs in Bastrop and Lee counties; hot springs near Gonzales; and tall-grass prairie remnants near Elgin. Some of the oldest rock formations in the state are found in the Llano Uplift region in Burnet, Llano, and Gillespie counties. Major cold-water springs emerge along faults in Austin, San Marcos, New Braunfels, and San Antonio, and there are numerous caves and other karst features in counties within and west of the Balcones Fault System. In addition, there are several long-extinct volcanoes in southern Travis County, Pilot Knob being the most widely known.

The Colorado River, with its origin in the Staked Plains region some 400 miles to the northwest, traverses the area northwest to southeast. Other rivers of the area include the Pedernales, Blanco, Guadalupe, San Marcos, Lampasas, Little, and San Gabriel, all draining southward and eastward off the Edwards Plateau. In addition, the entire chain of Highland Lakes on the Colorado River is included, as are seven other major reservoirs. These recreational waterways and the many oil fields, rock quarries, feedlots, wastewater treatment facilities, farmlands, pastures, small towns, and sprawling metropolitan centers have created additional habitats shunned by many species but frequented by others.

One of the intrinsic effects of land use is the development of a transportation network. Many plants have capitalized on the creation of roadway corridors with broad rights-of-way free from grazing. This is nearly the final refuge for some prairie species, whereas opportunistic "weedy" plants also take advantage of these open strips.

Nearly 2,000 of the more than 4,800 vascular plants of Texas have been documented in the nineteen counties of the South Central Texas area, and many species can be seen along the roadsides. Spring is a particularly delightful time to drive through the countryside. Two species of bluebonnets occur in the area, *Lupinus texensis,* which grows in clayey soils, and *L. subcarnosus,* a species found in sandy soils. In addition to bluebonnets, wildflowers such as Indian paintbrush, *Castilleja indivisa* and *C. purpurea;* Indian blanket or firewheel, *Gaillardia pulchella;* and greenthread, *Thelesperma filifolium,* are found in great abundance along roadways, particularly from mid-March to mid-April. Natural occurrences of these species are augmented along major highways with plantings by the Texas Department of Transportation. From mid-April through May, look for Mexican evening primrose, *Oenothera speciosa;* lazydaisies *Aphanostephus* spp.; goldenmane coreopsis, *Coreopsis basalis;* and phlox, *Phlox drummondii* and *P. roemeriana.* A few excellent roads for viewing wildflowers in spring are US 183 in Gonzales County, RR 1431 from Kingsland to SH 29 in Llano County, SH 29 from Burnet to Llano and beyond, and SH 71 between Austin and Bastrop. There are many other scenic routes, as well.

Throughout this book, the scientific and English (common) names of grasses conform to *The Grasses of Texas* (Gould 1975). Other plant names conform to the *Manual of the Vascular Plants of Texas* (Correll and Johnston 1970). There have been numerous revisions and corrections of plant names in the years since these references were published, and some of these changes affect species mentioned in this book. As an aid to the reader, we have compiled a list of those changes in scientific names of which we are aware, in the order in which these species are mentioned in the book (see following page). Note spelling differences.

In accordance with conventional usage, the English (common) names of birds are capitalized (for example, Mourning Dove and Blue Jay) throughout the text and in the bird checklist. A different convention has been adopted for other animals and all plants: English names for these species are not capitalized (for example, nine-banded armadillo and Texas bluebonnet) except in some taxonomic references. For this reason, English names of plants and all animals except birds are not capitalized in this handbook except in their respective checklists. Eventually, English names may become standardized for all organisms, allowing consistent treatment in publications of this kind.

Correll and Johnston (1970)	Gould (1975)	Hatch et al. (1990)	Johnston (1990)
Carya illinoinensis	Not listed	*C. illinioensis*	*C. illinoinensis*
Quercus fusiformis	Not listed	*Q. viriginana*	*Q. fusiformis*
Q. sinuata var. *breviloba*	Not listed	*Q. durandii* var. *breviloba*	*Q. sinuata* var. *breviloba*
Q. texana	Not listed	*Q. buckleyi*	*Q. buckleyi*
Bothriochloa saccharoides var. *longipaniculata*	*B.s.* var. *longipaniculata*	*B. longipaniculata*	*B. longipaniculata*
Fraxinus pensylvanica var. *integerrima*	Not listed	*F. pennsylvanica*	*F. pensylvanica* var. *subintegerrima*
Commelinantia anomala	Not listed	*Tinantia anomala*	*Commelinantia anomala*
Berberis trifoliolata	Not listed	*Mahonia trifoliolata*	*Berberis trifoliolata*

Throughout the text, particularly in Chapter 2, frequent reference is made to specific highways and roads. Conventional abbreviations for road types have been used. These road types and abbreviations include:

IH   Interstate or Interregional Highway
US   United States (Federal) Highway
SH   State (Texas) Highway
FM   Farm-to-Market Road
RR   Ranch Road
RM   Ranch-to-Market Road
CR   County Road
PR   Park Road

A publication of this kind results from the compilation of records and past experiences of a great many people (many unknown to the authors), and a debt of gratitude is due all of them. Everyone who has observed and reported a bird, mammal, reptile, amphibian, fish, land snail, or butterfly in the area has contributed directly or indirectly to this guide.

Persons who contributed directly are Ben Archer, Diane Birsner, Joye Johnson, Nan Hampton, Clark Hubbs, Pat Johnson, Raymond Neck, David Riskind, Ernest Roney, Willie Sekula, Rickard Toomey III, and Sue Wiedenfeld. Clifton Ladd reviewed the entire manuscript while Ernest Lundelius reviewed the checklist of mammals and Greg Lasley and Lawrence Buford reviewed the checklist of birds. A botanist who wished to remain anonymous reviewed Chapter 1. We thank these readers for their invaluable comments and insights. The authors are also indebted to the Austin Parks and Recreation Department, Lower Colorado River Authority, San Antonio Parks Department, Seguin Parks Department, Texas Department of Transportation, Texas Parks and Wildlife Department, Travis County Parks Department, U.S. Army Corps of Engineers, and U.S. Fish and Wildlife Service for maps and information requested. Additional acknowledgments accompany each of the species checklists in the following chapters.

Finally, thanks are due our wives, Amy and Kay, for their continued understanding and support.

E.A.K.

S.C.C.

*Birds and Other Wildlife
of South Central Texas*

CHAPTER I

Natural Features

SOUTH CENTRAL TEXAS includes portions of two major physiographic provinces, the Great Plains and the Gulf Coastal Plains. In South Central Texas, these provinces are separated by a prominent natural landmark, the Balcones Escarpment, which roughly bisects the South Central Texas area. Interregional Highway 35 is located just east of the escarpment through most of this area. The escarpment forms the common boundary of many eastern and western species whose ranges do not overlap. For other species, this borderland affords unique habitat conditions, and some of these plants and animals are found nowhere else in the world.

The Great Plains Province extends from central Canada southward through the west-central United States, east of the Rocky Mountains, and terminates in central Texas at the southern edge of the Edwards Plateau. The Edwards Plateau is the southernmost major subdivision of this province. The Gulf Coastal Plains Province lies adjacent to the Gulf of Mexico and extends from northern Mexico through Texas, up the Mississippi River valley as far as southern Illinois, and through the southeastern states to the southern tip of Florida. In Texas, the Gulf Coastal Plains comprise marshes, prairies, and woodlands from the coastline westward to the Balcones Escarpment. Strong east-to-west environmental contrasts (related to topographic, climatic, and pedologic differences) combine with a north-south temperature gradient and southward increase in the length of the growing season to enrich the area's overall ecological diversity. Within the area, the Edwards Plateau can be further divided into the Balcones Canyonlands or "Hill Country," the Llano Uplift, and the Lampasas Cut Plain. That portion of the Gulf Coastal Plains in the area encompasses parts of the Blackland Prairie (including the Fayette Prairie) and the Post Oak Savannah. Some authorities place southernmost Bexar County in the Rio Grande Plain (or South Texas Plain) section of the Gulf Coastal Plains Province, but we do not here subscribe to

1. South Central Texas

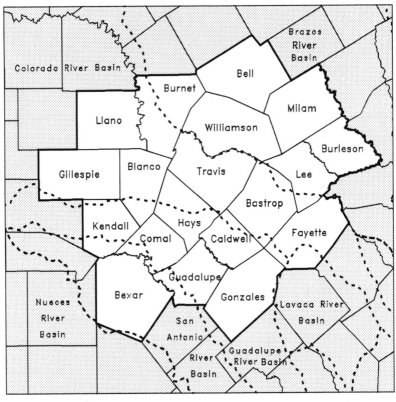

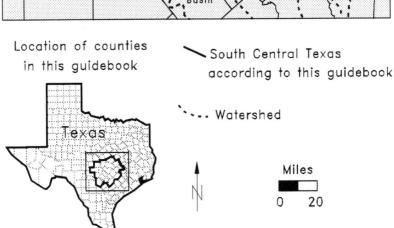

Location of counties
in this guidebook

South Central Texas
according to this guidebook

Watershed

Miles

0   20

2. Geographic Regions of South Central Texas

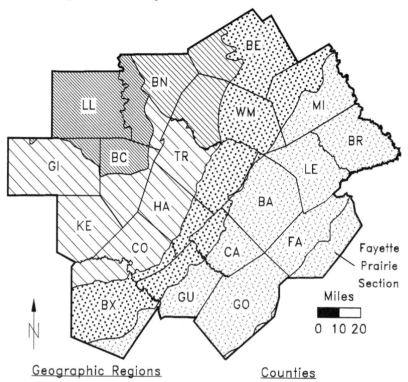

Fayette
Prairie
Section

Miles

0 10 20

Geographic Regions

Great Plains Province

▨ Llano Uplift

▧ Lampasas Cut Plain

◪ Balcones Canyonlands

Gulf Coastal Plains Province

▦ Blackland Prairie

▢ Post Oak Savannah

Counties

Bastrop: BA
Bell: BE
Bexar: BX
Blanco: BC
Burleson: BR
Burnet: BN
Caldwell: CA
Comal: CO
Fayette: FA
Gillespie: GI

Gonzales: GO
Guadalupe: GU
Hays: HA
Kendall: KE
Lee: LE
Llano: LL
Milam: MI
Travis: TR
Williamson: WM

(adapted from W. K. Ferguson, *The Geographic Provinces of Texas*
[Austin: Texas Mosaics, 1986])

that interpretation, instead treating southern Bexar County as part of both the Blackland Prairie and Post Oak Savannah regions. Each of these regions is discussed more fully below as is the escarpment itself.

Balcones Escarpment and Environmental Diversity

The Balcones Escarpment is a major environmental boundary separating the steep, rocky hills of the state's interior from the flat to rolling plains of the humid coastal region. The escarpment was produced by geologic processes operating over millions of years. During most of the Cretaceous and Early Tertiary periods of Earth's history (from roughly 140 million to 58 million years before the present), South Central and South Texas were covered by ocean waters. For some 82 million years, sediment was continually deposited on the sea floor throughout this area. The resulting horizontal layers of sand, clay, limey mud, and other materials later became rock strata of Cretaceous age, which in some places are collectively more than 3,000 feet thick. Plant and animal remains accumulated in the shallow seas and coastal flats and became fossilized, providing a glimpse of the distant past when dinosaurs and other extinct life forms thrived in South Central Texas.

The Tertiary Period was a time of transition throughout this area as elsewhere. Between 58 million and 37 million years ago, much of South Central Texas alternated between periods of marine inundation and emergence of coastal lowlands. Sediment accumulated in broad bays when ocean waters rose to their highest levels. During periods of low sea level, great rivers deposited vast quantities of sand and clay that ultimately became more than 4,000 feet of Tertiary sandstone and shale. Biological remains were once again preserved as fossils, which reveal the nature of environmental conditions at the time. Forests and swamplands were common on land while a wide variety of marine organisms thrived in the warm coastal waters. Since 37 million years ago, this area has remained above sea level. Rivers eroded older strata and deposited a veneer of sediment, much of which was later stripped away without a trace.

Then, about 20 million years ago, major faults fractured the strata along a line running roughly northeast to southwest through what are now the communities of Hillsboro, Waco, Temple, Austin, San Marcos, New Braunfels, and San Antonio, then westward to near Uvalde and Del Rio. Rock layers to the east and south of this line began to slip downward along the break, producing some 600 feet of vertical shifting, or *throw*, at the Main (or Mount Bonnell) Fault in Austin. A series of roughly parallel faults developed, producing a combined throw of more than 1,000 feet in some places. These faults compose the Balcones Fault System, and the area of intense faulting is known as the Balcones Fault Zone.

On the eastern and southern sides of the Balcones faults, relatively young rock formations consisting of Late Cretaceous–age strata were displaced downward into contact with older rock layers of Early Cretaceous age lying west and north of the faults. The older and harder Early Cretaceous limestone deposits contrast sharply with the younger, more easily eroded, soft Late Cretaceous limestones and shales. A long interval of intense weathering subsequently created the dramatic differences in landscape visible today: steep, rocky hills on the "up" side of the fault zone to the west and north were left in stark relief above low, rolling hills, and broad valleys cut into strata on the "down" side to the east and south. The transition is so abrupt, in fact, that in many areas a near vertical cliff, the Balcones Escarpment, has resulted. (An excellent point from which to view the Escarpment today is Mount Bonnell City Park in western Austin.) Rivers draining southward and eastward to the Gulf of Mexico cut deep, narrow canyons through the Balcones Escarpment as the rivers adjusted to the difference in elevation across the fault zone. Sand and gravel deposits were stranded at various levels along the valley walls, particularly in the areas immediately east and south of the fault zone, as the rivers cut ever deeper. The Generalized Geologic Map illustrates the surface geology of South Central Texas. Refer also to the generalized cross section (Figure 1) which depicts geologic, biologic, and topographic variations, as well as topographic features of the major physiographic provinces.

The hard Early Cretaceous–age limestones typically give rise to thin, stony soils, whereas the softer Late Cretaceous limestones and shales allow development of thick, arable soils. Differences in soil types influence both the natural vegetative cover and potential land use. Thick soils of the Gulf Coastal Plains support tillage agriculture, which has shaped much of the history of the region. In contrast, thin soils of the Edwards Plateau provide few opportunities for cultivation, such that most of the region has been given over to a ranching economy. Exceptions to this pattern are the vineyards and fruit orchards of the Llano Uplift, where sandy soils predominate, and the pecan groves of river bottoms, which have thick alluvial soils and shallow ground water. The Balcones faults were thus indirectly responsible for much of the present character of the area.

As is to be expected, variations in topography and other factors produced floristic differences across the area. The Gulf Coastal Plains were originally unbroken ribbons of riverside (riparian) forests and upland tallgrass prairies, brushlands, and woodlands, although few intact areas of natural vegetation remain. Plant associations of the Edwards Plateau include upland and riparian woodlands, particularly in spring-fed portions of the Balcones Canyonlands, and mixed-grass and short-grass prairies. These associations are discussed separately below.

3. Generalized Geologic Map of South Central Texas

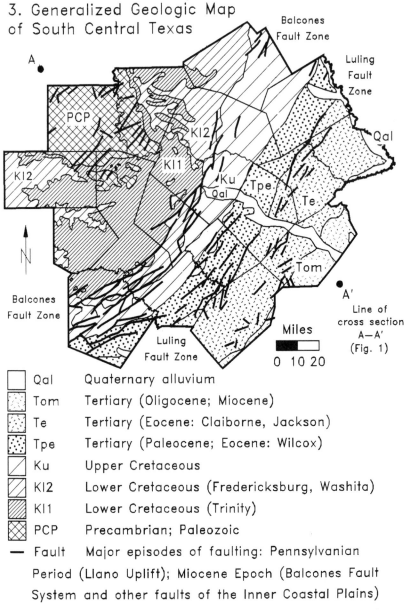

☐	Qal	Quaternary alluvium
▦	Tom	Tertiary (Oligocene; Miocene)
▦	Te	Tertiary (Eocene: Claiborne, Jackson)
▦	Tpe	Tertiary (Paleocene; Eocene: Wilcox)
◫	Ku	Upper Cretaceous
◩	Kl2	Lower Cretaceous (Fredericksburg, Washita)
◪	Kl1	Lower Cretaceous (Trinity)
▨	PCP	Precambrian; Paleozoic
—	Fault	Major episodes of faulting: Pennsylvanian Period (Llano Uplift); Miocene Epoch (Balcones Fault System and other faults of the Inner Coastal Plains)

(adapted from H. B. Renfro, D. E. Feray, and P. B. King, *Geological Highway Map of Texas* [Tulsa: American Association of Petroleum Geologists, 1973])

Figure 1. Geologic Cross Section through South Central Texas

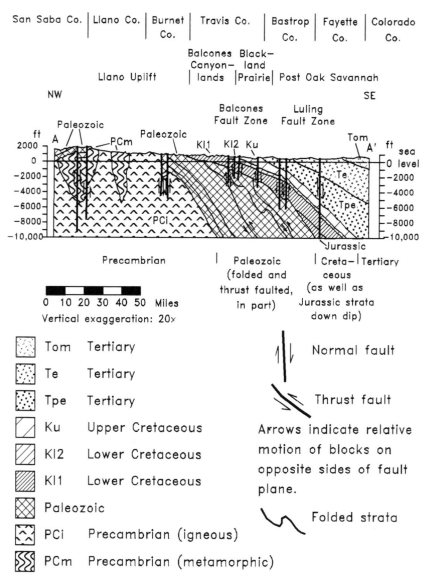

San Saba Co. | Llano Co. | Burnet Co. | Travis Co. | Bastrop Co. | Fayette Co. | Colorado Co.

Balcones Black-
Canyon- land
Llano Uplift | lands | Prairie | Post Oak Savannah

NW   SE

Precambrian | Paleozoic (folded and thrust faulted, in part) | Creta-ceous (as well as Jurassic strata down dip) | Tertiary

0 10 20 30 40 50 Miles
Vertical exaggeration: 20x

Tom   Tertiary   Normal fault

Te   Tertiary

Tpe   Tertiary   Thrust fault

Ku   Upper Cretaceous   Arrows indicate relative

Kl2   Lower Cretaceous   motion of blocks on

Kl1   Lower Cretaceous   opposite sides of fault
                                        plane.
Paleozoic

PCi   Precambrian (igneous)   Folded strata

PCm   Precambrian (metamorphic)

(adapted from H. B. Renfro, D. E. Feray, and P. B. King, *Geological Highway Map of Texas* [Tulsa: American Association of Petroleum Geologists, 1973])

Edwards Plateau

The Edwards Plateau is recognized as a distinct geologic and physiographic region characterized by limestones of the Lower Cretaceous Series and in the Llano Uplift, by rocks of varying composition and age (mostly pre-Cretaceous). In South Central Texas, the plateau can be divided into three subregions: the Llano Uplift (also called the Central Basin and the Central Mineral Region) west of Burnet; the Balcones Canyonlands (also known as the Hill Country) adjacent to and west of the Balcones Escarpment; and the Lampasas Cut Plain, that portion of the Edwards Plateau drained by tributaries of the Brazos River. The true plateau portion of the Edwards Plateau lies west of the South Central Texas area as here defined.

The most widely publicized vertebrates of the Edwards Plateau (all three local subregions) are the Golden-cheeked Warbler, *Dendroica chrysoparia,* and Black-capped Vireo, *Vireo atricapillus,* each of which is listed as an endangered species by the U.S. Fish and Wildlife Service. In South Central Texas, both are restricted to the Edwards Plateau. Golden-cheeked Warblers nest exclusively in Texas in a narrow band adjacent to and west of the Balcones Escarpment. See Chapter 3 for known locations both within and outside the nineteen-county area covered by this handbook where these two species can likely be observed in spring. Other vertebrates whose eastern boundaries occur at or near the Balcones Escarpment include Common Poorwill, *Phalaenoptilus nuttallii;* Golden-fronted Woodpecker, *Melanerpes aurifrons;* Ladder-backed Woodpecker, *Picoides scalaris;* Black-chinned Hummingbird, *Archilochus alexandri;* Ash-throated Flycatcher, *Myiarchus cinerascens;* Scrub Jay, *Aphelocoma coerulescens;* Verdin, *Auriparus flaviceps;* Canyon Wren, *Catherpes mexicanus;* Bell's Vireo, *Vireo bellii;* Canyon Towhee, *Pipilo fuscus;* Rufous-crowned Sparrow, *Aimophila ruficeps;* Black-throated Sparrow, *Amphispiza bilineata;* House Finch, *Carpodacus mexicanus;* Lesser Goldfinch, *Carduelis psaltria;* cave myotis, *Myotis velifer incautus;* Mexican ground squirrel, *Spermophilus mexicanus;* rock squirrel, *Spermophilus variegatus;* Merriam's pocket mouse, *Perognathus merriami;* white-ankled mouse, *Peromyscus pectoralis;* American badger, *Taxidea taxus;* cliff chirping frog, *Syrrhophus marnockii;* eastern green toad, *Bufo debilis debilis;* great plains skink, *Eumeces obsoletus;* Texas alligator lizard, *Gerrhonotus liocephalus infernales;* Texas night snake, *Hypsiglena torquata jani;* Texas longnose snake, *Rhinocheilus lecontei tessellatus;* and plains blackhead snake, *Tantilla nigriceps.* Numerous invertebrates are restricted to the Edwards Plateau or there reach the eastern limit of their range. See the checklists of land snails and butterflies later in this book and refer to publications cited in the Selected References.

Llano Uplift

The Llano Uplift area of Llano County and most adjacent counties is a tectonic uplift or dome of Paleozoic sedimentary strata and Precambrian igneous and metamorphic rocks. These rocks have been deeply eroded, forming an irregular topographic basin surrounded by hills of hard erosion-resistant Lower Cretaceous (Early Cretaceous–age) limestone. Approximately one billion years ago, molten rock, or magma was pushed toward the surface by pressures in the Earth's mantle and crust. The magma solidified into discrete masses of igneous rock called batholiths. Intrusion of the molten rock caused preexisting strata to be metamorphosed. These igneous and metamorphic rocks were gradually buried by marine sediment of Cambrian to Pennsylvanian age (570 million to 286 million years before present). The area was then uplifted, forming a broad dome with Precambrian batholiths and metamorphic rocks at its core and Paleozoic strata dipping away from the center of the uplift. Much later, after a long period of erosion, a sequence of Lower Cretaceous sandstones and limestones covered the entire area; eventually, however, this overburden was breached and stripped away by additional erosion, revealing the underlying Precambrian granites, gneisses, and schists and Paleozoic sandstones, limestones, and shales as well as the Lower Cretaceous sandstones and limestones at the borders of the Llano Uplift. Soils of the uplift are largely derived from these diverse rock types, which in weathering leave a calcareous sandy residue. The plants of this region are well adapted to these soils. Typical vegetation includes post oak, *Quercus stellata*; blackjack oak, *Q. marilandica*; cedar elm, *Ulmus crassifolia*; Arizona walnut, *Juglans major*; buffalograss, *Buchloe dactyloides*; common curlymesquite, *Hilaria belangeri*; Texas grama, *Bouteloua rigidiseta*; sideoats grama, *B. curtipendula*; and hairy grama, *B. hirsuta*. Peaches are a major agricultural product in soils developed on Lower Cretaceous sands in eastern Gillespie County, at the margin of the uplift, and grapes grown in this area support a flourishing wine industry. Several species of plant, such as rock quillwort, *Isoetes lithophylla*, and basin bellflower, *Campanula reverchonii*, are largely or exclusively confined to granite outcrops and their associated soils.

Balcones Canyonlands

The Balcones Canyonlands subregion is deeply dissected by streams and is noted for its scenic ruggedness and biological diversity. Much of the region is subject to severe erosion, even under the best land management. Nearly one-third of the Balcones Canyonlands consists of barren rock outcrops and rough, stony, steep slopes with little or no soil cover. The canyonlands are predominantly rangeland, with cultivation restricted to the deeper soils of river valleys. Except for the deep, fertile, clayey sands along streams, soils over virtually the entire region are stony, shallow, and highly calcareous. Bottomland soils may have low concentrations of lime in their topsoils, while their subsoils are calcareous, and they usually overlie limestone or marl. Many trees thrive in the bottomlands and spring-fed canyons, including cedar elm, *Ulmus crassifolia;* little walnut, *Juglans microcarpa;* Texas redbud, *Cercis canadensis;* sugar hackberry, *Celtis laevigata;* pecan, *Carya illinoinensis (C. illinioensis);* and baldcypress, *Taxodium distichum.* In contrast, the uplands sustain plateau live oak, *Quercus fusiformis (Q. virginiana);* shin oak, *Q. sinuata* var. *breviloba (Q. durandii* var. *breviloba);* Spanish oak, *Q. texana (Q. buckleyi);* Ashe juniper (commonly called cedar), *Juniperus ashei;* mescalbean (commonly called mountain laurel), *Sophora secundiflora;* and honey mesquite, *Prosopis glandulosa.* Common grasses include little bluestem, *Schizachyrium scoparium;* Texas grama, *Bouteloua rigidiseta;* Texas wintergrass, *Stipa leucotricha;* common curlymesquite, *Hilaria belangeri;* buffalograss, *Buchloe dactyloides;* and seep muhly, *Muhlenbergia reverchonii.*

The limestones of the Edwards Plateau are porous and contain numerous caves and vertical sinkholes. Enormous quantities of rainwater and runoff seep into and thus recharge the limestone aquifers, which serve as natural underground reservoirs. The most important of these is the Edwards Aquifer. A myriad of aquatic and nonaquatic cave-dwelling organisms occupy caverns throughout this aquifer. Long isolated from contact with other breeding populations, the Edwards Aquifer cave fauna includes a disproportionately large percentage of species known only from this region, including several endangered species. Springs discharging from the Edwards Aquifer supply the headwaters of countless streams and supplement the flow of several rivers. The aquifer is also an important source of well water. Major springs along the Balcones Escarpment include Comal Springs, the headwaters of the Comal River in Landa Park, New Braunfels; San Marcos Springs, which form Spring Lake at the head of the San Marcos River in San Marcos; San Pedro and other springs that are the headwaters of the San Antonio River in San Antonio; and Barton Springs, with an average flow of 37 million gallons per day, in Zilker Park, Austin. The communities that grew up near these springs and rivers were founded by early settlers who knew the value of a constant source of pure water.

Lampasas Cut Plain

Northeast of the Llano Uplift and north of the Colorado River basin is the region known as the Lampasas Cut Plain. The Lampasas Cut Plain is characterized by grass-covered low hills and oak-juniper woodlands, although much of the land has been cleared for grazing. There are many similarities between this region and the Balcones Canyonlands in terms of geology, soils, and physiography. In both regions, thin, stony soils cover broad hills, and narrow valleys cut into Lower Cretaceous limestones, although sandstones become more widespread to the north. There are, however, significant botanical differences. For example, Ashe juniper, *Juniperus ashei*, is common in the uplands of both regions, but the plateau live oak, *Quercus fusiformis (Q. virginiana)*, of the Balcones Canyonlands is gradually replaced northward by post oak, *Q. stellata*, and blackjack oak, *Q. marilandica*, which dominate the Cross Timbers near Dallas (north of South Central Texas). Canyon habitats, so important to the flora of the canyonlands, become less common northward, and most of the canyon species are progressively eliminated. Grasslands also change to the north, where remnants of once vast, treeless prairies provide a glimpse of the past. Although all of the grasses and many of the upland forbs that are found in the Balcones Canyonlands are present in the Lampasas Cut Plain, many of these species are more common to the north. The Lampasas Cut Plain is, therefore, an *ecotonal* or transitional region biologically, affording a bridge between the restricted species associations of the Edwards Plateau and the formerly widespread woodland and true prairie associations of the Central Lowland Province north of the Lampasas Cut Plain. Yet even the vegetational components of the two areas are becoming more alike because of progressive invasion of the grasslands by scrub species. The shallow soils of both the Lampasas Cut Plain and the Balcones Canyonlands are easily disturbed by human influence.

Gulf Coastal Plains

The Gulf Coastal Plains encompass a suite of habitats very different from those of the Great Plains. In South Central Texas, the major regions of the Gulf Coastal Plains are the Blackland Prairie and Post Oak Savannah. The Blackland Prairie is the down-faulted block of soft limestones and clays of Late Cretaceous age, which forms the low, mostly flat, formerly grass-covered terrain at the foot of the Balcones Escarpment. The escarpment thus serves as the western boundary of the prairie. East of the Blackland Prairie is a zone of Early Tertiary–age sandstones and shales, the Post Oak Savannah, which is a rolling landscape with dense woodlands. These regions form parallel bands extending through the South Central Texas area from northeast to southwest.

The Gulf Coastal Plains support a wide-ranging fauna. Vertebrates reaching their western range limits along or near the Balcones Escarpment include the Crested Caracara, *Polyborus plancus;* Ruby-throated Hummingbird, *Archilochus colubris;* Red-bellied Woodpecker, *Melanerpes carolinus;* Great Crested Flycatcher, *Myiarchus crinitus;* Eastern Kingbird, *Tyrannus tyrannus;* Blue Jay, *Cyanocitta cristata;* Prothonotary Warbler, *Protonotaria citrea;* Common Grackle, *Quiscalus quiscula;* eastern mole, *Scalopus aquaticus;* swamp rabbit, *Sylvilagus aquaticus;* eastern gray squirrel, *Sciurus carolinensis;* northern pygmy mouse, *Baiomys taylorii;* eastern woodrat, *Neotoma floridana;* smallmouth salamander, *Ambystoma texanum;* central newt, *Notophthalmus viridescens louisianensis;* Hurter's spadefoot, *Scaphiopus holbrookii hurterii;* green treefrog, *Hyla cinerea;* upland chorus frog, *Pseudacris feriarum feriarum;* southern leopard frog, *Rana utricularia utricularia;* western chicken turtle, *Deirochelys reticularia miaria;* three-toed box turtle, *Terrapene carolina triunguis;* western slender glass lizard, *Ophisaurus attenuatus attenuatus;* and broad-banded water snake, *Nerodia fasciata confluens.* The Balcones Escarpment provides an abrupt environmental transition, restricting the western distribution of these and many other species, including invertebrates and plants.

Blackland Prairie

Occupying a narrow zone from the Balcones Escarpment eastward for 20 to 30 miles is the Blackland Prairie, which is underlain by Upper Cretaceous clays and soft limestones. The Blackland Prairie extends from the Red River southward to near San Antonio. The soils of this region are deep, dark, and clay-rich and are among the most productive croplands in the state. Prior to the local advent of agriculture, the Gulf Coastal Plains were virtually uninterrupted grasslands. Honey mesquite, *Prosopis glandulosa;* sugar hackberry, *Celtis laevigata;* and other woody vegetation has invaded areas improperly farmed and overgrazed, resulting in the loss of almost all of the original prairie. The true prairie consisted of a mixed grassland dominated by little bluestem, *Schizachyrium scoparium.* Other important grasses were (and in a few places, remain) big bluestem, *Andropogon gerardii;* yellow indiangrass, *Sorghastrum nutans;* switchgrass, *Panicum virgatum;* sideoats grama, *Bouteloua curtipendula;* tall dropseed, *Sporobolus asper;* silver bluestem, *Bothriochloa saccharoides (B. longipaniculata);* and Texas wintergrass, *Stipa leucotricha.* A vast array of wildflowers cover remaining prairie remnants in season, including true prairie species and formerly uncommon plants that have become abundant in disturbed grasslands: Texas bluebonnet, *Lupinus texensis;* Texas paintbrush, *Castilleja indivisa;* obedient-plant, *Physostegia pulchella;* cobaea penstemon (commonly called foxglove), *Penstemon cobaea;* poppymallow or winecup, *Callirhoe involucrata;* and

Engelmann daisy, *Engelmannia pinnatifida*, among many others. Along major waterways, pecan, *Carya illinoinensis (C. illinioensis)*; American elm, *Ulmus americana*; red ash, *Fraxinus pensylvanica (F. pennsylvanica)*; sugar hackberry, *Celtis laevigata*; eastern cottonwood, *Populus deltoides*; American sycamore, *Platanus occidentalis*; boxelder, *Acer negundo*; and other woody vegetation are dominant.

Post Oak Savannah

In areas where sandy soils replace clayey soils on the inner Gulf Coastal Plains east of the Blackland Prairie, prairies give way to a savannah dominated by post oaks. This plant association is so conspicuous that its name is applied to the region as a whole. As its name implies, the Post Oak Savannah was originally a grassy plain where trees were isolated or confined to groves, or mottes. Woodlands of post oak, *Quercus stellata*, and blackjack oak, *Q. marilandica*, originally occupied only narrow strips throughout the region but extended laterally as the prairies were destroyed by cultivation and grazing. Yaupon, *Ilex vomitoria*, is a very common understory shrub. Important grasses, in addition to those of the Blackland Prairie, include Texas cupgrass, *Eriochloa sericea*; eastern gamagrass, *Tripsacum dactyloides*; rough tridens, *Tridens muticus*; Florida paspalum, *Paspalum floridanum*; and Canada wildrye, *Elymus canadensis*. American beautyberry, *Callicarpa americana*; coralbean, *Erythrina herbacea*; and spiderwort, *Tradescantia* spp., are among the more conspicuous wildflowers.

Within the Post Oak Savannah in Bastrop County, there is a population of loblolly pines, *Pinus taeda*, known as the "Lost Pines," which are separated from the main body of pines in the East Texas forests. Apparently, the deep, moist, acidic, sandy soil developed on sandstones of the Tertiary Carrizo, Reklaw, and Queen City formations provides the pines and associated biota with conditions suitable for their survival in an environment that today is otherwise unfavorable. Porous gravel deposited by the ancestral Colorado River covers the Tertiary formations of this area and may enhance storage and gradual infiltration of supplemental moisture. The Lost Pines provide some of the best habitat in the area covered by this guide for a number of vertebrate species, including the Houston toad, Pileated Woodpecker, and Pine, Hooded, Kentucky, and Swainson's warblers.

Climate

Part of the diversity that characterizes biogeographical regions of South Central Texas is the result of climatic variations. As is true in all

Thirty-Year Temperature and Rainfall Data, 1951—1980

County, Elevation of Reporting Station in Feet above Mean Sea Level	Average Annual Rainfall	Annual Mean	Temperature (degrees F) Means January High	January Low	August High	August Low	Number of Frost-Free Days
Bastrop (315)	36.5	68	62	38	98*	72	268
Bell (700)	33.8	67	57*	36	97	72	260
Bexar (788)	29.1	69	62	39	95	74*	265
Blanco (1350)	34.7	65*	60	33	95	69	234
Burleson (263)	39.1*	67	58	37	94	72	275
Burnet (1320)	30.4	65*	59	33	94	70	230
Caldwell (405)	34.7	68	61	37	96	72	275
Comal (718)	33.6	69	62	38	97	73	261
Fayette (425)	37.4	69	62	41*	96	72	277*
Gillespie (1747)	28.7	66	61	36	94	68	219*
Gonzales (406)	32.6	70*	64	41*	97	72	276
Guadalupe (505)	31.4	69	63*	40	97	72	267
Hays (600)	34.3	67	61	36	96	71	254
Kendall (1422)	32.2	65*	60	35	93*	68*	236
Lee (465)	35.1	67	58	38	94	72	273
Llano (1040)	26.6*	66	60	32*	97	71	229
Milam (393)	34.3	68	61	38	96	72	256
Travis (597)	31.5	68	59	39	95	74*	270
Williamson (570)	34.2	67	58	35	97	72	258

Adapted from "The Climate of Texas Counties," 1987, Natural Fibers Information Center, University of Texas, Austin.
*Extremes for area (duplicate values at some stations).

of Texas, average rainfall generally increases in the area from west to east and from south to north. The accompanying table provides a climatic summary of data from representative sites in the nineteen counties.

The highest recorded temperature in the area has been 113° F. (August 1953) and the lowest, − 6° F. (January 1949); both records were set in Llano County. Throughout the area, daily temperature variations in August generally range from the low 70's to the high 90's with readings over 100° occurring on a few days most summers. In January, temperatures usually vary between the mid-30's and about 60° F. Other modifying climatic factors include a high evaporation rate (potential evaporation exceeds the amount of precipitation in most years) and a growing season averaging 219 to 277 days per year in the northern and southern parts of the area, respectively.

In general, years of below-average rainfall are the rule and above-average rainfall the exception. Extended drouth is not uncommon and with very rapid runoff, especially to the west, effective aridity through much of the area is even greater than the normal rainfall amounts would seemingly indicate. Rainstorms along and west of the Balcones Escarpment are often intense but small and fast moving, which limits the rainfall received at any given site on an annual basis.

Most of the rainfall occurs in spring and early autumn. At these times of the year, warm, moist air from the Gulf of Mexico is blown inland by prevailing south-southeasterly winds. When the moisture-laden gulf air mass overrides the escarpment and meets a dry frontal system from the north or west, thunderstorms may be triggered supplying most of the spring rains for the area. Based on past records, rainstorms exceeding 10 inches in 24 hours occur, on average, once each decade, and 24-hour rains in excess of 6 inches occur once every two years. This record is based on data from existing reporting rain gauges; the actual frequency is probably higher because the network of gauges is sparse compared to the small size and uneven distribution of local, high-intensity rainstorms. There are also those times, mainly in the early fall, when hurricanes come ashore on the Texas coast, move inland a few hundred miles, then break up into individual storm cells depositing very large quantities of rain in a short period of time. The Edwards Plateau will experience a hurricane breakup of this type two or three times in a 10-year period.

The largest 24-hour rainfall total ever recorded in the area was measured near Thrall, Williamson County, where 38.2 inches fell in the storm of September 9–10, 1921. In the United States, this deluge is exceeded only by an unofficial record of 43 inches at Alvin in southeast Texas, July 25, 1979, during Hurricane Claudette. Heavy rainstorms occur in the area along the escarpment with greater frequency than is true elsewhere. Rains such as the above have produced heavy flooding and are responsible for intermittent stream flows greater here than in comparable watersheds anywhere else in the continental United States. Flooding on the Edwards Plateau is further accentuated by the steepness of the hills and valleys and by the spareness of vegetation that might otherwise retard the resulting rapid runoff. Also, inland hurricane-associated storms generally concentrate over a very small area, producing stream flows many times the normal carrying capacity of the natural drainage system. Hardly a year passes without loss of life, and extensive property damage, due to flash floods somewhere along the Balcones Escarpment. These conditions make development on floodplains particularly hazardous.

CHAPTER 2

Locations of Interest to Naturalists

THIS CHAPTER gives directions to and information about sixty-eight parks, preserves, lakes, and other areas which the authors consider of interest to residents and visitors wishing to study and enjoy the wide diversity of habitats and the flora and fauna of the nineteen counties of South Central Texas. Included are fourteen areas administered by the Texas Parks and Wildlife Department, seven owned by the Lower Colorado River Authority (most operated by others), twenty-two areas managed by cities, and nine areas operated by other entities, along with thirteen lakes, plus areas for locating wildlife in three cities. Twenty-six other locations are mentioned but not described in detail. Locations are grouped by counties, which are listed in alphabetical order. Special emphasis has been placed on bird-finding possibilities and on the types of facilities offered at each location. Most locations are readily accessible to the public. If fees or permission are required for entry, that information is included also.

Bastrop County

BASTROP STATE PARK, 3,500 acres, P.O. Box 518, Bastrop, TX 78602, (512) 321-2101, is 1 mile east of Bastrop. From Bastrop, drive east on SH 71/21; then go east on SH 21/95 a short distance, south on SH 21 to the top of the hill, and enter on Park Road 1. The park, along with Buescher State Park, encloses a large portion of the remaining "Lost Pines of Texas," an isolated stand of the loblolly pine approximately 180 miles west of their principal range.

Pine Warbler and Pileated Woodpecker are permanent residents. Other nesting birds include the Barred Owl, Yellow-throated Vireo, Northern Parula, Black-and-white Warbler, and Red-shouldered Hawk. Wintering species frequently found include Red-breasted Nuthatch, Solitary Vireo, Golden-crowned Kinglet, Purple Finch, and Hermit Thrush.

Facilities available include campsites, group barracks and mess hall, lodge, cabins, picnicking sites, restrooms with showers, playgrounds, swimming pool, nine-hole golf course, an outdoor sports area, a small lake, and an 8.5-mile hiking trail.

BUESCHER STATE PARK, 1,017 acres, P.O. Box 75, Smithville, TX 78957, (512) 237-2241, is 2 miles northwest of Smithville. From SH 71, drive north on FM 153 for 0.5 mile; enter on Park Road 1C.

The walk around the small lake at Buescher State Park is good in all seasons for seeking the Red-shouldered Hawk and Barred Owl. Northern Parula nests in spring and summer, and waterfowl can be found on the lake in winter.

Camping and picnicking areas, a group facility, recreational hall, shelters, restrooms with showers, and a playground are provided. A portion of the park has been redesignated as the University of Texas Environmental Science Park, a cancer research facility.

The scenic 13-mile drive between Bastrop and Buescher state parks on Park Road 1C through the pines is particularly rewarding. The only Hammond's Flycatcher recorded in the eastern half of Texas was found one February near where Alum Creek crosses Park Road 1C. Species which have nested along this creek include Swainson's, Kentucky, and Hooded warblers. Red Crossbill has been a very rare winter visitor.

LAKE BASTROP, 906 acres, created by the Lower Colorado River Authority to provide cooling water for power generation, is between SH 21 and SH 95, 3 miles north of Bastrop. At the present time, North Shore Park is operated by the Lower Colorado River Authority and is open to the public. To reach the park, drive north from Bastrop on SH 95 about 3 miles to FM 1441; then go east on FM 1441, 2.4 miles to the entrance sign. Features include camping, fishing, boat launching, swimming, and picnicking. There is also a small store for buying snacks. Formerly the authority operated a park on the south shore, but this facility has been leased to the Texas Parks and Wildlife Department and will be developed into a state park. North Shore Park will also become a state park after the south shore is opened to the public several years hence.

The lake is the winter home for a variety of water birds. Usually present are American Wigeon, Gadwall, and large numbers of American Coot. Osprey is found in fall, winter, and spring, and occasionally a Bald Eagle is spotted over the water. Check the brushy cover along the roads approaching the lake as well as around the lake for land birds.

The county roads in Bastrop County are favorable for observing resident Common Grackle. In winter, look for Brewer's and Rusty blackbirds. Also, Zone-tailed Hawks have been recorded on several Christmas Counts. One such road is an unpaved road from Elgin to Bastrop, west of and more or less parallel to SH 95 through Sayersville. Sayersville is more easily located on county maps than it is found from the road. From Elgin, drive south on SH 95 for 0.5 mile to County Road 49, which becomes County Road 179 at Sayersville; then after 4.8 miles, it becomes County Road 157, which leads to Bastrop. Through small land holdings and large ranches, the road traverses grasslands, brushy fence rows, pecan bottoms, woodlands with and without dense undergrowth, and several creek crossings. The variety of habitats make this an excellent drive in winter for a dozen or so sparrow species as well as a variety of other winter residents. The stream crossings can be especially productive for migrants in spring and fall. Red-shouldered Hawk and Crested Caracara are permanent residents. Painted Buntings are always present in spring and summer.

Another good bird-finding spot is the road along the Colorado River in Tahitian Village, a subdivision on SH 71 at the southeast edge of Bastrop. There is an abundance of riparian habitat along the river as well as grasslands and open woodlands. Pileated Woodpeckers are found occasionally along this road.

Bell County

STILLHOUSE HOLLOW LAKE, 6,430 acres, is located approximately 8 miles southwest of Belton on FM 1670. This U.S. Army Corps of Engineers impoundment on the Lampasas River is formed by a dam on the Lampasas River. Facilities include parks with boat ramps as well as camping and picnicking areas on the north and south shores. Depending on demand and budget constraints, some of the parks may be closed some seasons.

Bald Eagle, Osprey, American White Pelican, and Double-crested Cormorant can be seen roosting on dead trees in the middle of the reservoir throughout the winter months and during migrations. An excellent bird location especially in fall, winter, and spring is the wildlife management area on the south shore of the lake just east of River's Bend Park. To reach the wildlife management area, drive west on FM 2484 5.4 miles from its intersection with FM 1670. At the village of Union Grove, take the rightmost road to a locked gate. From there, park and walk to the shoreline. At the end of this road are extensive mudflats frequented by shorebirds during migration. Ring-billed Gulls and Forster's Terns, along with numerous waterfowl species, are usually present in winter. West of the mudflats are dense woods where Connecticut and Mourning warblers, Lazuli Bunting, and many other migrants have been seen.

Union Grove Park west of the wildlife management area is also a favorable birding area. Another place for birding is the area along the Lampasas River just below the dam. A nature trail leads through a riparian area with tall trees and dense undergrowth.

Not only is the area rich in wildlife, it also has a colorful local history. The cedar-covered, steep-walled canyons of the Edwards Plateau and the Lampasas Cut Plain offered excellent hiding places for moonshiners during the Prohibition Era of the 1920's and 1930's. Many "stillhouses" were operated here during this period. Thus the name Stillhouse Hollow Lake is especially appropriate.

BELTON LAKE, 12,300 acres at conservation pool level, is approximately 3 miles north of Belton and 14 miles northwest of Temple. The lake is a U.S. Army Corps of Engineers impoundment on the Leon River. The corps has thirteen parks around the lake, most offering boat ramps and camping and picnicking areas. Some offer a fishing barge, restaurant, snack bar, and showers, besides camping and picnicking.

OWL CREEK PARK on the north side of Belton Lake affords many birding opportunities. To reach Owl Creek Park from Belton, drive north on SH 317; or from Temple, drive north on SH 36 to the intersection of SH 317 and SH 36. Then go north on SH 36 approximately 6.5 miles to the Owl Creek Park sign, turn left and drive 1.1 miles on the road to the "Y"; then turn left and drive 2.2 miles to the Owl Creek Nature Area. The area, a cooperative effort of the Twin Lakes Audubon Society and the corps, is characterized by lake frontage, fallow fields, and mixed hardwood-juniper woodlands. Extensive native plantings are currently in progress, and a nature trail is planned. Also, a guidebook is being prepared to enhance hikes along the trail.

Painted Buntings are common summer residents here. The extensive marshes are excellent for sparrows in fall and winter, including Field, Vesper, Lark, Fox, Song, Lincoln's, White-crowned, and Harris'. In the wooded uplands look for Red-bellied, Ladder-backed, and Downy woodpeckers, along with the Yellow-bellied Sapsucker, Northern Flicker, Hermit Thrush, Orange-crowned Warbler, Rufous-sided Towhee, Chipping Sparrow, and American Goldfinch. The water should be checked for gulls, terns, and waterfowl. The area is excellent for recording spring and fall migrants.

TEMPLE LIONS PARK is located in southwest Temple and is operated by the Temple Parks and Recreation Department. To drive to the park from IH 35, take the Midway Drive Exit, Exit 297; drive east on Midway Drive 1.4 miles, then south on Hickory Road 1.0 mile to the Lions Park sign. Turn right and drive down the hill past the baseball fields to the picnic area. Permanent residents in the pecan bottoms include the Great Horned Owl, Red-bellied and Downy woodpeckers, Carolina Wren, and Eastern Bluebird. In summer watch for the Great Crested Flycatcher and

Yellow-crowned Night-Heron. The marsh area should be checked when water is present. Watching for migrants in spring and fall can be very rewarding. There are lots of warblers to see (thirty species have been recorded in the county) as well as *Empidonax* flycatchers, and with good fortune, Peregrine Falcon, Broad-winged Hawk, and Sora. White-breasted Nuthatch has been a recent summer resident. Wintering species include Golden-crowned and Ruby-crowned kinglets, American Kestrel, Red-tailed and Cooper's hawks, and Ring-billed Gull, along with ten or so sparrow species.

CAMP TAHUAYA is on the Lampasas River between Belton and Salado. It is operated by the Boy Scouts of America. From Belton, drive south on IH 35 approximately 5 miles to Exit 289A, then west 1.0 mile to the camp. From Salado, drive north on IH 35 about 5 miles to Exit 289A. Several trails through open hardwood-juniper woodlands wind between the camping areas. The woodlands along the main trail, which leads to the river, are good for locating Carolina Wren, Brown Creeper, and Red-bellied Woodpecker in fall and winter. There is a pond which can be good for finding ducks, including Wood Duck and Green-winged Teal in fall, winter, and spring. Migrants and sparrows are sometimes abundant in the open areas near camp headquarters. PERMISSION IS REQUIRED FOR BIRDING. Call (817) 947-5525 for information.

Bexar County

Bexar County is at or near the convergence of three very distinct natural areas. The southern part of the county is the northern extension of the South Texas Plains, or Tamaulipan Plains. West is the Balcones Canyonlands, and east, the southern portion of the Blackland Prairies. Several lakes, some described later, are areas of special interest to naturalists. As always, the variety of landscapes provides a broad range of available habitats, which means a diverse flora and fauna.

SAN ANTONIO is one of the oldest cities in Texas. The city played a vital role in early Texas history, and there are many historic places open to visitors. The San Antonio Parks and Recreation Department maintains 136 parks in the city, ranging in size from less than an acre to over 1,000 acres. Birding locations include the San Antonio River along Mission Parkway, where one can not only visit the old missions but also follow the road along the river, several stretches of which are wooded. Barred Owls have been recorded regularly where Somerset Road crosses the Medina River. Somerset Road is south of San Antonio about 1 mile east of the intersection of IH 35 South and Loop 410. Green Kingfishers have been found along the Medina River.

DWIGHT D. EISENHOWER PARK, 317 acres (50 developed), 19399 NW Military Highway (FM 1535), is operated by the San Antonio Parks and Recreation Department. From the intersection of IH 10 and Loop 1604, drive 2 miles east on Loop 1604 to FM 1535, then north of FM 1535 2 miles to the park. There are restrooms, group and individual picnicking and camping areas, and 5.89 miles of well-marked trails, some paved for the mobility-impaired. Common birds include Scrub Jay, Chipping Sparrow, and House Finch. The habitat is typical of the Balcones Canyonlands with a variety of Edwards Plateau trees, including oaks and Ashe juniper, as well as shrubs and herbaceous plants. The area appears to be favorable for Golden-cheeked Warblers.

BRACKENRIDGE PARK, 343 acres, 500 North St. Mary's, is located north of downtown San Antonio between North St. Mary's and Broadway, either of which will lead to the park. It is near the headwaters of the San Antonio River and is operated by the San Antonio Parks and Recreation Department. This heavily wooded park has concessions, a golf course, picnicking areas, playgrounds, and the Sunken Gardens. The variety of plant species at the Japanese Tea Gardens attract Black-chinned Hummingbirds in spring and summer and Ruby-throated and Rufous hummingbirds in migration. Broad-tailed and Anna's hummingbirds have also been sighted.

SAN ANTONIO ZOO is adjacent to Brackenridge Park. In addition to one of the best displays in Texas of other animals from around the world, the zoo features approximately seven hundred bird species. Of special interest to birders are the F. C. Hixon Tropical Bird House and the African Flight Cage, both of which have free-flying birds in an enclosed aviary. Waterfowl from around the world are on display; with them are free-flying Wood Ducks and Black-bellied Whistling-Ducks in summer and several North American species in winter. A Yellow-crowned Night-Heron rookery is located on the zoo grounds. The woodlands in both the park and the zoo can be very good locations during spring and fall migration. In winter, look for Golden-crowned and Ruby-crowned kinglets, Brown Thrasher, sparrows, and woodpeckers.

SOUTHSIDE LIONS PARK, 900 Hiawatha, and SOUTHSIDE LIONS PARK EAST, 2800 Roland, 599 acres (275 developed), are operated by the San Antonio Parks and Recreation Department. From the intersection of IH 37 and IH 10, drive south on IH 37 about 3 miles to Pecan Valley Drive, then north on Pecan Valley Drive approximately 2 miles to the park. There are playgrounds, picnicking areas, fishing spots, trails, and camping sites. The lake in Southside Lions Park is the wintering home for Pied-billed Grebe, Gadwall, American Wigeon, Green-winged Teal, Northern Shoveler, Lesser Scaup, American Coot, and other waterfowl.

The undeveloped portion of the park is typical South Texas brush where Curve-billed and Long-billed thrashers, Cactus Wren, and Pyrrhuloxia occur. All these South Texas species are near the northern limit of their range. Many sparrow species spend the winter here, and Salado Creek, which flows through a portion of the park, can be good for spring and fall migrants.

W. W. MCALLISTER PARK, 856 acres, 13102 Jones-Maltsberger, is operated by San Antonio Parks and Recreation Department. From NE Loop 410 at the San Antonio International Airport, drive north on US 281, 3.2 miles to Bitters Road; turn right (east) on Bitters Road to the junction with Starcrest, and continue straight ahead on Starcrest (Bitters Road veers to the right). At Jones-Maltsberger (0.9 mile from US 281), turn left (north) and drive 0.8 mile to the entrance on the right. Facilities offered include a nature trail, hike and bike trail, campsites, playgrounds, restrooms, and picnic areas. Vegetational areas include live oak groves, mesquite grasslands, and prairies. In spring and fall migrating shorebirds can be found at the lake; also look for wintering waterfowl. The lake may be dry during drought years. The woodlands should be checked for wintering passerines. This is a good place for recording wintering sparrows, including Fox Sparrow, and is a favorable spring and fall migration location. The park is usually crowded on nice weekends.

EMILIE AND ALBERT FRIEDRICH PARK, 232 acres, 21480 Milsa, is operated by the San Antonio Parks and Recreation Department. The park preserves a portion of the Balcones Canyonlands. To reach the park from the intersection of Loop 410 and IH 10 northwest of the city, go 12 miles on IH 10 to the Camp Bullis Exit; drive west (left) at the underpass, then drive 1 mile north on the west access to the park sign. The park is about 0.5 mile from IH 10. In 1990, twenty-two pairs of Golden-cheeked Warblers and two pairs of Black-capped Vireos nested in the park. Other nesting species include Greater Roadrunner, Golden-fronted Woodpecker, Ladder-backed Woodpecker, Ash-throated Flycatcher, Verdin, Bell's Vireo, Yellow-breasted Chat, Rufous-crowned Sparrow, Northern (Bullock's) Oriole, and Lesser Goldfinch. A stop at headquarters to get literature and information on which of the seven trails to hike is recommended. Facilities include restrooms. The park is open from 9:00 AM to 5:00 PM Wednesday through Sunday, with no admission after 4:00 PM.

JACK JUDSON NATURE TRAIL, 10 acres, is located in Alamo Heights. Because of vandalism and other problems, visitors must obtain permission from the Alamo Heights Police Department, (210) 822-3321, before entering. To reach the area from Austin Highway and Broadway, drive north on Broadway for 3 blocks to Ogden Lane, then west on Ogden, 5 blocks to Greely, and south a block or so to the entrance on the right.

The Alamo Heights Swimming Pool is adjacent to the nature trail acreage. This heavily wooded area with thick underbrush is in a floodplain. Nesting species include Yellow-crowned Night-Heron, Chuck-will's-widow, Golden-fronted Woodpecker, Verdin, and House Finch. Wintering species include Brown Creeper, Blue-gray Gnatcatcher, Solitary Vireo, Rufous-sided Towhee, and Common Grackle. The undergrowth is excellent for wintering sparrows, also. From time to time, the San Antonio Audubon Society, (210) 733-8306, conducts bird walks at this location.

JOHN JAMES PARK, 89 acres (40 developed), 1300 Rittiman Road, is operated by the San Antonio Parks and Recreation Department. Rittiman Road crosses IH 35 approximately 8 miles south of the intersection of Loop 410 and IH 35 northeast. In the park, there are playgrounds, a picnic area, and a nature trail. The trail leads from the mesquite-hackberry uplands to Salado Creek. The extensive riparian area along the creek is a favorable location for spring and fall migrants. Many species of seasonal wildflowers can be found along the trail, some in abundance.

SAN ANTONIO BOTANICAL CENTER, 555 Funston Place, is operated by the San Antonio Parks and Recreation Department with guidance from the San Antonio Botanical Society, a nonprofit support group. There are extensive formal gardens, greenhouses, the new Lucile Halsell Conservatory Complex with approximately 0.5 acre under glass, featuring ferns, palms, cycads, western cacti, tropical fruits, and flowering tropicals (well worth a visit by itself), a winding trail with buildings, soils and plantings representing three vegetational areas of Texas (Hill Country, East Texas Pineywoods, and South Texas Plains), and a large gift shop and bookstore. The pond in the middle of the Texas section is a very reliable location in San Antonio for Black-bellied Whistling-Ducks. Also, Verdin and Bell's Vireo are summer residents. There is an entrance fee.

MITCHELL LAKE, 660 surface acres, formerly was a part of the San Antonio wastewater treatment process. The lake is located on Moursund Boulevard, 0.6 mile south of the southern portion of Loop 410. Moursund Boulevard is between SH 16 and US 281. The gate may be locked to the general public. Birders can gain entry by calling the San Antonio Audubon Society, (210) 733-8306, a day or two ahead of time. This is the most popular birding spot in Bexar County for wading birds, waterfowl, wintering raptors, and shorebirds. Most of the sixteen species of wading birds, thirty geese and ducks, thirty-eight shorebirds, and fifteen gulls and terns on the Bexar County bird checklist have been found here. Rarities recorded at Mitchell Lake include Brown Pelican, Glossy Ibis, Great Kiskadee, Red Knot, Curlew Sandpiper, and Ruff. Nesting rarities include Cinnamon Teal, Groove-billed Ani, Lesser Nighthawk, and American Avocet. Pelagic and coastal species recorded as a result of hurricanes from the Gulf of Mexico include Sooty and Royal terns, Black Skimmer, Magnificent Frigatebird, and Parasitic Jaeger.

BRAUNIG LAKE, 1,350 surface acres, is operated by the City Public Service Board of San Antonio to provide cooling water for a power generation plant. It is located south of the city on IH 37. Recreational opportunities include fishing, boating, and picnicking. This is a good spot for gulls, terns, Double-crested and Neotropic cormorants, and Osprey. There is an entrance fee, which is also good for same-day entry to Calaveras Lake.

CALAVERAS LAKE, 3,450 surface acres, is operated by the City Public Service Board of San Antonio. It is located 15 miles southeast of San Antonio with entry from Loop 1604. Many rarities have been recorded here, including California Gull (March 1991), Mew Gull (December 1990–January 1991), Western Grebe, Black-legged Kittiwake, and Pacific and Red-throated loons. Gulf storms have blown in Black Skimmers, Royal Terns, and Magnificent Frigatebirds. Some South Texas species that have been recorded in the brushy areas include Long-billed Thrasher, Black-throated Sparrow, Lesser Nighthawk, Brown-crested Flycatcher, Common Ground-Dove, Cactus Wren, and Bronzed Cowbird. There is an entrance fee, which is also good for same-day entry to Braunig Lake.

OLMOS BASIN PARK, 1,010 acres (617 developed), 800 Olmos Drive East, is operated by the San Antonio Parks and Recreation Department and has a golf course, group and general picnic areas, playgrounds, and restrooms. A large part of the park is heavily wooded near the river. The large picnic area on Jones-Maltsberger Road has huge live oaks where migrants occur in spring and fall. The park has been a good location for migrating Mississippi Kites. The park is bisected north to south by the McAllister Freeway and east to west by Basse Road. Most of the development is north of Basse Road.

Blanco County

PEDERNALES FALLS STATE PARK, 4,851 acres, Route 1, Box 31A, Johnson City, TX 78636, (210) 868-7304, is located on the Pedernales River about 9 miles east of Johnson City. From Johnson City, drive east on RR 2766, or from Austin, drive west on US 290 for 32 miles. Then go north on RR 3232 for 6 miles. The varied habitats are typical of the eastern Edwards Plateau, or Balcones Canyonlands, varying from the luxuriant baldcypress–lined banks of the Pedernales River, to localized, botanically rich, wet canyons, springs, and seeps, to dry upland grasslands, cedar brakes, live oak mottes, and post oak, mesquite, and Ashe juniper–elm woodlands. Most of the park is retained in a natural condition with development at a minimum. White-tailed deer, rock squirrel, and Wild Turkey are plentiful.

The falls, the main attraction of the park, were formed by the fault juxtaposition of rock strata of differing resistance to erosion. The more easily eroded layers lie downstream from the point at which the faults cross the riverbed and are more rapidly removed. The upstream side was left higher, thus creating the falls. A short walk from the parking lot at the north end of the road leads to a scenic overlook above the falls. These limestones belong to the Marble Falls formation of the Pennsylvanian geologic period, and with an age of over 300 million years, they are the oldest rock exposed in the park. In this area, the elevation of the river drops about 50 feet over a distance of 3,000 feet.

The park includes more than 6 miles of Pedernales River frontage. The spectacular falls, which give the park its name, are located in the northwestern corner of the park. Continuous erosion of the riverbed has carved a deep, steep-walled canyon. Spring-fed tributaries of the river create a scenic and ecologically important microhabitat for a wide variety of uncommon plants and animals. Overall, the park provides a prime example of the vegetation and environments characteristic of the eastern Edwards Plateau.

The name *Pedernales* is Spanish for "flint"; much of the gravel in the river channel is composed of the mineral chert which is popularly called flint. The plunge pool beneath the falls has long been known by local residents to be a favored spawning ground for large catfish.

Here, nesting birds include Ash-throated Flycatcher, Painted Bunting, Verdin, Bell's Vireo, Blue Grosbeak, Canyon Wren, Rufous-crowned Sparrow, Greater Roadrunner, and Scrub Jay. This park is one of only a very few public areas where the Golden-cheeked Warbler, an endangered species, is easily found. They are usually heard and seen from mid-March to the end of June along the Pedernales Hill Country Nature Trail, above the overlook at the falls, and along Wolf Mountain Trail. It helps greatly to learn their song. Bushtits are uncommon in the dry uplands. Look for Osprey along the river in spring and autumn.

Activities include camping, picnicking, swimming, fishing, and hiking. The 7.5-mile Wolf Mountain Trail leads to the primitive camping area, which is approximately 2.5 miles from the trailhead. Campers must bring in their own water. The quarter-mile Pedernales Hill Country Trail is adjacent to the campground. A guide for the latter is available at headquarters.

BLANCO STATE PARK, 110 acres, P.O. Box 493, Blanco, TX 78606, (210) 833-4333, is located on the Blanco River 1 mile south of Blanco or 14 miles south of Johnson City on US 281. Features offered include swimming in the Blanco River, camping, and picnicking. Structures include a group facility, restrooms with hot showers, a playground, and a hiking trail. Also, the area is rich in fossils that, of course, may not be collected in the park.

Burleson County (See Lee County)

Burnet County

INKS LAKE STATE PARK, 1,200 acres, Box 117, Buchanan Dam, TX 78609, (512) 793-2223, is located on the east shore of Inks Lake on Park Road 4. From Burnet, drive west on SH 29 to Park Road 4. Activities here include camping, picnicking, primitive camping, boating, water skiing, sailing, swimming, fishing, hiking, and golfing. Facilities include a marina, two fishing piers, a beach (unsupervised), 7.5 miles of hiking trails, and a nine-hole golf course. In addition, there is a concessionaire store for groceries and picnic supplies. Also, motorboats, paddleboats, and canoes can be rented for recreation. With its variety of activities and impressive scenery, the park is one of the most popular Texas parks in summer. Inks Lake, 803 acres, is a constant-level lake surrounded by the formations of the Llano Uplift. Valley Spring Gneiss is the predominant rock type cropping out in the park. Granite Mountain and quarry at Marble Falls, 15 miles south, furnished material for the Texas State Capitol.

Bell's Vireo, Verdin, Orchard Oriole, Painted Bunting, and Golden-fronted Woodpecker nest throughout the park. Winter residents include Common Loon, Horned Grebe, Red-breasted Merganser, and numerous duck species. Bald Eagles are regular winter visitors from nearby Lake Buchanan. Ringed Kingfisher has been recorded.

The Federal Fish Hatchery, a short distance south of the park on Park Road 4, is recommended highly for finding wintering ducks as well as numerous land birds in the brushy areas adjacent to the creeks and the Colorado River.

Burnet and Llano Counties

LAKE BUCHANAN, 23,060 acres at operating level, is the largest of the Highland Lakes in surface acres. The dam is just north of SH 29 about 12 miles west of Burnet. Construction of the stair-stepped system of dams forming the Highland Lakes commenced in 1895, when work began on the Austin Dam.

The Highland Lakes provide flood control, electricity generation, municipal and agricultural water, and recreation. They are maintained and managed by the Lower Colorado River Authority. Lake Travis is the flood control unit.

Wintering birds on Lake Buchanan include Common Loon, Red-breasted Merganser, Bald Eagle, Horned Grebe, Forster's Tern and Herring, Ring-billed and Bonaparte's gulls. Look for Greater Roadrunner, Canyon Towhee, Cactus Wren, Verdin, and Black-throated Sparrow in brushy areas around the Lake.

The Vanishing Texas River Cruise, P.O. Box 901, Burnet, TX 78611, (512) 756-6986, conducts tours on the lake to view wintering Bald Eagles from November to March and scenic cruises year-round.

An especially pleasurable drive from Austin through the Highland Lakes area, away from the major highways, is to take RR 2222 west from Austin to RR 620, cross RR 620, to Anderson Mill Road, then take RR 2769 to the community of Volente. From RR 2769, follow Big Sandy Creek Road to RR 1431 and continue northwestward on RR 1431 through Jonestown, Marble Falls, and Kingsland in Llano County to SH 29 just west of Lake Buchanan. Bluebonnets and many other wildflowers are outstanding in the Kingsland area in early April.

Caldwell County

LOCKHART STATE PARK, 257 acres, Route 3, Box 69, Lockhart, TX 78644, (512) 398-3479, is on Plum Creek southwest of Lockhart. To reach the park, drive 1 mile south of Lockhart on US 183 to FM 20, then southward on FM 20 2 miles to Park Road 10, and finally, 1 mile south on Park Road 10. There are campsites, a group recreation hall, picnic tables, a group picnic area, restrooms with hot showers, a swimming pool, nine-hole golf course, playground, and hiking trail. Nearby is the site of the Battle of Plum Creek where early settlers and Comanche Indians fought in 1840.

Comal County

NEW BRAUNFELS DUMP is a city sanitary landfill operation where Sandhill Crane have been wintering for many years. To drive to the dump from New Braunfels, go north on IH 35 four miles to Exit 193, then east on Kohlenburg Road one mile; turn left on FM 1101, and drive 1.5 miles to the dump at the top of the hill. Take the county road just right of the dump entrance, where a large pond can be seen on the left. Or from San Marcos, drive 11 miles south on IH 35 to Exit 193. The cranes are usually present at this location from October through March, especially at dawn and dusk. During the day, they forage in fields mostly south and east of this spot and are usually easily heard and seen flying to and from their feeding and roosting areas. Look for waterfowl on the pond in winter.

GUADALUPE RIVER STATE PARK, 1,900 acres, Route 2, Box 2087, Bulverde, TX 78163, (210) 438-2656, is on the Guadalupe River between New Braunfels and Boerne. From New Braunfels, drive west on SH 46 to US 281, then continue on SH 46, 8 miles to Park Road 31, which leads to the park. From Boerne, drive west on SH 46 13 miles to Park Road 31. From downtown San Antonio, drive north on US 281 to SH 46, then west as just described. The Comal-Kendall county line bisects the park southwest to northeast.

Divided more or less east to west by the clear, flowing waters of the Guadalupe River, the ruggedness and scenic beauty of the park is typical of the Texas Hill Country. Pending development, only the area south of the river is open to the public.

On its winding path through the park, the river courses over four natural rapids, and two steep limestone bluffs reflect its awesome erosive power. The huge baldcypress trees along the bank, some snapped off by floods, are ample evidence of this power. There are three major terrestrial plant communities in the park and adjacent Honey Creek State Natural Area: Ashe juniper/Texas oak woodlands, post oak/cedar elm woodlands, and riparian woodlands. Small grasslands and savannahs exist throughout these community types and provide additional habitats. All habitats are easily accessible by trail. Trees in lower elevations and bottomlands include sycamore, elm, basswood, pecan, walnut, persimmon, willow, and hackberry. In the uplands away from the river, the limestone terrain is typical of the Balcones Canyonlands and has oak and juniper woodlands with interspersed grasslands.

Birds that nest in the park include Common Poorwill, Scrub Jay, Yellow-throated Vireo, Rufous-crowned Sparrow, and Lesser Goldfinch. Golden-cheeked Warblers have been recorded and may nest here. Fourteen sparrow species, twenty-four warblers, and one hundred sixty-eight bird species have been found in the park and the natural area.

In addition to numerous species of birds, the park supports a wide variety of wild animals including white-tailed deer, coyote, gray fox, skunk, raccoon, opossum, bobcat, and armadillo. Other smaller species abound, and the efforts of wildlife observers are usually well rewarded.

Activities include swimming, hiking, picnicking, and camping. There are also playgrounds. In addition, tubing, canoeing, and rafting are popular on the Guadalupe, but the park does not rent or offer any of the equipment. Inquire at headquarters for location of rental companies nearby.

HONEY CREEK STATE NATURAL AREA, 1,825 acres, is east of and adjacent to Guadalupe River State Park. Guided tours to the natural area are usually scheduled at 9:00 AM on Saturdays. Honey Creek is a pristine stream, fed by a large spring, where nesting species include Acadian Flycatcher, Yellow-throated Warbler, Louisiana Waterthrush, Northern Parula, and Green Kingfisher.

CYPRESS BEND PARK is maintained and operated by the New Braunfels Parks and Recreation Department. From "The Square" in New Braunfels drive 1 mile east on Common Street to Peach Avenue, then south on Peach Avenue to the entrance. The park has camping facilities. Cypress Bend is on a scenic bend of the Guadalupe River.

CANYON LAKE, 8,240 surface acres, is a U.S. Army Corps of Engineers impoundment on the Guadalupe River north of New Braunfels. It provides flood control along with many recreational activities including boating, fishing, and swimming. The lake is a very popular South Central Texas recreational area. From New Braunfels, drive north on either FM 306 or the River Road. The River Road is a county road which follows the meanderings of the Guadalupe River from SH 46 north of New Braunfels to the dam. It is a very scenic drive in all seasons. Both roads lead to the dam where the headquarters for the corps are located. Across the road from headquarters are picnic tables and a path which can be hiked and will lead to the top of the dam. All the species (listed below) for the lake have been recorded in this area. A Pacific Loon was seen from the dam in January 1987.

The corps has several parks on both the north and south sides of the lake. The parks offer campsites, picnic tables, restrooms, and boat ramps. Canyon Park, Jacobs Creek Park, and Potters Creek Park are on the north and can be reached from FM 306. Comal Park and Cranes Mill Park are on the south off FM 2673, which dead-ends at FM 306 south of the dam. The parks offer a variety of habitats: woodlands, grasslands, thick underbrush, beach areas near the shoreline, and the lake itself.

Permanent resident birds include Rufous-crowned Sparrow, Bewick's Wren, Scrub Jay, Lesser Goldfinch, Ladder-backed Woodpecker, and House Finch. Species that can be found in summer are Yellow-billed Cuckoo, Scissor-tailed Flycatcher, and Orchard Oriole. Scott's Oriole has summered in the area. In winter look for Pied-billed, Eared, and Horned grebes, Osprey, American Pipit, Double-crested Cormorant, ducks, and sparrows. Occasionally, a Common Raven can be seen with the soaring Turkey and Black vultures. Winter rarities at Comal Park include Pyrrhuloxia and LeConte's Sparrow.

Fayette County

MONUMENT HILL/KREISCHE BREWERY STATE HISTORIC PARKS, Route 1, Box 699, La Grange, TX 78945, (409) 968-5658, is located at the southern edge of La Grange near the Colorado River. To reach the park from La Grange, drive south on US 77 about 2 miles to Spur 92. The facilities are open every day from 8:00 AM to 5:00 PM for day use only. There are picnic areas with fire grills, an exhibit center, and scenic overlooks. Guided tours of the brewery are on weekends at 2:00 and 3:30 PM. Each tour lasts an hour.

Most park visitors come to see Monument Hill, the burial site for the remains of Texans who died in the battle of Salado Creek in 1842, and on the ill-fated Mier expedition in 1843; they also come to see the brewery complex where Heinrich L. Kreische conducted his beer business in the late nineteenth century. However, the flora and fauna also deserve the attention of the visiting naturalist.

The limestone that forms the resistant cap of the Oakville Escarpment, locally called the La Grange Bluff, yields a soil which, when combined with the topography, supports numerous plant species which are characteristic of the Edwards Plateau some 60 miles northwest. These "displaced" species intermix with the vegetation that predominates on uplands of the La Grange area, the Post Oak Savannah. Little bluestem, *Schizachyrium scoparium*, is the dominant grass on the grasslands, which has apparently not been overgrazed here. Other plants include big bluestem, *Andropogon gerardii* (one of the better stands in South Central Texas); yellow Indiangrass, *Sorghastrum nutans*; inland ceanothus, *Ceanothus herbaceus*; button snakeroot, *Eryngium yuccifolium*; rosinweed, *Silphium laciniatum*; and numerous other grasses and forbs. Typical Edwards Plateau plants include false dayflower, *Commelinantia anomala (Tinantia anomala)*; Lindheimer beargrass, *Nolina lindheimeriana*; agarito, *Berberis trifoliolata (Mahonia trifoliolata)*; Texas kidneywood, *Eysenhardtia texana*; fragrant mimosa, *Mimosa borealis*; mescalbean, *Sophora secundiflora*; Mexican-buckeye, *Ungnadia speciosa*; Texas persimmon, *Diospyros texana*; and elbowbush, *Forestiera pubescens*. There is a nature trail where the flora and fauna can be observed.

PARK PRAIRIE PARK, 5 acres, is on the western side of Cedar Creek Reservoir, 2,420 acres, owned by the Lower Colorado River Authority and operated by Fayette County. The lake provides cooling water for a power generation facility. The park can be reached from La Grange by driving northeast on FM 159 about 7 miles to County Road 196, then 0.9 mile southeast on CR 196 to the park. Features include a boat ramp, campsites, picnic areas, a sandy beach, skiing area, and chemical toilets. In the adjoining woodlands, look for the resident land birds of the area. There are usually cormorants present, Neotropic in summer and Double-crested in winter and both in other seasons. Also look for Ospreys. Ducks are in the coves in fall, winter, and spring.

OAK THICKET PARK is on the north shore of Cedar Creek Reservoir just south of SH 159 approximately 12.5 miles east of La Grange or 3.4 miles west of Fayetteville. Facilities include a boat ramp, picnic sites, and chemical toilets. There is no potable water. Adjoining the park are 20 acres, to be preserved as natural habitat. The Rice-Osborne Bird and Natural Trail, 5 acres, leads through woods, grasslands, and marsh in the sanctuary. Future plans include labeling vegetation along the trail, establishing an open-air classroom, and building benches for birders and hikers. The presence of more woodlands, grasslands, and marsh here provide better birding opportunities than at Park Prairie Park. One of the authors has recorded Wood Stork (summer) and Green Kingfisher near this site. The park is open Saturday and Sunday, 5:00 AM to 5:00 PM.

Gillespie County

LADY BIRD JOHNSON PARK, 190 acres, owned and operated by the City of Fredericksburg, is 3.5 miles south of Fredericksburg on SH 16. Facilities include campsites with hookups, a golf course, swimming pool, playgrounds, picnic areas, and hiking trails. There is a 17-acre lake for sailboats, canoes, and pedal boats.

Gonzales County

PALMETTO STATE PARK, 263 acres, P.O. Box 4, Ottine, TX 78658, (210) 672-3266, is located on the San Marcos River between Luling and Gonzales. From Gonzales, drive northwest 13 miles on US 183 to FM 1586, then west on FM 1586 2 miles to Ottine, and south on Park Road 11 to the entrance. From Luling, drive southeast 6 miles on US 183, then southeast on Park Road 11 for 3 miles.

The park is located in the Post Oak Savannah vegetational area. Several plant communities occur in this small park including hardwood bottomlands along the San Marcos River, wet grasslands with occasional palmetto-filled swales, an oxbow lake, and several lagoons fed by an artesian well. The swamp area, formerly known as the Ottine Swamp, features a botanical garden seemingly lifted from the tropics. The unique variety of plants and animal life has attracted many naturalists, professional and amateur. In the park are seven species of oak. Over eighty species of amphibians and reptiles, nearly 100 butterflies, and 276 birds have been reported in the Palmetto area.

Park Road 11 from US 183 to the park has a spectacular overlook of the San Marcos River Valley, wooded uplands, heavily wooded lowlands, and cultural areas where a wide diversity of plants and birds can be encountered. In winter, look for American Woodcock amid leaf litter beneath trees on the south side of the road at the bottom of this hill. The River Trail along the San Marcos River, the Palmetto Trail through the swamps near the old water tower, and the trail around the oxbow lake offer particularly rewarding birding opportunities. Trail guides are available at headquarters.

Resident birds include Pileated and Downy woodpeckers, Red-shouldered Hawk, Crested Caracara, Eastern Bluebird, Eastern Screech-Owl, and Great Horned and Barred owls. Indigo and Painted buntings are summer residents. Brown Thrasher, Rufous-sided Towhee, and Purple Finch spend the winter. Where water is present in the swamps, look for Winter Wren in winter and Kentucky, Hooded, and Prothonotary warblers in spring. Northern Parula are usually easy to find in spring and summer near the recreation building. Hairy Woodpecker, Green Kingfisher, and American Woodcock have been found on recent Christmas Counts. A rare Christmas Count sighting was a Cape May Warbler. Without too much effort, a dozen species of sparrows including Fox, White-throated, White-crowned, and Lincoln's sparrows can be found from December through February. This is an excellent area for birding during both the spring and fall migrations.

Facilities offered include campsites, picnic areas, a group recreation building, restrooms with showers, fishing piers, and playgrounds.

Guadalupe County

MAX STARKE AND RIVERSIDE PARK, 190 acres, is located at the south edge of Seguin on both sides of SH 123 Business adjacent to the Guadalupe River. Facilities include an eighteen-hole golf course, swimming pool, picnicking sites, and playgrounds. A winding drive along the river among tall oaks and pecan trees and the brushy areas near the riverbank offer the best birding opportunities.

GOVERNOR IRELAND PARK is maintained and operated by the Guadalupe-Blanco River Authority. To reach the park from Seguin, drive west on US 90A about 0.5 mile from the intersection with SH 46; then drive south on Lake View 1 mile to the park. Lake Placid, a reservoir on the Guadalupe River, adjoins the park. Extensive riparian woodlands, marshlands, the river below, and the lake above the dam provide a variety of habitats. Campsites are provided. The park is named for John Ireland, Texas governor from 1883 to 1887.

Hays County

CITY PARK, maintained and operated by the San Marcos Parks and Recreation Department, is located on C. M. Allen Parkway between University Drive (Loop 82) and Hopkins Street (RR12) in downtown San Marcos. The San Marcos River bisects the park, which extends downstream from Spring Lake, the river's headwaters. Activities include camping, picnicking, and swimming; playgrounds and restrooms are provided. The park offers ready access to the fast-flowing, clear waters of the San Marcos River, one of the most scenic places in South Central Texas. The upper reaches of the river, including Spring Lake, are home to rare and endangered salamanders, fish, an endangered freshwater shrimp, and Texas wildrice, *Zizania texana,* an endangered plant. To observe wildlife, the best time to visit this busy park is very early in the morning before the crowds arrive.

WIMBERLEY, a small community on RR 12 about 15 miles northwest of San Marcos, has become a mecca for visitors seeking crafts and antiques on weekends. Located in a beautiful portion of the Hill Country on Cypress Creek, it also is a favorable birding locality. One location is the old bridge just east of RR 12 where the road crosses the Blanco River about 1 mile south of town. Park at either the north or south end of the old road leading to the bridge. The river can be searched from the old bridge for Summer Tanager, Yellow-throated and Red-eyed vireos in summer, Green Kingfisher, and spring and fall migrants. North of the town, the riparian area along Cypress Creek can be good for the same species as well as land birds in the tall trees adjoining the creek. Scarlet Tanager in migration and a wandering Groove-billed Ani have been found along the creek. On at least two occasions in the past, Green Violet-Ear, a large Mexican hummingbird, has visited the Wimberley area.

Kendall County

BOERNE CITY LAKE is reached by driving north from Boerne on IH 10 to Exit 573 (Boerne, US 87 N Business). From Exit 573, drive northwest on the west access road approximately 0.8 mile to Boerne City Lake Road. The lake was formed for flood control and to provide water for the City of Boerne. Along the entrance road, watch for resident land birds and wintering sparrows. Many waterfowl are found on the lake in winter and during spring and fall migration. A walk along the creek is also excellent for locating land birds including Lesser Goldfinch. Birds recorded in a couple of hours in November include Pied-billed Grebe, Double-crested Cormorant, Gadwall, American Wigeon, Redhead, Lesser Scaup, Bufflehead, Ruddy Duck, dozens of American Coots, and a Solitary Vireo in the live oaks. There are no facilities at the lake.

CITY PARK, 150 acres, owned and maintained by the City of Boerne, is at the eastern edge of the city adjacent to and south of SH 46 on Cibolo

Creek. The north portion of the park has soccer and baseball fields, a swimming pool, an agricultural museum, picnic areas, and restrooms, with the south 70-plus acres set aside as the Cibolo Wilderness Trail whose purpose is "to preserve a section of land that will remain undeveloped and in its natural state so that people from the community and abroad can sample the natural country wildlife habitat." There is a marsh with boardwalk, grasslands, and huge baldcypress trees along the creek and upland woodlands. Resident birds include Red-shouldered Hawk, Golden-fronted and Ladder-backed woodpeckers, Eastern Phoebe, Carolina Chickadee, Tufted Titmouse, Carolina Wren, and House Finch. Purple Finch has been recorded in winter along with numerous sparrows. On a fall visit, one of the authors recorded thirty-two bird species in an hour or so including Common Snipe, Song and Lincoln's sparrows at the marsh, and Golden-fronted Woodpecker, Yellow-breasted Sapsucker, Northern Flicker, Eastern Phoebe, Winter Wren, Golden-crowned Kinglet, Hermit Thrush, and Rufous-sided Towhee on the trail which follows the creek. *A Birder's Checklist of the Boerne Area* is available from the Boerne Chamber of Commerce, 1209 South Main St., #1, Boerne, TX 78006, (210) 249-9373.

OLD TUNNEL WILDLIFE MANAGEMENT AREA, 5-plus acres, is operated by the Texas Parks and Wildlife Department. At the present time limited tours are conducted daily when bats are present; a more comprehensive tour starts one hour before sunset. A Texas Conservation Passport is required for the comprehensive tour. Call park headquarters (512) 389-4800 or (210) 896-2500 for current entry policy. To reach the site, drive east from Comfort on RR 473 approximately 4.5 miles to a road known locally as Old No. 9, then north about 9 miles. There is no road sign indicating Old No. 9, but the turn is where RR 473 turns sharply to the right. The area is best known for its railroad history and the large number of bats that summer in the tunnel. Most are Brazilian free-tailed bats; however, cave myotis have been recorded, and continuing research will likely find additional species. The bats arrive in late April and fly south in late October. Adjacent to the park site is a canyon with thermals which favor soaring hawks including Golden Eagle in winter. Other hawks recorded are Red-tailed, Red-shouldered, and Cooper's, which not only like the thermals but find ample feeding opportunities as the bats leave and enter the tunnel.

Lee and Burleson Counties

LAKE SOMERVILLE STATE PARK contains 5,200 acres in three units along the western side of Lake Somerville. Birch Creek Unit, 640 acres,

Route 1, Box 499, Somerville, TX 77879, (409) 535-7763, is on the north side of the lake; Nails Creek Unit, 300 acres, Route 1, Box 61C, Ledbetter, TX 78946, (409) 289-2392, on the south side; and the Trailway's Unit, 4,260 acres, connects the units around the western end of the lake. To reach the Birch Creek Unit, drive west from Lyons on FM 60 about 12 miles west to Park Road 57, which leads to the entrance. For the Nails Creek Unit, drive east on US 290 from Giddings about 7 miles to FM 180, then north 15 miles to the park.

The park is within the Post Oak Savannah vegetation area of east-central Texas. Numerous habitats occur within the park. Aquatic, wetland, and/or floodplain habitats include (1) open water; (2) shallow marshy flats; (3) mudflats during low-water periods; (4) saline grassy flats; (5) riparian woodlands along the creeks; and (6) an extensive cleared pastureland on the floodplain. Upland habitats in the park include (1) oak-hickory woodlands; (2) little bluestem dominated grasslands; and (3) yaupon thickets.

Nesting birds are more or less the common species of the area; however, spring and fall migrants and winter residents bring the bird list for the lake to 270 species. Migrants include seven vireo species, eighteen hawks, twenty-eight shorebirds, and twenty-eight warblers. Winter species include a large population of American White Pelican and Double-crested Cormorant, seventeen sparrow species along with twenty-seven species of waterfowl. Neotropic Cormorant and Bald Eagle are often present as well. Late summer is the prime time for large numbers of herons and egrets with eleven species recorded, along with Roseate Spoonbill, Wood Stork, and Anhinga.

Activities include camping, picnicking, swimming (no lifeguard), fishing, and boating. There are also playgrounds and hiking, bicycling, and horseback riding trails.

LAKE SOMERVILLE, 11,460 surface acres, is a U.S. Army Corps of Engineers impoundment on Yegua Creek, a major tributary of the Brazos River. In addition to the state parks just discussed, the corps has several parks on the lake as well. Big Creek, Overlook, Rocky Creek, and Yegua Creek are open all year, offering campsites, boat ramps, picnic areas, and sanitary facilities. In general, these parks are highly developed; however, some good birding opportunities are available along the fringes.

Llano County

ENCHANTED ROCK STATE NATURAL AREA, 1,643 acres, is located 18 miles north from Fredericksburg on RR 965 or 22 miles south from Llano via SH 16 for 14 miles; then west on RR 965 for 8 miles. The extreme southern section of the park is in Gillespie County. Facilities include about 6 miles of trails for hiking and backpacking, an area for tent camping, restrooms with showers, primitive campsites (no water or facilities), picnic tables, and a group picnic area. There are programs for nature study. The natural area is a mecca for rock climbers, with climbs varying from easy to very difficult. The different climbs are described in detail in a guidebook which is available at park headquarters.

Enchanted Rock proper is a well-known geological feature of the Llano Uplift area. The pink granite has an estimated age of over one billion years and is among the oldest exposed rocks in North America. It is but one small exposed part of a 100-square-mile batholith. The dome occupies approximately 70 acres and rises 425 feet above the bed of Sandy Creek 0.6 mile below.

The four major plant communities of Enchanted Rock are open oak woodland, mesquite grassland, floodplain, and granite rock community. Rare plants which occur here are the basin bellflower, *Campanula reverchonii,* and rock quillwort, *Isoetes lithophylla,* both endemic to the Llano Uplift, and a tropical fern, *Blechnum occidentale,* not found elsewhere in Texas. White-tailed deer, black-tailed jackrabbits, cottontail rabbits, eastern fox and rock squirrels, armadillos, skunks, lizards, and snakes typical of the Balcones Canyonlands occur here.

Common permanent resident birds include Wild Turkey, Northern Bobwhite, Golden-fronted and Ladder-backed woodpeckers, Eastern Phoebe, and Lark Sparrow. Less common are Inca Dove, Greater Roadrunner, Belted Kingfisher, Scrub Jay, Common Raven, Verdin, Bushtit, Canyon Wren, and Black-throated Sparrow. Nesting species in addition to the above are Yellow-billed Cuckoo, Common Poorwill, Vermilion and Scissor-tailed flycatchers, Rock Wren, Blue-gray Gnatcatcher, Bell's Vireo, Summer Tanager, Painted Bunting, Orchard Oriole, and Lesser Goldfinch. Fifteen sparrow species winter in the park.

Natural history books and other information of interest can be purchased at park headquarters. Trail guides, bird checklist, and other materials are available at no charge. The address for park headquarters is Route 4, Box 170, Fredericksburg, TX 78624, (915) 247-3903.

BLACK ROCK PARK, 10 acres, is maintained and operated by the Lower Colorado River Authority. The park can be reached by driving 16 miles east of Llano or 14 miles west of Burnet on SH 29 to SH 261; then go north for 3 miles. Facilities include campsites, a dump station, a playground, restrooms, picnic areas, and a boat ramp. The park is on the west shore of Lake Buchanan, the highest in the chain of Highland Lakes on the Colorado River.

SHAW ISLAND PARK, 4 acres on the west side of Lake Buchanan, is maintained and operated by the Lower Colorado River Authority. From the intersection of SH 29 and SH 261, drive north 8.4 miles, then right (east) on CR 225 about 5 miles to the park. The park has picnic sites and restrooms. County Road 225 is an excellent road for viewing birds in all seasons. A variety of habitats—wooded areas, grassy fields, and several arms of Lake Buchanan—can be seen from the road.

CEDAR POINT RESOURCE AREA, 400 acres on the west side of Lake Buchanan, is owned and operated by the Lower Colorado River Authority. The area is about 0.5 mile north of Tow on RR 3014. Plans are to have the area preserved in a natural state with a minimum of improvements. The area is predominately woodlands. In winter, look for Bald Eagles perched around and flying over the lake.

Milam County

ALCOA LAKE, 880 acres, owned and operated by the Aluminum Company of America to provide cooling water for power generation, is located 7 miles southwest of Rockdale. From Rockdale, drive west on US 79 5.6 miles to FM 1786, then south approximately 5 miles. The lake is at the end of FM 1786. To reach the northeast side, drive south from Rockdale on FM 487 about 3 miles; then go west on FM 2116 to the lake. Double-crested Cormorant, Pied-billed Grebe, Northern Pintail, Ring-necked Duck, American Coot, Gadwall, Bufflehead, Lesser Scaup, and American Wigeon all winter on this lake, most of which can be viewed from the highways. In migration, look for Blue-winged Teal, American White Pelican, and Common Goldeneye. Land birds can also be found on FM 1786 as well as numerous sandy land wildflowers. The Oklahoma Plum, *Prunus gracilis*, is common on this road.

A very favorable birding road in Milam County is County Road 421. From Thorndale, drive north on FM 486 to San Gabriel. County Road 421 is the road west from San Gabriel. The road parallels the San Gabriel River with riparian woodlands south of the road and farmlands north. The woodlands are excellent for resident and migrating land birds. White-breasted Nuthatch has been recorded along this road.

Travis County

AUSTIN is bisected by the Balcones Escarpment from north to south and by the Colorado River from northwest to southeast and offers a wide variety of habitats to the naturalist. The Austin Parks and Recreation Department oversees over 160 parks with more than 11,800 acres. Included are eight metropolitan parks, ten nature preserves, and twenty-one greenbelts adjacent to about that many creeks. Many eastern and western species are near or at the periphery of their range in the city. In addition, the city is an excellent area for spring migration, which peaks between mid-April and mid-May. As many as twenty warbler species have been recorded at one time as well as Philadelphia and Warbling vireos, Swainson's and Gray-cheeked thrushes, Summer and Scarlet tanagers, Northern (Baltimore and Bullock's) orioles, and Rose-breasted Grosbeak. Spring warbler migration, March to May, offers the highest concentrations of individuals; however, fall migration, August to October, can be rewarding as well, even though the birds do not move in large flocks as sometimes happens in a spring "fall-out."

Any of the numerous wooded creeks in the city are good places to be during migration. The Shoal Creek Hike and Bike Trail, Northwest Park, and the Town Lake Hike and Bike Trail are rewarding birding areas. Waller Creek has the Elizabet Ney Museum, Eastwoods Park, and Waterloo Park. Blunn Creek Wilderness Area between St. Edwards Drive and Oltorf Street, Stacy Park between Live Oak Street and Riverside Drive on Blunn Creek, and the Rosewood-Zaragosa Greenbelt on Boggy Creek are other favorable spots. The grounds of the Laguna Gloria Art Museum and Mayfield Park at the west end of 35th Street and the capitol grounds at the intersection of Congress Avenue and 11th Street are particularly good during migration.

ZILKER PARK, 365 acres, is operated by the Austin Parks and Recreation Department and is highly developed but still offers a variety of habitats along Barton Creek and Town Lake. From downtown Austin, drive south on Congress Avenue, turn right (west) on Barton Springs Road, the first street south of the Colorado River, which leads to the park. The central feature of the park is the spring-fed Barton Springs Swimming Pool. Other facilities include the Austin Garden Center, playgrounds, soccer fields, picnic areas, and the Austin Nature Center with a small zoo and an outdoor theatre. The greenbelt, which follows Barton Creek from just above the swimming pool to well past Loop 360, is good in all seasons for seeking Canyon Wren, rock squirrel, and other Edwards Plateau species. Every spring and summer, there is a very large colony of Cliff Swallow under the MoPac (Loop 1) highway bridge over Town Lake at Stratford Drive. Where Barton Creek flows into Town Lake is always good for finding wintering waterfowl. Near the soccer fields, thirteen-lined ground squirrels are always present.

HORNSBY BEND WASTEWATER TREATMENT PLANT is maintained by the City of Austin for sewage treatment. The plant is located on FM 973, east of Austin. Drive east on Martin Luther King, Jr. Boulevard (becomes FM 969), about 8 miles to FM 973; turn right (south) and go 3.3 miles to the entrance. The plant can also be reached from SH 71 by driving north on FM 973 about 1 mile. FM 973 crosses SH 71 about 2 miles east of the intersection of SH 71 and US 183.

For years this location has been the most popular birding location in the Austin area. Entry regulations are subject to change. At the time of writing, birders are welcome during daylight hours. First-time visitors should check at the office for current policy. Southbound shorebird migration starts the first week of July, tapering off about the end of October; northbound begins in March and lasts until mid-June. It is not unusual to record ten to fifteen shorebird species in an hour or so during migration. Water levels and food supply for birds are variable from year to year, but most years there are favorable conditions. Ducks and other waterfowl are usually abundant in autumn, winter, and spring. In summer, Black-necked Stilt, Wood Duck, and Black-bellied Whistling-Duck with young are occasionally seen. The ponds are adjacent to the Colorado River, with extensive riparian woodlands that are frequented in all seasons by a wide variety of passerine birds. Many accidentals and other rarities have been recorded including Glaucous and Sabine's gulls, Ruff, Curlew Sandpiper, Northern Jacana, Glossy and White ibises, and Roseate Spoonbill.

LAKE WALTER E. LONG METROPOLITAN PARK, 3,800 acres, at 6614 Blue Bluff Road, is located at the eastern limit of the city. From Austin, drive east on either US 290 or FM 969. From US 290, drive south on FM 3177 (Decker Lane), then east on Decker Lake Road south of the power plant to the entrance. From FM 969, drive north on FM 3177 to Decker Lake Drive. The 1,269-acre lake provides cooling water for a municipal power plant. Woodlands and grasslands surrounding the lake attract and support a variety of wildlife. Post oak–live oak forests alternate with invaded croplands, marshes, and small impoundments along the lake shore. The drive around the perimeter of the park on Decker Lane (FM 3177), Lindell Road, Blue Bluff Road, Bloor Road, FM 973, and Loyola Drive is excellent for seeing wintering Red-tailed Hawk as well as Vesper, White-crowned, Lincoln's, White-throated, Grasshopper, and Harris' sparrows. Great Horned Owl can be heard from the road at night starting in January. The wooded sections along the drive and in the park are best during migrations. Former farm ponds, visible from the roads, are good for wintering waterfowl. Birds recorded, mostly in migration, in the marshes below the dam include Swamp Sparrow, Sora, Virginia Rail, Common Yellowthroat, and Marsh Wren. Flying over the water during migration are American White Pelican, Franklin's Gull, and Black Tern. Nesting species include Pied-billed Grebe, Orchard and Northern (Bullock's) orioles, Ladder-backed Woodpecker, Eastern Bluebird, and occasionally Least Bittern and Blue Grosbeak. Crested Caracara (all seasons), Double-crested Cormorant, and Common Snipe (winter) are frequently found. A family of bobcats has been observed on at least two occasions here. Hiking, picnicking, fishing, and boating are permitted. There are restrooms available. An entrance fee is charged.

TOWN LAKE METROPOLITAN PARK, 534 acres, is approximately 7 miles long and is located on the Colorado River in downtown Austin. The lake provides cooling water for power plants. There are marshy areas, grasslands, and woodlands. Waterfowl are present in large numbers in winter all along the lake from Red Bud Isle near Tom Miller Dam to Longhorn Dam on Pleasant Valley Road. Where Barton, Shoal, and Waller creeks enter the lake and near the Holly Street Power Plant are locations usually favorable for birding. Wood Duck nest between Barton Creek and Tom Miller Dam. Red Bud Isle near Tom Miller Dam can be a productive spot for locating migrants. In spring and summer, Yellow-crowned Night-Heron are always present. Monk Parakeet are well established at the ball fields behind the Austin Parks and Recreation Department offices near Lamar Boulevard. The extensive hike and bike trails, which are adjacent to most of the shoreline, are also excellent places to view the birds on the lake. Rare winter visitors include Common Loon, White-winged Scoter, and Oldsquaw. Ringed Kingfisher has been recorded nearly every other year in the recent past.

EMMA LONG METROPOLITAN PARK, or City Park, 1,147 acres, maintained and operated by the Austin Parks and Recreation Department, is located on Lake Austin 6 miles west of Austin on RR 2222. The entrance is at the end of City Park Road, which is off RR 2222 a short distance north of Loop 360. Lake Austin is the original impoundment on the Colorado River and is now part of the Highland Lakes chain upstream along with Town Lake downstream in downtown Austin. The original Austin Dam, as it was then called, was completed in 1900, and at the time, it was the largest masonry structure of its kind in the world; the reservoir it impounded was called Lake McDonald, which became the scene of international regattas and much public attention. But in the year of its completion, the Austin Dam collapsed during a flood, resulting in deaths and considerable property loss. Portions of the dam can still be seen at Red Bud Isle in Austin. In the intervening years, the dam was repeatedly rebuilt and subsequently destroyed until the present facility, Tom Miller Dam, was completed in 1935. At Emma Long Metropolitan Park, camping and picnicking sites, a group facility, restrooms, an enclosed swimming area, lighted fishing piers, and two boat ramps are provided. This large municipal park is heavily wooded except along the waterfront, where recreational facilities are maintained. Golden-cheeked Warblers nest along Turkey Creek, the only stream on City Park Road.

Look for waterfowl on the lake and sparrows in the uplands in winter. There are entrance and camping fees.

MARY QUINLAN PARK, 58 acres, and SELMA HUGHES PARK, 5 acres, are on Lake Austin at the end of Quinlan Park Road, which is south of RR 620 and about 2 miles east of Mansfield Dam. Most resident land birds can be found at one or both of these parks. Wild Turkey can sometimes be found in early morning and at dusk. In spring, listen for Common Poorwill and Chuck-will's-widow at night throughout the Highland Lakes area. Picnic areas and restrooms are at both parks, with a boat ramp at Mary Quinlan Park.

WILD BASIN PRESERVE, 227 acres, 1515 South Capital of Texas Highway (Loop 360), P.O. Box 13455, Austin, TX 78711, (512) 327-7622, is owned by Travis County but managed and operated by the Committee for Wild Basin Wilderness, Inc. The entrance is on Loop 360 1.5 miles north of Bee Caves Road (RR 2244) or 3.2 miles south of the bridge on Lake Austin.

There are hiking trails and an interpretive center where educational programs are offered for school children, teachers, volunteers, and the general public interested in learning about the natural history of the Hill Country. One of the objectives is to keep the 227 acres in as undisturbed a state as possible; the programs offered are consistent with this objective. Regular programs include stargazing, bird walks, the Wild Basin walk (an overview of the preserve), moonlight walks, nature sketching, and education on native plants.

Permanent resident bird species include Ladder-backed Woodpecker, Eastern Meadowlark, Bewick's and Carolina wrens, Carolina Chickadee, Tufted Titmouse, Scrub and Blue jays, and Rufous-crowned, Field, and Chipping sparrows. In addition to the above, Golden-cheeked Warbler, Black-capped and White-eyed vireos, Painted Bunting, Great Crested Flycatcher, and Common Nighthawk can be found in the preserve in summer. In winter, be on the watch for Ruby-crowned Kinglet, Dark-eyed Junco, and American Goldfinch.

MCKINNEY FALLS STATE PARK, 726 acres, 7102 Scenic Loop, Austin, TX 78744, (512) 234-1643, is between IH 35 and US 183 at the south edge of Austin. It can be reached by driving east on William Cannon Drive to Scenic Loop, or from US 183 by driving west on Scenic Loop.

The park is located in a transition area between the Edwards Plateau to the west and the Blackland Prairie to the east; however, the park landscape is mostly characteristic of the Edwards Plateau. Local physiography has evolved largely as the result of volcanic activity at Pilot Knob, just east of the park, during the Late Cretaceous Period, as well as from the subsequent erosional and depositional events associated with Onion and Williamson creeks and their ancient counterparts.

The park bird checklist lists 224 species that have been recorded. Most of the bird habitats of the park can be visited by walking the 3.8 mile hike and bike trail. As the trail goes south from Smith Visitor Center, it wanders through riparian woodlands along Onion Creek, an area where Red-bellied Woodpecker, Eastern Phoebe, Carolina Chickadee, Tufted Titmouse, and Carolina Wren are found year-round. In winter, Yellow-bellied Sapsucker, Brown Creeper, Brown Thrasher, Hermit Thrush, Golden-crowned and Ruby-crowned kinglets, Cedar Waxwing, Solitary Vireo, Yellow-rumped Warbler, and Harris', Lincoln, and White-throated sparrows are commonly found in this riparian area. Nearly every winter, American Woodcock and Winter Wren are found where the trail nears the southern park boundary, before the trail climbs the bluff. During spring migration, many passerines can be found along this section of the trail. This dense riparian area is an excellent location for vocalizing *Empidonax* flycatchers flying north in May and often in August moving south.

Above the bluff, the hike and bike trail winds through woodlands and mesquite-invaded fields, areas where Yellow-billed Cuckoo and Painted and Indigo buntings are common summer residents. In winter, many species of sparrows are often abundant in these upland areas. Greater Roadrunner are permanent residents in the open areas along this part of the trail and in the campgrounds.

Eastern Screech-Owl and Blue Jay nest in the large campground trees. Canyon Wren are permanent residents along Onion Creek, north of the Smith Visitor Center. Wood Duck are found on Onion Creek, and in winter, other waterfowl are sometimes present. During spring and fall migration, wading birds and shorebirds often frequent the marshy areas at the confluence of Williamson and Onion creeks above McKinney Falls. This area also seems to attract the unexpected wanderers—an immature Reddish Egret and a Groove-billed Ani have been recorded at this spot.

The low hills approximately 1.7 miles southeast of the park are the remains of Pilot Knob, an extinct volcano which erupted approximately 80 million years ago when the area was covered by a shallow sea. The rock formations at Upper and Lower (McKinney) Falls in the park consist of limestones deposited on ancient beaches surrounding the former volcanic island. Pilot Knob is one of nine such eruptions in southern Travis County.

The Smith Visitor Center has exhibits (including the story of Pilot Knob), slide shows, and interpretive information; other park features are campgrounds with hookups, restrooms with hot showers, picnic areas and a group section with shelters and dining room.

PACE BEND PARK, 1,520 acres, owned by Lower Colorado River Authority and operated by Travis County, is located on a peninsula of Lake

Travis at the eastern end of RR 2322. RR 2322 is in northwest Travis County off SH 71 just south of the Pedernales River. The park is mostly an undeveloped wooded upland with camping and picnicking areas and restrooms adjacent to the lake. Gentle slopes on the eastern side provide broad areas for swimming and boating activities. With over 9 miles of lakefront, Pace Bend is a popular and attractive recreation area.

The center of the park, approximately 1 mile wide by 2 miles long, serves as a natural wildlife preserve where no vehicular access is permitted. There is abundant cover for white-tailed deer, raccoon, opossum, eastern cottontail and black-tailed jackrabbit. The limestone cliffs along its western edge are the best areas for Canyon Wren calling in spring and summer. Other Edwards Plateau bird species which have been recorded include Golden-fronted Woodpecker, Ash-throated Flycatcher, Scrub Jay, Verdin, Cactus Wren, Bell's Vireo, Canyon Towhee, Lesser Goldfinch, and Rufous-crowned and Black-throated sparrows.

Facilities provided include picnicking areas, campsites, with and without hookups, boat launch ramps, and restrooms. There is an entrance fee.

MANSFIELD DAM PARK, 65 acres, is owned by the Lower Colorado River Authority and operated by Travis County. The park is just west of Mansfield Dam on RR 620, 6 miles west of RR 2222. Camping and picnicking sites, restrooms, and a boat ramp are provided. There is an entrance and camping fee.

WEBBERVILLE PARK, 135 acres, is operated by the Travis County Parks Department and is located on the Colorado River about 4 miles east of the community of Webberville on FM 969, near the Bastrop county line. Facilities provided are restrooms, playgrounds, picnicking areas, and a boat ramp. With numerous large pecan trees as well as a woody section along the river, birds which are usually present are Red-shouldered Hawk, Eastern Bluebird, and Red-bellied and Downy woodpeckers as well as most permanent resident perching birds. Summer residents include Eastern Kingbird and Red-eyed and Yellow-throated vireos. Ducks, osprey, herons, and egrets are sometimes found along the river. Rarities recorded include Groove-billed Ani and Yellow-green Vireo. This is a very good spring and fall migration location.

HAMILTON POOL PARK, 232 acres, operated by the Travis County Parks Department is in northwest Travis County. From Austin, drive north on SH 71 past the village of Bee Caves to RM 3238, then about 13 miles to the park. The park offers swimming, hiking, nature study, and picnicking. There are restrooms available. Currently, the park is being preserved and restored to a natural condition—with park activities compatible with this goal. Most visitors are attracted to the natural swimming pool formed when the dome of an underground river collapsed thousands of years ago. The Pedernales River forms the western boundary of the park. The pool itself is below a 65-foot waterfall on Hamilton Creek and is surrounded by a unique grotto. A variety of plants and animals are found in the grotto and along the creek between the pool and the river. Summer residents include Acadian Flycatcher, Cliff Swallows, Yellow-throated, Red-eyed, and White-eyed vireos, Summer Tanager, Yellow-billed Cuckoo, Ash-throated Flycatcher, and Blue Grosbeak. Scrub Jay and Canyon Wren can be found in all seasons. There is an entrance fee. Call (512) 264-2740 for current information on hours of operation, swimming regulations, and other information.

Williamson County

GRANGER LAKE, 4,400 acres, a U.S. Army Corps of Engineers impoundment on the San Gabriel River, is located about 4 miles east of SH 95 between Taylor and Granger. From SH 95, drive east on FM 971 to reach Friendship Park on the north shore, or take FM 1331 to reach Taylor and/ or Wilson H. Fox parks on the south shore. Take County Road 346 east from SH 95 to reach Willis Creek Park. In addition to the parks, there are four wildlife management areas where hunting is allowed in season. Hiking along the San Gabriel River and/or Willis Creek in the wildlife management areas will usually be very productive for recording land birds. Facilities are available for boat launching, picnicking, swimming, camping, and fishing.

Birding is best in fall, winter, and spring when Double-crested Cormorants in large numbers, American White Pelicans in good numbers, Ring-billed Gulls, Forster's Terns, Ospreys, and several waterfowl species are present. Hawks seem to prefer the Pecan Grove Wildlife Management Area below the dam in winter where Red-tailed, Ferruginous and Rough-legged hawks and Northern Harrier are often present. Bald Eagle and Harris' Hawk are rare visitors. One winter a Little Gull was recorded flying over the lake near the dam. The brushy areas in the Texas Parks and Wildlife management areas are excellent for wintering sparrows, with sixteen species found. Nesting birds include Wood Duck, Eastern Screech-Owl, and Barn, Great Horned and Barred owls. Horned Lark, Mountain Plover, and Chestnut-collared, McCown's, and Lapland longspurs can sometimes be found in winter in the fields west of the lake, both east and west of SH 95.

LAKE GEORGETOWN, 1,310 surface acres, a U.S. Army Corps of Engineers lake, is on the North San Gabriel River west of Georgetown. To reach the lake, drive west of Georgetown 3.5 miles on FM 2338, then south to the dam. In March, April, and May, Golden-cheeked Warblers nest in Cedar Breaks Park and can usually be heard and seen from the Good Water Trail. The trail winds through 16 miles of the Texas countryside and features lakeside recreation and camping. A hiking guide is available at headquarters. Rock Wren have nested in the riprap below the dam. To reach this area from Georgetown, drive west on FM 2338 1.3 miles, then south on Bootys Road to the dam. County Road 258 at the extreme western end of the lake is an excellent birding road in winter. There are three developed parks along the shoreline offering boat ramps and featuring camping, picnicking, swimming, and fishing.

Maps

4. Bastrop County

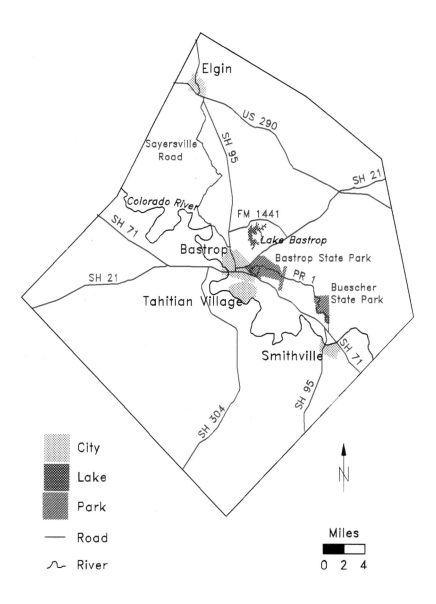

Elgin

US 290

SH 95

Sayersville
Road

SH 21

Colorado River

FM 1441

SH 71

Lake Bastrop

Bastrop

Bastrop State Park

SH 21

PR 1

Buescher
State Park

Tahitian Village

Smithville

SH 71

SH 95

SH 304

City

Lake

Park

—— Road

∿ River

N

Miles

0 2 4

5. Bell County

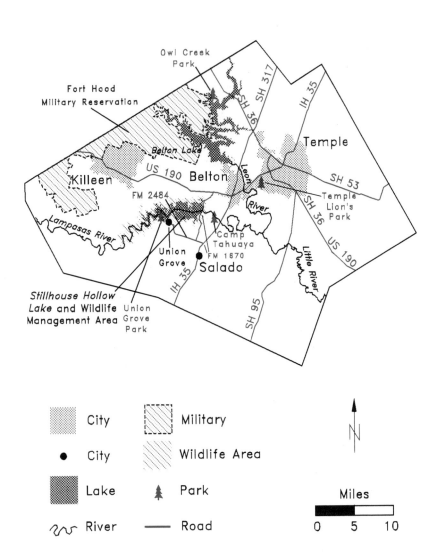

City   Military

City   Wildlife Area

Lake   Park

River   Road

N

Miles

0   5   10

6. Bexar County

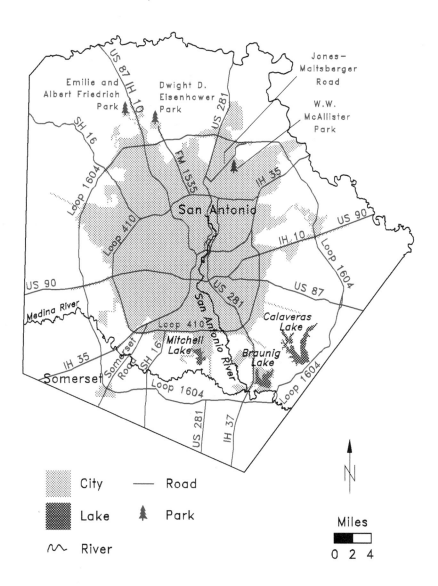

Jones–
Maltsberger
Road

Emilie and
Albert Friedrich
Park

Dwight D.
Eisenhower
Park

W.W.
McAllister
Park

US 87 IH 10

SH 16

US 281

FM 1535

IH 35

Loop 1604

Loop 410

San Antonio

US 90

IH 10

Loop 1604

US 90

US 87

Medina River

San Antonio River

US 281

Loop 410

Calaveras
Lake

IH 35

Somerset Road

SH 16

Mitchell
Lake

Braunig
Lake

Loop 1604

Somerset

Loop 1604

US 281

IH 37

City — Road

Lake ♠ Park

River

N

Miles
0 2 4

7. San Antonio Detail

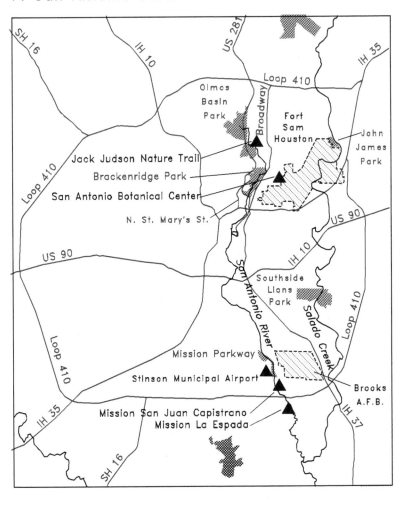

Legend:

- Lake
- Military
- ▲ Other
- ∿ River
- Park
- — Road

N ↑

Miles
0 1 2

8. Blanco County

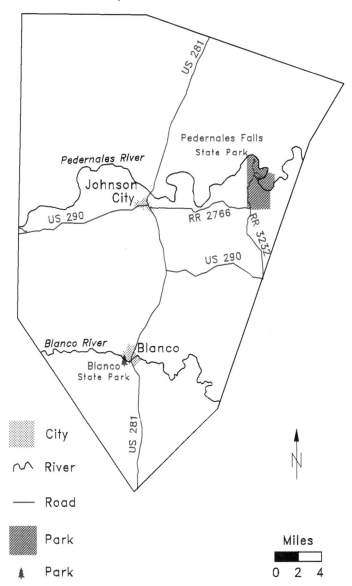

US 281

Pedernales Falls
State Park

Pedernales River

Johnson
City

US 290

RR 2766

RR 3232

US 290

Blanco River

Blanco

Blanco
State Park

US 281

N

City

River

Road

Park

Park

Miles

0 2 4

9. Burnet County

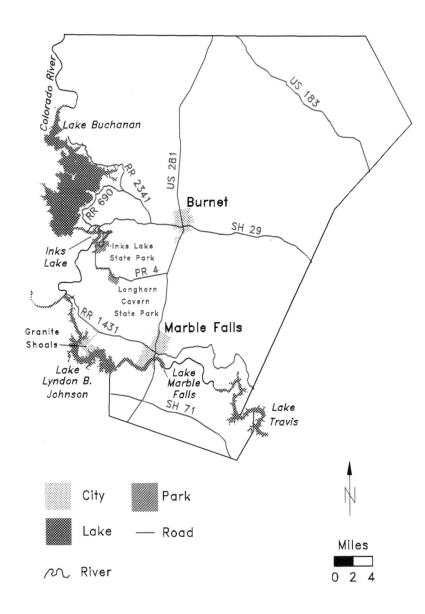

Colorado River

Lake Buchanan

US 183

RR 2341

RR 690

US 281

Burnet

SH 29

Inks
Lake

·Inks Lake
State Park

PR 4

Longhorn
Cavern
State Park

RR 1431

Marble Falls

Granite
Shoals

Lake
Lyndon B.
Johnson

Lake
Marble
Falls

SH 71

Lake
Travis

City   Park

Lake   — Road

River

N

Miles
0 2 4

10. Caldwell County

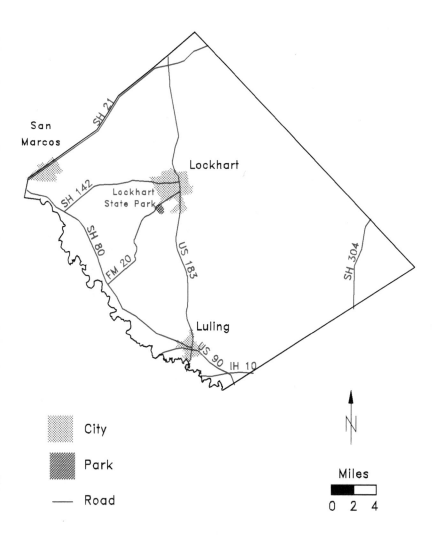

San Marcos

SH 21

Lockhart

SH 142

Lockhart State Park

SH 80

FM 20

US 183

SH 304

Luling

US 90   IH 10

City

Park

— Road

N

Miles

0   2   4

11. Comal County

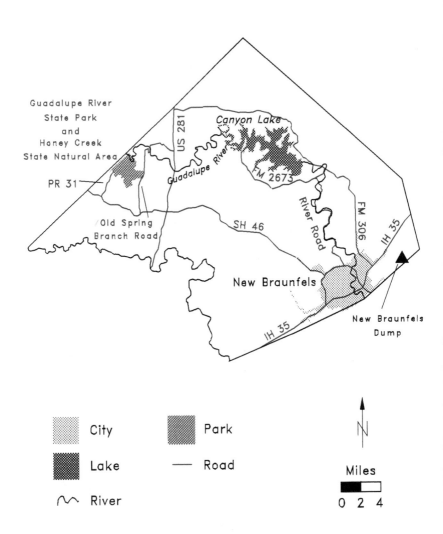

Guadalupe River
State Park
and
Honey Creek
State Natural Area

PR 31

US 281

Canyon Lake

Guadalupe River

FM 2673

River Road

FM 306

IH 35

Old Spring
Branch Road

SH 46

New Braunfels

IH 35

New Braunfels
Dump

City   Park

Lake   — Road

River

N

Miles
0 2 4

12. Canyon Lake

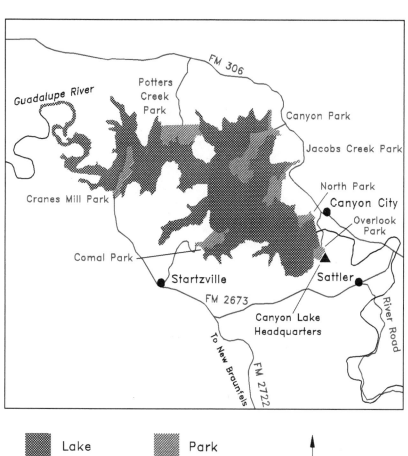

▨ Lake	▨ Park	↑ N
● City	— Road	
▲ Headquarters		Miles
ᔕ River		0 1 2

13. Fayette County

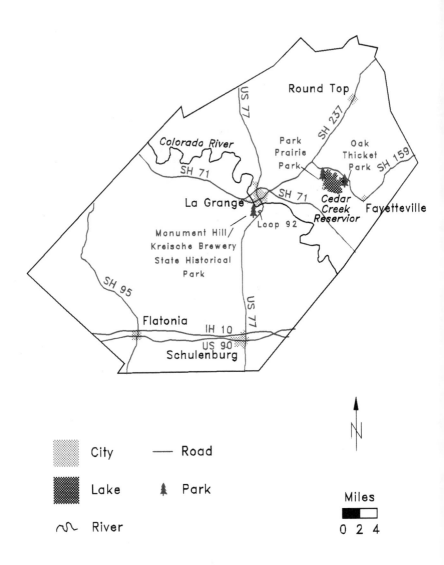

Round Top

US 77

Colorado River

SH 237

Park
Prairie
Park

Oak
Thicket
Park SH 159

SH 71

SH 71

La Grange

Cedar
Creek
Reservior

Fayetteville

Loop 92

Monument Hill/
Kreische Brewery
State Historical
Park

SH 95

US 77

Flatonia

IH 10

US 90
Schulenburg

City   —— Road

Lake   🌲 Park

River

N

Miles
0 2 4

14. Gillespie County

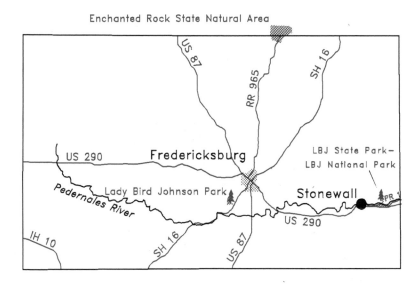

Enchanted Rock State Natural Area

US 87   RR 965   SH 16

US 290   Fredericksburg

LBJ State Park—
LBJ National Park

Pedernales River   Lady Bird Johnson Park   Stonewall   PR

IH 10   SH 16   US 87   US 290

City   Park

City   Park

River   Road

N

Miles
0 2 4

15. Gonzales County

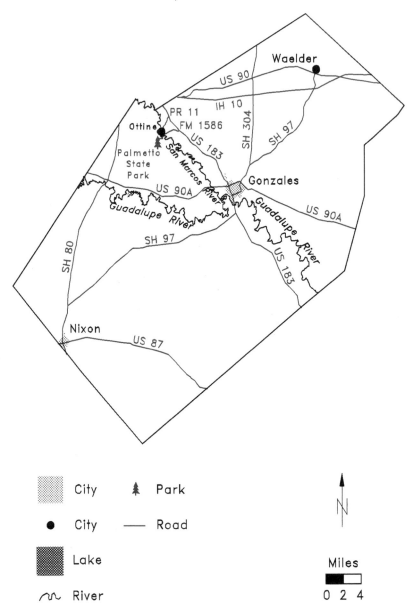

▓ City	♣ Park
● City	— Road
▓ Lake	
∿ River	

N

Miles
▰▱
0 2 4

16. Guadalupe County

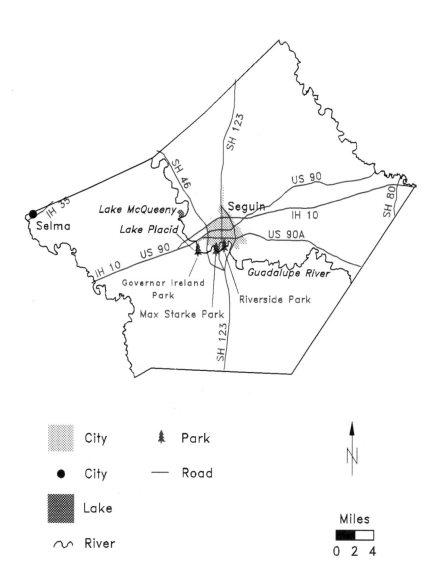

City (shaded)	♣ Park		N ↑
● City	— Road		
Lake (dark)			
～ River			Miles 0 2 4

17. Hays County

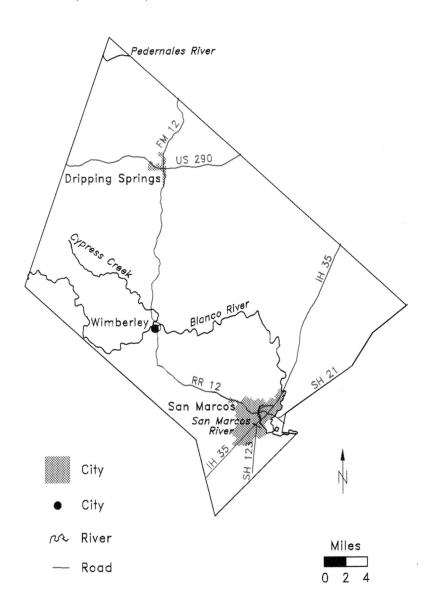

Pedernales River

FM 12

US 290

Dripping Springs

Cypress Creek

IH 35

Wimberley

Blanco River

RR 12

SH 21

San Marcos
San Marcos
River

IH 35

SH 123

City

City

River

Road

N

Miles

0 2 4

18. San Marcos

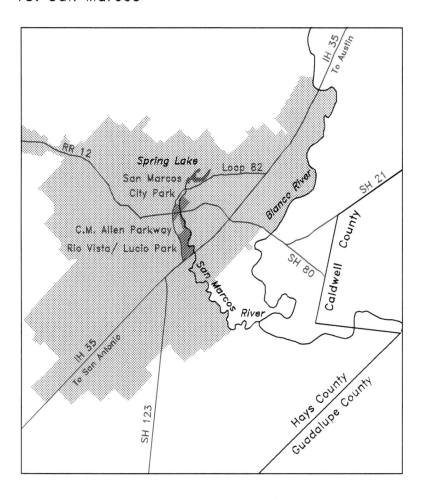

City   Park

Lake   — Road

River

19. Kendall County

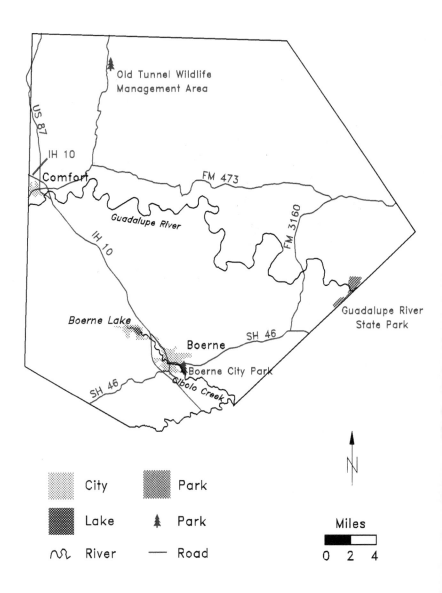

Old Tunnel Wildlife
Management Area

US 87

IH 10

Comfort

FM 473

Guadalupe River

FM 3160

IH 10

Boerne Lake

Guadalupe River
State Park

Boerne

SH 46

Boerne City Park

SH 46

Cibolo Creek

City   Park

Lake   Park

River   — Road

N

Miles

0   2   4

20. Lee and Burleson Counties

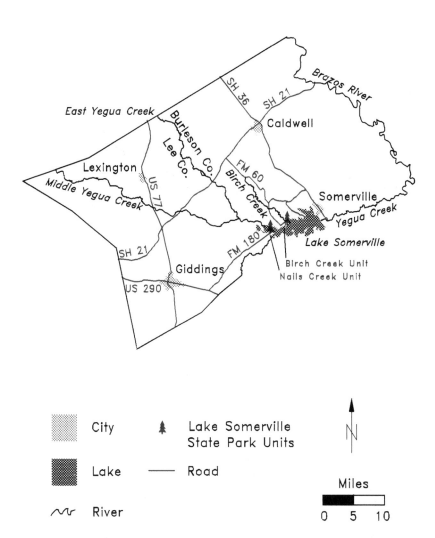

East Yegua Creek

SH 36

SH 21

Brazos River

Caldwell

Burleson Co.

Lee Co.

Lexington

Middle Yegua Creek

US 77

FM 60

Birch Creek

Somerville

Yegua Creek

Lake Somerville

Birch Creek Unit
Nails Creek Unit

SH 21

FM 180

Giddings

US 290

City

Lake

River

Lake Somerville
State Park Units

Road

N

Miles

0   5   10

21. Lake Somerville

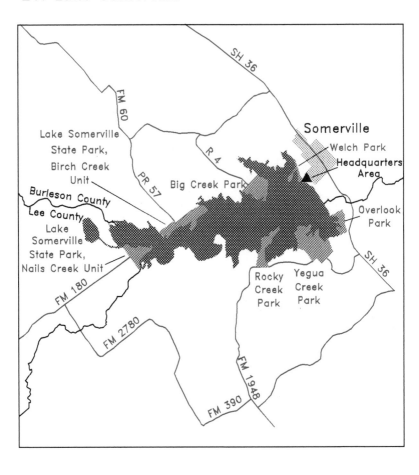

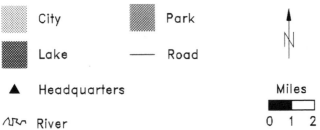

22. Llano County

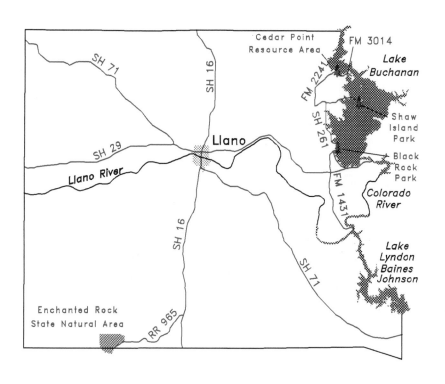

Cedar Point Resource Area

FM 3014

Lake Buchanan

SH 71

SH 16

FM 2241

SH 29

FM 261

SH 261

Llano

Llano River

Shaw Island Park

Black Rock Park

Colorado River

FM 1431

SH 16

Lake Lyndon Baines Johnson

SH 71

Enchanted Rock State Natural Area

RR 965

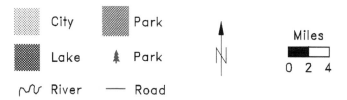

City

Park

Lake

Park

River

Road

Miles

0 2 4

N

23. Milam County

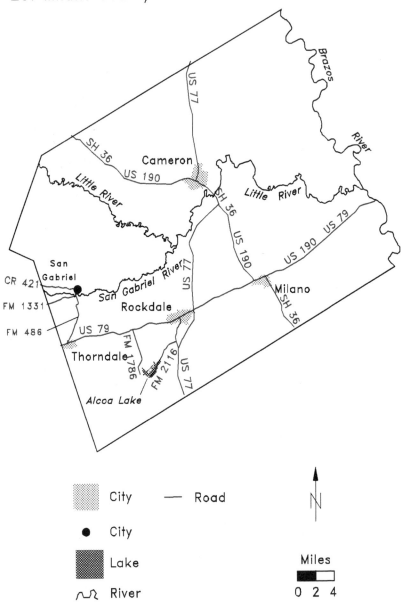

Brazos River

US 77

SH 36

US 190

Cameron

Little River

Little River

SH 36

US 190

US 190 US 79

San Gabriel

CR 421

San Gabriel River

US 77

Milano

FM 1331

SH 36

Rockdale

FM 486

US 79

Thorndale

FM 1786

FM 2116

US 77

Alcoa Lake

City — Road

N

City

Lake

Miles

River

0 2 4

24. Travis County

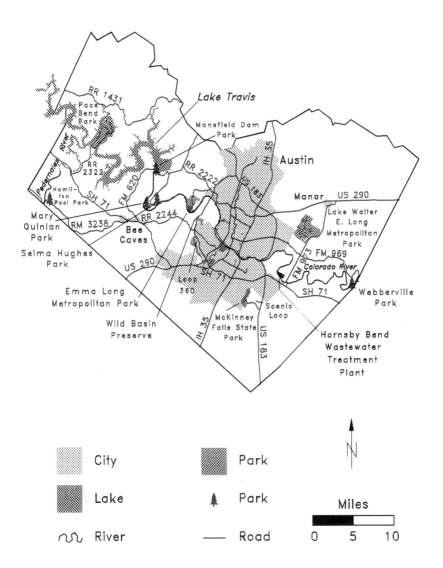

RR 1431
Pace Bend Park
Lake Travis
Mansfield Dam Park
Pedernales River
RR 2322
RR 2222
IH 35
Austin
US 183
Hamil-ton Pool Park
SH 71
FM 620
Manor US 290
Mary Quinlan Park
RM 3238
RR 2244
Bee Caves
Lake Walter E. Long Metropolitan Park
Selma Hughes Park
FM 973 FM 969
US 290
Colorado River
Emma Long Metropolitan Park
Loop 360
SH 71
FM 973
Webberville Park
Wild Basin Preserve
IH 35
McKinney Falls State Park
Scenic Loop
US 183
Hornsby Bend Wastewater Treatment Plant

City   Park

Lake   Park

River   — Road

N

Miles

0   5   10

25. Austin Detail

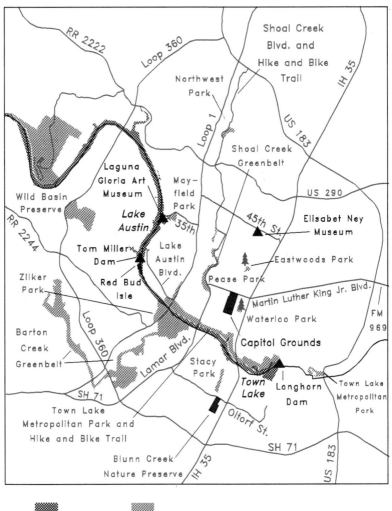

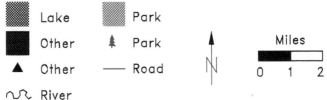

26. Williamson County

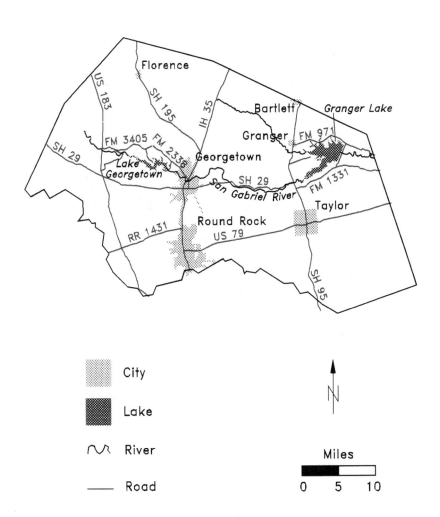

City

Lake

River

Road

Miles

0   5   10

27. Granger Lake

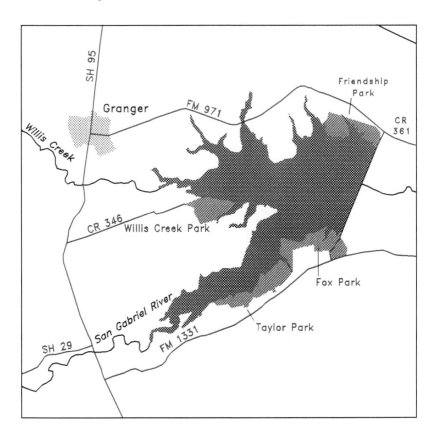

City   Park

Lake   —— Road

▲ Headquarters

∿ River

N

Miles

0   1   2

28. Lake Georgetown

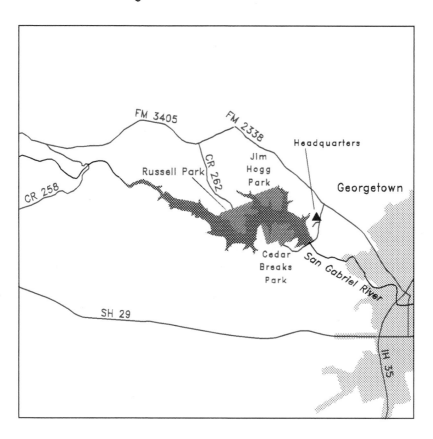

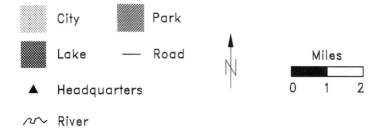

City

Park

Lake

—— Road

▲ Headquarters

〜 River

N

Miles

0   1   2

CHAPTER 3

Birds

EDWARD A. KUTAC

THE BIRD LIST which follows has 445 species; of these, 74 are accidental, 7 hypothetical, and 15 formerly recorded, leaving 349 species which are found with some degree of regularity. This list attempts to include all species that have occurred in the area in historic times as well as the present. The large number of species results, not only from the variety of habitats described in Chapter 1, but also from the fact that the area is wholly within the Central Flyway, one of the four major avifaunal migration routes in North America. Migration begins in early July, when the shorebirds begin to arrive on their way south, and continues until the end of May, when passerines and some shorebirds are still seen going north. The peak of the spring warbler migration, when more than 20 species may be recorded at one spot in one day, is usually the last week in April or the first half of May; however, warbler migration in the spring actually starts during the middle of March and continues to the first of June.

East meets west for several bird species within the area covered by this guide: for example, the Blue Jay is found to the east; to the west, the Scrub Jay rapidly replaces its eastern counterpart. Eastern and Western kingbirds, White-eyed and Bell's vireos, and Red-bellied and Golden-fronted woodpeckers are all at or near their eastern and western limits, respectively. Birds approaching their western breeding limits are Barred Owl, Ruby-throated Hummingbird, Carolina Chickadee and Field Sparrow; western birds near their eastern breeding limits are the Black-chinned Hummingbird, Ash-throated and Vermillion flycatchers, Canyon Wren, Curve-billed Thrasher, and Rufous-crowned, Cassin's, and Black-throated sparrows.

Birding visitors to South Central Texas most often inquire about where to find the Golden-cheeked Warbler, Black-capped Vireo, and to a lesser extent, Green Kingfisher. The Balcones Canyonlands is and historically has been the principal breeding area for the warbler and the vireo, and both have been designated as endangered species by the U.S. Fish and Wildlife Service. Green Kingfishers are found on streams of the Edwards Plateau as well as along the Rio Grande farther south.

At the present time the Golden-cheeked Warbler is found in thirty-one Texas counties, most in the Balcones Canyonlands or in nearby areas with similar geology. They nest only in Texas. Ideal nesting habitat is found in juniper-oak woodlands distributed along steep scarps and canyons. Prime habitat has a diverse mixture of Ashe juniper and hardwood trees, especially Texas, Lacey, or scaleybark (shin) oaks. Arizona walnut, sycamore, escarpment choke-cherry, madrone, coma, cedar elm, and big-tooth maple are often lesser components of this unique habitat. The steep narrow canyons of the Balcones Canyonlands, with tall, deciduous trees along the drainage bottoms and junipers on the slopes, provide an ideal mix of vegetation for this bird. Apparently, the female Golden-cheeked Warbler will not build her nest unless very long strips of mature Ashe juniper bark are available. The oaks probably harbor an important source of food, mainly insect larvae.

Golden-cheeked Warblers are not easily located, and the nests can be very difficult to find. They seem to prefer the upper margins of canyons and ravines where the terrain is roughest. The best time to look for this endemic bird is from the middle of March to the end of May, while the males are singing. Migration south to southern Mexico and Central America begins in June, and they are hard to find in South Central Texas after July 1.

Locations accessible to the public in the area where the warbler may be found include Turkey Creek in Emma Long Metropolitan Park (City Park) in Travis County, Cedar Brakes Park at Lake Georgetown on the San Gabriel River west of Georgetown, Friedrich Park in Bexar County, and Pedernales Falls State Park in Blanco County. The Travis Audubon Society has established a sanctuary for the Golden-cheeked Warbler in Travis County. Regulations for entry change from time to time. Call (512) 483-0952 at least 24 hours in advance for current entry policy. Public locations outside the area covered by this handbook where Golden-cheeked Warblers can be found are Colorado Bend State Park, Dinosaur Valley State Park, Meridian State Park, Garner State Park, Lost Maples State Natural Area, and Kerr Wildlife Management Area.

The historic summer home of the Black-capped Vireo extended from Mexico northward into Kansas. With removal of nesting habitat, the range has been greatly reduced. Recent records in Texas extend from Dallas County to Big Bend National Park, with most on the Edwards Plateau. At the present time, the bird does not regularly nest in any public locations in the area covered by this book except for Friedrich Park in Bexar County and Hippie Hollow Park in Travis County. The Wild Basin, (512) 327-7622, has provided information and tours to find vireos in the past, but it is not known if this practice will continue. Public lands outside the area covered by this book where the vireo has been recorded recently include Big Bend National Park, Colorado Bend State Park in San Saba County, Dinosaur Valley State Park in Somervell County, Meridian State Park in Bosque County, Kickapoo Cavern State Natural Area in Kinney County, South Llano River State Park and Walter Buck Wildlife Management Area in Kimble County, Devil's River State Natural Area in Val Verde County, Hill Country State Natural Area in Bandera and Medina counties, Lost Maples State Natural Area in Bandera County, and Kerr Wildlife Management Area in Kerr County. In the Balcones Canyonlands, the breeding habitat is a subclimax between grasslands and woodlands of mature oak and/or juniper, characterized by clumps of low shrubs growing close to the ground (oaks, sumac, and others), adjoining open grassy areas.

Two projects underway to protect the Golden-cheeked Warbler and the Black-capped Vireo are the Balcones Canyonlands Conservation Plan and the Balcones Canyonlands National Wildlife Refuge. The Balcones Canyonlands Conservation Plan is a cooperative effort of conservationists, developers, landowners, and governmental agencies to develop a regional plan to protect the ecosystem, thereby ensuring protection of endangered and endemic species. The plan attempts to resolve land-use conflicts, to preserve and enhance water quality (especially on Barton Creek and Lake Austin), and to conserve the habitat, not only of these two birds, but also the rare plants and invertebrates of the area. It seeks to protect 29,000 acres through voluntary restrictions and a preserve system. The U.S. Fish and Wildlife Service, as its part of the plan, is acquiring land for the Balcones Canyonlands National Wildlife Refuge in northwest Travis County as well as portions of Burnet and Williamson Counties. At present, 10,000 acres, plus or minus, has been purchased, with plans for the refuge to eventually contain about 40,000 acres. Due to lack of facilities, personnel, and funding, the refuge is not now open to visitors, but it is hoped there will be at least limited access to the general public by 1995. These projects, when implemented, should ensure preservation of significant habitat for a wide range of canyonland animal and plant species, including breeding territory for both the Golden-cheeked Warbler and Black-capped Vireo.

On the Edwards Plateau, Green Kingfishers should be looked for on clear streams. Favorable locations in the past, although not in every year, include the Blanco River west of IH 35 to its source in Kendall County; the Pedernales River below Pedernales Falls State Park; the creeks flowing into the Pedernales River in Hays and Travis counties; in Wimberley, both the Blanco River and Cypress Creek; Honey Creek adjacent to Guadalupe River State Park in Comal County; and Onion Creek in Hays County near Driftwood. Canoeing affords ready access to these areas and offers a high probability of success.

To assist bird seekers wanting to keep abreast of the many unusual birds which show up from time to time in South Central Texas, there are two rare bird alert numbers: in San Antonio—(210) 733-8306; in Austin—(512) 483-0952. All records of Accidental and Hypothetical species should be reported to the Bird Records Committee of the Texas Ornithological Society, in care of Gregory W. Lasley, 305 Loganberry Court, Austin, TX 78745. Give complete details, and if possible, send a photo of the bird and tape of voice.

There are twelve bird checklists for the nineteen counties covered by this guide. All have been used extensively in preparing the list that follows. All checklists for state parks are available at the park or from Texas Parks and Wildlife Department, 4200 Smith School Road, Austin, TX 78744. The checklists are as follows:

AUSTIN

Check-List and Seasonal Distribution: Birds of the Austin, Texas Region, 7th ed., May 1989, is published by Travis Audubon Society. Available from Travis Audubon Society, 5401 Martin Luther King, Jr. Boulevard, Austin, TX 78722. Covers a circle within a 60-mile radius of Austin, Texas.

BASTROP

Birds of Buescher and Bastrop State Parks, Texas Parks and Wildlife Department, November 1988.

BELL

Birds of Bell County, Texas, Twin Lakes Audubon Society and U.S. Army Corps of Engineers, undated. To obtain a copy send addressed, stamped envelope to Twin Lakes Audubon Society, Department of Biology, University of Mary Hardin-Baylor, UMHB Station, Belton, TX 76513. Checklist is free.

BEXAR

Birds of Bexar County, Texas: A Seasonal Checklist, San Antonio Audubon Society, 1986. Available by mail from San Antonio Au-

dubon Society, 3006 Belvoir, San Antonio, TX 78230, for 25 cents
plus addressed, stamped envelope or may be purchased at the San
Antonio Zoo. Envelope must accommodate 4" × 7", 16-page
checklist.

BURNET
Bird Check List of Highland Lakes Birding Society, Burnet, TX,
December 1987. Available from Highland Lakes Birding Association, Burnet County Library, Burnet, TX 78611, for 25 cents plus
an addressed, stamped envelope.

ENCHANTED ROCK
Birds of Enchanted Rock State Natural Area: A Field Checklist,
Texas Parks and Wildlife Department, August 1989.

GUADALUPE RIVER
Birds of Guadalupe River State Park, Texas Parks and Wildlife
Department, April 1984.

LAKE SOMERVILLE
*Birds of Lake Somerville State Recreation Area: A Field Check-
list,* Texas Parks and Wildlife Department, June 1989.

LEE
Bird Checklist—Hugh Brown's Land, Lee County, June 1992.
Available from Hugh Brown, Route 1, Box 291A, Lexington, TX
78947, for 25 cents plus an addressed, stamped envelope.

MCKINNEY FALLS
Birds of McKinney Falls State Park, Texas Parks and Wildlife Department, December 1988.

PALMETTO
Birds of Palmetto State Park: A Field Checklist, Texas Parks and
Wildlife Department, June 1988.

PEDERNALES FALLS
Birds of Pedernales Falls State Park: A Field Checklist, Texas
Parks and Wildlife Department, January 1992.

After each species account on the following pages, the checklists on
which the bird appears are listed in italics; however, many of the records are hypothetical or accidental and therefore, not expected. The individual checklists should be consulted for exact status. Birds on one or
more of the above checklists, not included in the species accounts are
American Black Duck, Barrow's Goldeneye, Chukar, Black Rail, Ringed

Turtle-Dove, Budgerigar, Orange-fronted Parakeet, Phainopepla, Northern Shrike, Gray Vireo, and Bachman's Sparrow. These are not included for lack of documentation or because the species is an exotic not yet established. Recent literature has addressed the apparent recent occurrence of parrot species in Texas, particularly, far south Texas. Red-crowned Parrots have been found nesting in San Marcos, Hays County, in very limited numbers and Green Parakeets may be nesting in Bexar County. These are presumed to be escapees (though this is not certain) and time will tell whether these Mexican species become a permanent part of the South Central Texas avifauna.

The authors are from Austin; therefore, many locations given in the species accounts are near Austin. This should not be taken to mean these birds do not occur just as regularly elsewhere in the area. No effort has been made to show all places a bird has occurred or can occur.

Where no specific location is given, it means the birds are either very easy to find or very difficult.

Some descriptions such as "east of Balcones Escarpment" are meant to describe where birds can usually be found within the area covered by this guide only and not outside the area.

Locations listed are generally those belonging to a governmental agency, such as parks and large lakes and areas observed from public roads. There are many excellent birding spots on private property or property where permission must be obtained for entry, but these are not considered within the province of this guide.

Nomenclature

The names of birds follow the *Check-List of North American Birds,* sixth edition, American Ornithologists' Union, (1983), as amended through the Thirty-Eighth Supplement (August 1991). English names that have been changed in recent years are shown in parentheses.

The birds are listed in phylogenetic order, that is, in the order in which it is believed they evolved, and is the same order that appears in practically all popular field guides and checklists. For each species, the following information is provided: (1) current English name; (2) current scientific name; (3) relative abundance by seasons in the nineteen-county area; (4) habitat(s); (5) selected locations (not intended to be comprehensive); (6) other comments; (7) checklists. The symbol ‡ means the species has nested after 1969, more or less; † means nested before 1970, more or less; * means introduced. See the Appendix for definitions of terms used in the species accounts and Selected References for specific references.

Class AVES: Birds
Subclass NEORNITHES: True Birds
Superorder NEOGNATHAE: Typical Birds
Order GAVIIFORMES: Loons

Family GAVIIDAE: Loons

Red-throated Loon, *Gavia stellata:* Accidental in winter. Perennial
waterways. Calaveras Lake. *Austin, Bexar*
Pacific Loon, *Gavia pacifica:* Accidental in fall and winter. Perennial
waterways, wastewater ponds. Bell, Bexar, and Travis counties.
Austin, Bell, Bexar
Common Loon, *Gavia immer:* Uncommon winter resident; rare in
spring and fall. Perennial waterways, small impoundments. Lake
Buchanan, Lake Somerville. *Austin, Bastrop, Bell, Bexar, Burnet, Lake
Somerville*

Order PODICIPEDIFORMES: Grebes

Family PODICIPEDIDAE: Grebes

Least Grebe, *Tachybaptus dominicus*[+]: Rare, all seasons. Perennial waterways, especially if marshy; wastewater ponds. Burnet, Gonzales, and Travis counties. Has nested in Bexar County. *Austin,
Bexar, Burnet, Palmetto*
Pied-billed Grebe, *Podilymbus podiceps*[+]: Common fall, winter, and
spring resident; uncommon summer resident. Perennial waterways, wastewater ponds, small impoundments. Has nested at
Lake Walter E. Long and in Bexar County. *Austin, Bastrop, Bell,
Bexar, Burnet, Enchanted Rock, Lake Somerville, Lee, McKinney Falls, Pal-
metto, Pedernales Falls*
Horned Grebe, *Podiceps auritus:* Rare fall and winter resident; acciden-
tal in spring and summer. Perennial waterways, wastewater
ponds. Throughout. Lake Buchanan, Town Lake. *Austin, Bastrop,
Bexar, Burnet, Lake Somerville, Palmetto*
Red-necked Grebe, *Podiceps grisegena:* Hypothetical. Bexar County.
Bexar (May 1957, May 1979)
Eared Grebe, *Podiceps nigricollis*[†]: Uncommon fall, winter, and spring
resident; rare in summer. Perennial waterways, wastewater ponds.
Throughout. Highland Lakes. Has nested in Bexar County.
Austin, Bastrop, Bell, Bexar, Burnet, Lake Somerville, Palmetto, Pedernales Falls

Western Grebe, *Aechmophorus occidentalis:* Accidental in spring, fall, and winter. Perennial waterways. Calaveras Lake, Lake Buchanan, Lake Georgetown, Granger Lake.   *Austin, Bexar, Burnet*

Order PROCELLARIIFORMES: Tube-nosed Swimmers

Family HYDROBATIDAE: Storm-Petrels

Band-rumped Storm-Petrel, *Oceanodroma castro:* Accidental in summer. Mitchell Lake.   *Bexar*

Order PELECANIFORMES: Totipalmate Swimmers

Suborder PELECANI: Boobies, Pelicans, Cormorants, and Darters

Family PELECANIDAE: Pelicans

American White Pelican (White Pelican), *Pelecanus erythrorhynchos:* Common spring and fall migrant in large flocks; rare in winter. Perennial waterways, wastewater ponds, small impoundments. Throughout. Some years a few winter at Granger Lake.   *Austin, Bastrop, Bell, Bexar, Burnet, Lake Somerville, Lee, McKinney Falls, Palmetto*

Brown Pelican, *Pelecanus occidentalis:* Accidental, all seasons. Probably blown in by gulf storms. Bexar and Travis counties.   *Austin, Bexar*

Family PHALACROCORACIDAE: Cormorants

Double-crested Cormorant, *Phalacrocorax auritus:* Abundant fall, winter, and spring resident; rare in summer. Perennial waterways, wastewater ponds, small impoundments. All area lakes. No nest records.   *Austin, Bastrop, Bell, Bexar, Burnet, Guadalupe River, Lake Somerville, Lee, McKinney Falls, Palmetto*

Neotropic Cormorant (Olivaceous Cormorant), *Phalacrocorax olivaceus*[†]: Rare spring, summer, and fall resident; occasional in winter. Perennial waterways, small impoundments. Bell, Bexar, Burnet, Gonzales and Lee counties. May nest.   *Austin, Bell, Bexar, Burnet, Lake Somerville, Palmetto*

Family ANHINGIDAE: Darters

Anhinga, *Anhinga anhinga*[†]: Uncommon spring and fall visitor; rare summer visitor. Perennial waterways. Mostly east of Balcones

Escarpment. *Austin, Bastrop, Bexar, Burnet, Lake Somerville, Lee, Palmetto, Pedernales Falls*

Suborder FREGATAE: Frigatebirds

Family FREGATIDAE: Frigatebirds

Magnificent Frigatebird, *Fregata magnificens:* Accidental in summer and fall. Probably blown in by gulf storms. Bexar and Travis counties. *Austin, Bexar*

Order CICONIIFORMES: Herons, Ibises, Storks, and Allies

Suborder ARDEAE: Bitterns, Herons, and Allies

Family ARDEIDAE: Bitterns and Herons

Tribe BOTAURINI: Bitterns

American Bittern, *Botaurus lentiginosus:* Rare spring and fall migrant; accidental in winter. Marshes, wastewater ponds, perennial waterways. Throughout. *Austin, Bexar, Burnet, Lake Somerville, Lee, Palmetto*
Least Bittern, *Ixobrychus exilis*‡: Rare summer resident; rare spring and fall migrant. Marshes. Has nested at Lake Walter E. Long and Bexar County. *Austin, Bexar, Lake Somerville, Palmetto*

Tribe ARDEINI: Typical Herons

Great Blue Heron, *Ardea herodias*‡: Common permanent resident. Intermittent waterways, perennial waterways, small impoundments. Throughout. *Austin, Bastrop, Bell, Bexar, Burnet, Enchanted Rock, Guadalupe River, Lake Somerville, Lee, McKinney Falls, Palmetto, Pedernales Falls*
Great Egret, *Casmerodius albus*‡: Uncommon permanent resident. Perennial waterways, wastewater ponds. Has nested in Cattle Egret rookeries. *Austin, Bastrop, Bell, Bexar, Burnet, Lake Somerville, Lee, McKinney Falls, Palmetto*
Snowy Egret, *Egretta thula:* Uncommon in spring and summer; common in fall; rare in winter. Perennial waterways, wastewater ponds. Throughout. Granger Lake, Shipp Lake. *Austin, Bastrop, Bell, Bexar, Lee, McKinney Falls, Palmetto*
Little Blue Heron, *Egretta caerulea*‡: Uncommon spring and summer resident; common fall migrant; accidental in winter. Perennial waterways, wastewater ponds, small impoundments. Throughout.

Has nested in Cattle Egret rookeries.   *Austin, Bastrop, Bell, Bexar, Burnet, Guadalupe River, Lake Somerville, Lee, McKinney Falls, Palmetto, Pedernales Falls*

Tricolored Heron (Louisiana Heron), *Egretta tricolor:* Uncommon in summer and fall; accidental in spring. Perennial waterways, wastewater ponds. Throughout. Hornsby Bend Ponds, Granger Lake.   *Austin, Bastrop, Bell, Bexar, Lake Somerville, Lee, McKinney Falls, Palmetto*

Reddish Egret, *Egretta rufescens:* Accidental in summer, fall, and winter. Creeks, wastewater ponds. McKinney Falls State Park, Lake Somerville, Mitchell and Braunig lakes.   *Austin, Bexar, Lake Somerville, McKinney Falls*

Cattle Egret, *Bubulcus ibis*‡: Abundant spring, summer, and fall resident; rare in winter. Perennial waterways, range and pastures, small impoundments. Throughout, often seen with grazing cattle. Has nested in Travis and Williamson counties, Round Rock, and Taylor. Immigrant from Africa by way of South America.   *Austin, Bastrop, Bell, Bexar, Burnet, Lake Somerville, Lee, McKinney Falls, Palmetto, Pedernales Falls*

Green-backed Heron (Green Heron), *Butorides striatus*‡: Common spring, summer, and fall resident; rare in winter. Intermittent waterways, wastewater ponds, small impoundments. Throughout.   *Austin, Bastrop, Bell, Bexar, Burnet, Enchanted Rock, Guadalupe River, Lake Somerville, Lee, McKinney Falls, Palmetto, Pedernales Falls*

Tribe NYCTICORACINI: Night-Herons

Black-crowned Night-Heron, *Nycticorax nycticorax*‡: Rare, all seasons. Perennial waterways, wastewater ponds. Mostly east of the Balcones Escarpment. Town Lake. Nests in Bexar County.   *Austin, Bell, Bexar, Lake Somerville, McKinney Falls, Palmetto*

Yellow-crowned Night-Heron, *Nycticorax violaceus*‡: Uncommon spring, summer, and fall resident. Intermittent waterways, marshes, small impoundments. Throughout. Creeks, Town Lake, Brackenridge Park.   *Austin, Bastrop, Bell, Bexar, Burnet, Guadalupe River, Lake Somerville, Lee, McKinney Falls, Palmetto*

Suborder THRESKIORNITHES: Ibises and Spoonbills
Family THRESKIORNITHIDAE: Ibises and Spoonbills
Subfamily THRESKIORNITHINAE: Ibises

White Ibis, *Eudocimus albus:* Rare, all seasons. Wastewater ponds, perennial waterways. Mostly east of Balcones Escarpment.   *Austin, Bexar, Burnet, Lake Somerville, Lee, Palmetto*

Glossy Ibis, *Plegadis falcinellus:* Accidental in spring. Wastewater ponds. Mitchell Lake and Hornsby Bend Ponds.

White-faced Ibis, *Plegadis chihi:* Uncommon spring and fall migrant; rare in summer and winter. Wastewater ponds, perennial waterways. Throughout.   *Austin, Bastrop, Bell, Bexar, Lake Somerville, Lee, Palmetto, Pedernales Falls*

Subfamily PLATALEINAE: Spoonbills

Roseate Spoonbill, *Ajaia ajaja:* Rare spring, summer, and fall visitor. Wastewater ponds, perennial waterways. Mostly east of Balcones Escarpment.   *Austin, Bastrop, Bell, Bexar, Lake Somerville, Lee, Palmetto*

Suborder CICONIAE: Storks

Family CICONIIDAE: Storks

Tribe MYCTERIINI: Wood Storks

Wood Stork, *Mycteria americana:* Accidental in spring and summer; rare fall visitor. Perennial waterways. Mostly east of Balcones Escarpment. Lake Somerville.   *Austin, Bexar, Lake Somerville, Lee, Palmetto*

Order ANSERIFORMES: Screamers, Swans, Geese, and Ducks

Suborder ANSERES: Swans, Geese, and Ducks

Family ANATIDAE: Swans, Geese, and Ducks

Subfamily ANSERINAE: Whistling-Ducks, Swans, and Geese

Tribe DENDROCYGNINI: Whistling-Ducks

Fulvous Whistling-Duck (Fulvous Tree Duck), *Dendrocygna bicolor:* Occasional, all seasons. Perennial waterways, wastewater ponds. Mostly east of Balcones Escarpment. Hornsby Bend Ponds, Lake Somerville, Bexar County.   *Austin, Bexar, Lake Somerville, Lee*

Black-bellied Whistling-Duck (Black-bellied Tree Duck), *Dendrocygna autumnalis*[+]: Uncommon spring, summer, and fall resident; rare in winter. Perennial waterways, wastewater ponds. Reported from Lee and Gonzales counties, has nested in Bexar and Travis counties. Apparently extending range northward.   *Austin, Bexar, Lake Somerville, Lee, McKinney Falls, Palmetto*

Tribe CYGNINI: Swans

Tundra Swan (Whistling Swan), *Cygnus columbianus:* Occasional in winter. Farm ponds. Bell, Bexar, and Hays counties.   *Austin, Bell, Bexar*

Tribe ANSERINI: Geese

Greater White-fronted Goose (White-fronted Goose), *Anser albifrons:* Rare fall and winter visitor; accidental in spring. Wastewater ponds, small impoundments. Mostly east of Balcones Escarpment. Heard overhead during spring and fall migrations.   *Austin, Bastrop, Bell, Bexar, Lake Somerville, Lee, Palmetto*

Snow Goose, *Chen caerulescens:* Rare fall, winter, and spring visitor. Croplands, range and pastures, perennial waterways, wastewater ponds. Throughout. Heard overhead during spring and fall migrations.   *Austin, Bastrop, Bell, Bexar, Burnet, Lake Somerville, Lee, McKinney Falls, Palmetto*

Ross' Goose, *Chen rossii:* Occasional in spring, fall, and winter. Wastewater ponds, perennial waterways. Mostly east of Balcones Escarpment.   *Austin, Bell, Bexar, Burnet, Lake Somerville, Palmetto*

Canada Goose, *Branta canadensis:* Rare fall, winter, and spring visitor. Croplands, range and pastures, small impoundments. Throughout. Heard overhead during spring and fall migrations.   *Austin, Bastrop, Bell, Bexar, Burnet, Lake Somerville, Lee, McKinney Falls, Palmetto*

Subfamily ANATINAE: Ducks

Tribe CAIRININI: Muscovy Ducks and Allies

Wood Duck, *Aix sponsa*[‡]: Uncommon permanent resident. Perennial waterways, riparian woodlands, wastewater ponds, small impoundments. Throughout. Town Lake.   *Austin, Bastrop, Bell, Bexar, Burnet, Guadalupe River, Lake Somerville, Lee, McKinney Falls, Palmetto, Pedernales Falls*

Tribe ANATINI: Dabbling Ducks

Green-winged Teal, *Anas crecca:* Common fall, winter, and spring resident. Intermittent waterways, perennial waterways, wastewater ponds, small impoundments. Throughout.   *Austin, Bastrop, Bell, Bexar, Burnet, Enchanted Rock, Lake Somerville, Lee, McKinney Falls, Palmetto, Pedernales Falls*

Mottled Duck, *Anas fulvigula:* Rare visitor, all seasons. Small impoundments, perennial waterways. Mostly east of Balcones Escarpment. Granger Lake, Shipp Lake, Lake Somerville. *Austin, Bexar, Lake Somerville, Lee*

Mallard, *Anas platyrhynchos*[‡]: Common spring, fall, and winter resident; uncommon summer resident. Perennial waterways, small impoundments. Throughout. Highland Lakes. *Austin, Bastrop, Bell, Bexar, Burnet, Enchanted Rock, Guadalupe River, Lake Somerville, Lee, McKinney Falls, Palmetto, Pedernales Falls*

Northern Pintail (Pintail), *Anas acuta:* Common spring, fall, and winter resident. Intermittent waterways, perennial waterways, wastewater ponds, small impoundments. Throughout. *Austin, Bastrop, Bell, Bexar, Burnet, Enchanted Rock, Lake Somerville, Lee, McKinney Falls, Palmetto, Pedernales Falls*

Blue-winged Teal, *Anas discors*[‡]: Abundant spring and fall migrant. Rare in summer and winter. Perennial waterways, wastewater ponds, small impoundments. Throughout. Has nested in Bexar County. *Austin, Bastrop, Bell, Bexar, Burnet, Enchanted Rock, Lake Somerville, Lee, McKinney Falls, Palmetto, Pedernales Falls*

Cinnamon Teal, *Anas cyanoptera*[‡]: Uncommon spring visitor; rare in fall and winter. Perennial waterways, wastewater ponds, small impoundments. Never more than a few at a time. Throughout. Has nested in Bexar County. *Austin, Bell, Bexar, Burnet, Lake Somerville, McKinney Falls, Palmetto, Pedernales Falls*

Northern Shoveler, *Anas clypeata:* Abundant spring, fall, and winter. Wastewater ponds, small impoundments. Throughout. Hornsby Bend Ponds, Inks Lake Fish Hatchery. Has nested in Bexar County. *Austin, Bastrop, Bell, Bexar, Burnet, Enchanted Rock, Lake Somerville, Lee, McKinney Falls, Palmetto, Pedernales Falls*

Gadwall, *Anas strepera*[‡]: Common spring, fall, and winter; rare in summer. Intermittent waterways, perennial waterways, wastewater ponds, small impoundments. Throughout. Found in more different habitats in winter than any other duck. Has nested at Mitchell Lake. *Austin, Bastrop, Bell, Bexar, Burnet, Enchanted Rock, Guadalupe River, Lake Somerville, Lee, McKinney Falls, Palmetto, Pedernales Falls*

Eurasian Wigeon (European Wigeon), *Anas penelope:* Accidental in spring, fall, and winter. Small impoundments, wastewater ponds. *Austin*

American Wigeon, *Anas americana:* Common spring, fall, and winter resident; rare in summer. Perennial waterways, wastewater ponds, small impoundments. Throughout. Lake Somerville, Inks Lake Fish Hatchery. *Austin, Bastrop, Bell, Bexar, Burnet, Enchanted Rock, Lake Somerville, Lee, McKinney Falls, Palmetto, Pedernales Falls*

Tribe AYTHYINI: Pochards and Allies

Canvasback, *Aythya valisineria:* Uncommon spring, fall, and winter resident. Perennial waterways, wastewater ponds, small impoundments. Throughout.   *Austin, Bastrop, Bell, Bexar, Burnet, Enchanted Rock, Lake Somerville, Palmetto*

Redhead, *Aythya americana:* Uncommon spring, fall, and winter resident. Perennial waterways, wastewater ponds, small impoundments. Throughout. Hornsby Bend Ponds, below Mansfield Dam, Inks Lake Fish Hatchery.   *Austin, Bastrop, Bell, Bexar, Burnet, Lake Somerville, Lee, Palmetto*

Ring-necked Duck, *Aythya collaris:* Uncommon spring, fall, and winter resident; accidental in summer. Perennial waterways, wastewater ponds, small impoundments. Throughout.   *Austin, Bastrop, Bell, Bexar, Burnet, Enchanted Rock, Lake Somerville, Lee, McKinney Falls, Palmetto, Pedernales Falls*

Greater Scaup, *Aythya marila:* Accidental, all seasons. Perennial waterways, wastewater ponds. Throughout. Hornsby Bend Ponds.   *Austin, Bastrop, Bell, Bexar, Burnet, Lake Somerville, McKinney Falls, Palmetto*

Lesser Scaup, *Aythya affinis:* Abundant spring, fall, and winter resident. Perennial waterways, wastewater ponds, small impoundments. Throughout. Town Lake, Inks Lake Fish Hatchery.   *Austin, Bastrop, Bell, Bexar, Burnet, Enchanted Rock, Lake Somerville, Lee, McKinney Falls, Palmetto, Pedernales Falls*

Tribe MERGINI: Eiders, Scoters, Mergansers, and Allies

Oldsquaw, *Clangula hyemalis:* Occasional in spring, fall, and winter. Perennial waterways, wastewater ponds. Town Lake, Inks Lake Fish Hatchery, Bexar County.   *Austin, Bastrop, Bexar*

Black Scoter, *Melanitta nigra:* Formerly recorded. Bexar County (1957).   *Bexar*

Surf Scoter, *Melanitta perspicillata:* Rare fall and winter visitor. Perennial waterways, wastewater ponds, small impoundments. Hornsby Bend Ponds.   *Austin, Bexar*

White-winged Scoter, *Melanitta fusca:* Rare winter visitor. Perennial waterways, small impoundments. Town Lake, Bexar County.   *Austin, Bexar*

Common Goldeneye, *Bucephala clangula:* Uncommon winter resident; occasional in spring and summer. Wastewater ponds, perennial waterways. Mostly east of Balcones Escarpment, Hornsby Bend Ponds.   *Austin, Bastrop, Bell, Bexar, Burnet, Lake Somerville, Palmetto*

Bufflehead, *Bucephala albeola:* Common fall, winter, and spring resident. Perennial waterways, wastewater ponds, small impoundments. Hornsby Bend Ponds, Inks Lake Fish Hatchery. *Austin, Bastrop, Bell, Bexar, Burnet, Lake Somerville, Lee, Palmetto, Pedernales Falls*

Hooded Merganser, *Lophodytes cucullatus:* Uncommon fall and winter resident. Accidental in spring. Perennial waterways, wastewater ponds, small impoundments. Hornsby Bend Ponds, farm ponds. *Austin, Bastrop, Bell, Bexar, Burnet, Lake Somerville, Lee, Palmetto, Pedernales Falls*

Common Merganser, *Mergus merganser:* Occasional in winter. Perennial waterways, wastewater ponds. Bastrop, Bexar, Burnet, and Travis counties. *Austin, Bastrop, Bexar, Burnet*

Red-breasted Merganser, *Mergus serrator:* Uncommon fall and winter resident. Perennial waterways, wastewater ponds. Lake Buchanan, Inks Lake State Park. *Austin, Bastrop, Bell, Bexar, Burnet, Lake Somerville, Palmetto*

Tribe OXYURINI: Stiff-tailed Ducks

Ruddy Duck, *Oxyura jamaicensis*[‡]: Common fall, winter, and spring resident; rare in summer. Perennial waterways, wastewater ponds, small impoundments. Has nested in Bexar County. Hornsby Bend Ponds, Town Lake. *Austin, Bastrop, Bell, Bexar, Burnet, Lake Somerville, Palmetto*

Masked Duck, *Oxyura dominica:* Accidental in spring, fall, and winter. Small impoundments. Probably blown in by gulf storms. Hays and Bexar counties. *Austin, Bexar, Burnet*

Order FALCONIFORMES: Diurnal Birds of Prey

Suborder CATHARTAE: American Vultures

Superfamily CATHARTOIDEA: American Vultures

Family CATHARTIDAE: American Vultures

Black Vulture, *Coragyps atratus*[‡]: Common permanent resident. Wooded uplands. Throughout. Usually seen overhead. *Austin, Bastrop, Bell, Bexar, Burnet, Enchanted Rock, Guadalupe River, Lake Somerville, Lee, McKinney Falls, Palmetto, Pedernales Falls*

Turkey Vulture, *Cathartes aura*[‡]: Abundant permanent resident. Wooded uplands. Throughout. Usually seen soaring overhead. *Austin, Bastrop, Bell, Bexar, Burnet, Enchanted Rock, Guadalupe River, Lake Somerville, Lee, McKinney Falls, Palmetto, Pedernales Falls*

Suborder ACCIPITRES: Secretarybirds, Kites, Eagles, Hawks, and Allies

Superfamily ACCIPITROIDEA: Kites, Eagles, Hawks, and Allies

Family ACCIPITRIDAE: Kites, Eagles, Hawks, and Allies

Subfamily PANDIONINAE: Ospreys

Osprey, *Pandion haliaetus:* Uncommon fall, winter, and spring resident; occasional in summer. Perennial waterways. All area lakes. *Austin, Bastrop, Bell, Bexar, Burnet, Lake Somerville, Lee, McKinney Falls, Palmetto, Pedernales Falls*

Subfamily ACCIPITRINAE: Kites, Eagles, Hawks, and Allies

American Swallow-tailed Kite (Swallow-tailed Kite), *Elanoides forficatus:* Accidental in spring and summer. Bexar and Travis counties. *Austin, Bexar*

Black-shouldered Kite, *Elanus caeruleus*[‡]: Rare spring, summer, and fall resident; accidental in winter. Wooded uplands. Bastrop and Caldwell counties. Has nested.   *Austin, Bastrop, Bexar, Guadalupe River, Lake Somerville, Lee, Palmetto*

Mississippi Kite, *Ictinia mississippiensis:* Uncommon spring and fall migrant. Croplands, invaded fields, range and pastures. Throughout.   *Austin, Bastrop, Bell, Bexar, Burnet, Enchanted Rock, Guadalupe River, Lake Somerville, Lee, McKinney Falls, Palmetto*

Bald Eagle, *Haliaeetus leucocephalus*[†]: Uncommon winter resident. Perennial waterways. Lake Buchanan, Lake Somerville, Lake Bastrop.   *Austin, Bastrop, Bell, Bexar, Burnet, Lake Somerville, Pedernales Falls*

Northern Harrier (Marsh Hawk), *Circus cyaneus:* Common fall, winter, and spring resident. Croplands, invaded fields, range and pastures. Throughout. Typically, the low-flying hawk during the winter months.   *Austin, Bastrop, Bell, Bexar, Burnet, Enchanted Rock, Guadalupe River, Lake Somerville, Lee, McKinney Falls, Palmetto, Pedernales Falls*

Sharp-shinned Hawk, *Accipiter striatus:* Uncommon spring and fall migrant; rare in winter; occasional in summer. Riparian woodlands, wooded uplands, cultural areas. Throughout. Usually seen overhead.   *Austin, Bastrop, Bell, Bexar, Burnet, Enchanted Rock, Guadalupe River, Lake Somerville, Lee, McKinney Falls, Palmetto, Pedernales Falls*

Cooper's Hawk, *Accipiter cooperii*[‡]: Rare in fall, winter, and spring; occasional in summer. Riparian woodlands, wooded uplands. Throughout. Nests on Edwards Plateau.   *Austin, Bastrop, Bell, Bexar,*

Burnet, Enchanted Rock, Guadalupe River, Lake Somerville, Lee, McKinney
Falls, Palmetto, Pedernales Falls

Northern Goshawk, *Accipiter gentilis:* Accidental in spring and summer. Bexar and Travis counties. *Austin, Bexar*

Common Black-Hawk, *Buteogallus anthracinus:* Hypothetical. Bexar and Travis counties. *Austin, Bexar*

Harris' Hawk, *Parabuteo unicinctus*‡: Rare fall and winter visitor. Invaded fields, wooded uplands. Throughout but mostly east and south of Austin. Has nested in Bexar County. *Austin, Bell, Bexar, Burnet, McKinney Falls, Palmetto*

Red-shouldered Hawk, *Buteo lineatus*‡: Uncommon permanent resident. Riparian woodlands, wooded uplands. Throughout. Palmetto State Park, Buescher State Park, Enchanted Rock State Natural Area. *Austin, Bastrop, Bell, Bexar, Burnet, Enchanted Rock, Guadalupe River, Lake Somerville, Lee, McKinney Falls, Palmetto*

Broad-winged Hawk, *Buteo platypterus*‡: Uncommon spring and fall migrant; rare in summer. Throughout during migration, often in large flocks. May have nested in Travis County near Lake Austin. *Austin, Bastrop, Bell, Bexar, Burnet, Enchanted Rock, Guadalupe River, Lake Somerville, Lee, McKinney Falls, Palmetto, Pedernales Falls*

Swainson's Hawk, *Buteo swainsoni*†: Uncommon spring and fall migrant; rare in summer; occasional in winter. Croplands, invaded fields, range and pastures. Throughout. Sometimes migrates in large flocks. *Austin, Bastrop, Bell, Bexar, Burnet, Enchanted Rock, Guadalupe River, Lake Somerville, Lee, McKinney Falls, Palmetto, Pedernales Falls*

White-tailed Hawk, *Buteo albicaudatus:* Occasional fall, winter, and spring visitor. Croplands, invaded fields, range and pastures. Bastrop and Bexar counties. *Austin, Bexar*

Zone-tailed Hawk, *Buteo albonotatus*†: Occasional in winter and spring. Most records from Bastrop County near Colorado River. *Austin, Bastrop, Bexar, Palmetto*

Red-tailed Hawk, *Buteo jamaicensis*‡: Common fall, winter, and spring resident; uncommon summer resident. Croplands, invaded fields, range and pastures. Throughout. Most common buteo in winter. *Austin, Bastrop, Bell, Bexar, Burnet, Enchanted Rock, Guadalupe River, Lake Somerville, Lee, McKinney Falls, Palmetto, Pedernales Falls*

Ferruginous Hawk, *Buteo regalis:* Rare spring, fall, and winter resident. Croplands, invaded fields, range and pastures. Bastrop, Bell, Bexar, Gonzales and Lee counties. *Austin, Bell, Bexar, Lake Somerville, Palmetto*

Rough-legged Hawk, *Buteo lagopus:* Occasional spring, fall, and winter resident. Croplands, invaded fields, range and pastures. Enchanted

Rock State Natural Area; Bastrop, Bell, Bexar, and Lee counties. *Austin, Bell, Bexar, Enchanted Rock, Lake Somerville*

Golden Eagle, *Aquila chrysaetos:* Occasional visitor, all seasons. Usually flying by overhead. Throughout. *Austin, Bastrop, Bell, Bexar, Burnet, Lake Somerville, Pedernales Falls*

Suborder FALCONES: Caracaras and Falcons

Family FALCONIDAE: Caracaras and Falcons

Tribe POLYBORINI: Caracaras

Crested Caracara (Caracara), *Polyborus plancus*‡: Uncommon permanent resident. Croplands, invaded fields, wooded uplands. Throughout. Usually south and east of Austin. Sometimes flocks in winter. *Austin, Bastrop, Bell, Bexar, Burnet, Guadalupe River, Lake Somerville, Lee, McKinney Falls, Palmetto*

Tribe FALCONINI: True Falcons

American Kestrel, *Falco sparverius:* Abundant spring, fall, and winter resident. Wooded uplands, range and pastures. Throughout. Often seen perched on utility lines and fences. *Austin, Bastrop, Bell, Bexar, Burnet, Enchanted Rock, Guadalupe River, Lake Somerville, Lee, McKinney Falls, Palmetto, Pedernales Falls*

Merlin, *Falco columbarius:* Rare spring, fall, and winter visitor. Wooded uplands, range and pastures. Throughout. Erratic. *Austin, Bastrop, Bell, Bexar, Burnet, Guadalupe River, Lake Somerville, Lee, Palmetto*

Prairie Falcon, *Falco mexicanus:* Occasional winter visitor. Croplands, invaded fields. Bell and Hays counties. *Austin, Bell*

Peregrine Falcon, *Falco peregrinus:* Rare spring and fall migrant; occasional summer and winter visitor. Perennial waterways, small impoundments. Throughout. *Austin, Bastrop, Bell, Bexar, Burnet, Lake Somerville, Lee*

Order GALLIFORMES: Gallinaceous Birds

Superfamily PHASIANOIDEA: Partridges, Grouse, Turkeys, and Quail

Family PHASIANIDAE: Partridges, Grouse, Turkeys, and Quail

Subfamily PHASIANINAE: Partridges and Pheasants

Tribe PHASIANINI: Pheasants

Ring-necked Pheasant, *Phasianus colchicus:* Rare in Williamson County. Native of Asia. Introduced at Granger Lake. Status uncertain. *Austin, McKinney Falls*

Subfamily TETRAONINAE: Grouse

Greater Prairie-Chicken, *Tympanuchus cupido:* Extirpated. Travis County (1878). *Austin*

Subfamily MELEAGRIDINAE: Turkeys

Wild Turkey (Turkey), *Meleagris gallopavo*[‡]: Uncommon permanent resident. Croplands, range and pastures, riparian woodlands, wooded uplands. Throughout. Pedernales Falls State Park, Enchanted Rock State Natural Area. *Austin, Bell, Bexar, Burnet, Enchanted Rock, Guadalupe River, Lee, McKinney Falls, Palmetto, Pedernales Falls*

Subfamily ODONTOPHORINAE: Quail

Montezuma Quail, *Cyrtonyx montezumae*[†]: Formerly recorded. Bexar County (1901). *Bexar*

Northern Bobwhite (Bobwhite), *Colinus virginianus*[‡]: Abundant permanent resident. Range and pastures, fence rows. Throughout. *Austin, Bastrop, Bell, Bexar, Burnet, Enchanted Rock, Guadalupe River, Lake Somerville, Lee, McKinney Falls, Palmetto, Pedernales Falls*

Scaled Quail, *Callipepla squamata:* Accidental in summer, fall, and winter. Bexar County. *Austin, Bexar*

Order GRUIFORMES: Cranes, Rails, and Allies

Family RALLIDAE: Rails, Gallinules, and Coots

Subfamily RALLINAE: Rails, Gallinules, and Coots

Yellow Rail, *Coturnicops noveboracensis:* Hypothetical. Travis County (October 1984). *Austin*

King Rail, *Rallus elegans*[†]: Rare spring and fall migrant. Small impoundments, marshes. Lake Somerville; Bexar and Travis counties. *Austin, Bexar, Lake Somerville*

Virginia Rail, *Rallus limicola:* Rare spring and fall migrant; occasional in winter. Marshes. Mostly east of Balcones Escarpment. Bell, Bexar, Gonzales, Lee, and Travis counties. *Austin, Bell, Bexar, Lake Somerville, Lee, Palmetto*

Sora, *Porzana carolina:* Rare spring and fall migrant; occasional in winter. Marshes, small impoundments. Mostly east of Balcones Escarpment. Lake Walter E. Long. *Austin, Bastrop, Bell, Bexar, Lake Somerville, Lee, McKinney Falls, Palmetto*

Purple Gallinule, *Porphyrula martinica*[‡]: Rare summer resident; occasional fall visitor. Small impoundments, perennial waterways with water hyacinths. Throughout. Has nested at Lake Gonzales.

Austin, Bell, Bexar, Burnet, Lake Somerville, Lee, McKinney Falls, Palmetto

Common Moorhen, *Gallinula chloropus*‡: Rare spring, summer, and fall resident; occasional in winter. Intermittent waterways, small impoundments. Throughout.   *Austin, Bell, Bexar, Burnet, Lake Somerville, McKinney Falls, Palmetto*

American Coot, *Fulica americana*‡: Abundant spring, fall, and winter resident; uncommon summer resident. Perennial waterways, wastewater ponds, small impoundments. Throughout. Lake Walter E. Long in summer; all area lakes spring, fall, and winter.

Austin, Bastrop, Bell, Bexar, Burnet, Enchanted Rock, Lake Somerville, Lee, McKinney Falls, Palmetto

Family GRUIDAE: Cranes

Subfamily GRUINAE: Typical Cranes

Sandhill Crane, *Grus canadensis:* Uncommon spring, fall, and winter resident. Croplands, invaded fields. Throughout. Winters at farm pond adjacent to New Braunfels dump. Often seen and heard migrating in spring and fall.   *Austin, Bastrop, Bell, Bexar, Burnet, Enchanted Rock, Guadalupe River, Lake Somerville, Lee, McKinney Falls, Palmetto, Pedernales Falls*

Whooping Crane, *Grus americana:* Occasional fall migrant. Small impoundments. Throughout.   *Austin, Bell, Bexar, Burnet, Lee*

Order CHARADRIIFORMES: Shorebirds, Gulls, Auks, and Allies

Suborder CHARADRII: Plovers and Allies

Family CHARADRIIDAE: Plovers and Lapwings

Subfamily CHARADRIINAE: Plovers

Black-bellied Plover, *Pluvialis squatarola:* Uncommon spring and fall migrant; occasional in summer. Wastewater ponds. Hornsby Bend Ponds, Lake Somerville, and Bell and Bexar counties.   *Austin, Bell, Bexar, Lake Somerville, McKinney Falls*

Lesser Golden-Plover (American Golden Plover), *Pluvialis dominica:* Uncommon spring migrant; rare fall migrant; occasional in summer. Riparian baregrounds, wastewater ponds. Hornsby Bend Ponds, Lake Somerville, Bell and Bexar counties.   *Austin, Bell, Bexar, Lake Somerville*

Snowy Plover, *Charadrius alexandrinus:* Occasional spring and fall migrant. Riparian baregrounds, wastewater ponds. Hornsby Bend Ponds, Bell, Bexar, and Burnet counties. *Austin, Bell, Bexar, Burnet*

Wilson's Plover, *Charadrius wilsonia:* Accidental in summer and fall. Wastewater ponds. Mitchell Lake. *Bexar*

Semipalmated Plover, *Charadrius semipalmatus:* Uncommon spring and fall migrant. Riparian baregrounds, wastewater ponds. Lake Somerville, Hornsby Bend Ponds, Bell and Bexar counties. *Austin, Bell, Bexar, Lake Somerville, Lee*

Piping Plover, *Charadrius melodus:* Occasional fall migrant; accidental in spring. Wastewater ponds. Hornsby Bend Ponds, Bell and Bexar counties. *Austin, Bell, Bexar*

Killdeer, *Charadrius vociferus*[‡]: Abundant permanent resident. Wastewater ponds, perennial waterways, small impoundments, range and pastures, cultural areas (parking lots, flat roof buildings). Throughout. *Austin, Bastrop, Bell, Bexar, Burnet, Enchanted Rock, Guadalupe River, Lake Somerville, Lee, McKinney Falls, Palmetto, Pedernales Falls*

Mountain Plover, *Charadrius montanus:* Rare winter resident; occasional spring and fall migrant. Croplands, range and pastures. Williamson County west of Granger Lake; Guadalupe County east of New Braunfels Airport; Bell County. *Austin, Bell, Bexar*

Family RECURVIROSTRIDAE: Stilts and Avocets

Black-necked Stilt, *Himantopus mexicanus*[‡]: Uncommon spring and summer resident. Wastewater ponds, small impoundments. Hornsby Bend Ponds, Mitchell Lake, and Bell and Burnet counties. Has nested regularly in recent years at Mitchell Lake and Hornsby Bend Ponds. *Austin, Bell, Bexar, Burnet*

American Avocet, *Recurvirostra americana*[‡]: Uncommon spring and fall migrant. Wastewater ponds. Lake Somerville, Hornsby Bend Ponds, and Bell, Bexar, Burnet, and Gonzales counties. Has nested at Mitchell Lake. *Austin, Bell, Bexar, Burnet, Lake Somerville, Palmetto*

Suborder SCOLOPACI: Sandpipers, Jacanas, and Allies
Superfamily JACANOIDEA: Jacanas
Family JACANIDAE: Jacanas

Northern Jacana, *Jacana spinosa*[†]: Accidental in spring, fall, and winter. Range and pastures, wastewater ponds. Hornsby Bend Ponds, Gonzales County. *Austin, Bexar, Palmetto*

Superfamily SCOLOPACOIDEA: Sandpipers, Phalaropes, and Allies

Family SCOLOPACIDAE: Sandpipers, Phalaropes, and Allies

Subfamily SCOLOPACINAE: Sandpipers and Allies

Tribe TRINGINI: Tringine Sandpipers

Greater Yellowlegs, *Tringa melanoleuca:* Uncommon spring and fall migrant; rare in late summer and winter. Perennial waterways, wastewater ponds, small impoundments. Hornsby Bend Ponds, all area lakes.   *Austin, Bastrop, Bell, Bexar, Burnet, Lake Somerville, Lee, McKinney Falls, Palmetto, Pedernales Falls*

Lesser Yellowlegs, *Tringa flavipes:* Common spring and fall migrant; rare in winter. Perennial waterways, wastewater ponds, small impoundments. All area lakes, Hornsby Bend Ponds.   *Austin, Bastrop, Bell, Bexar, Burnet, Lake Somerville, Lee, McKinney Falls, Palmetto, Pedernales Falls*

Solitary Sandpiper, *Tringa solitaria:* Uncommon spring and fall migrant; occasional in winter. Wastewater ponds, riparian baregrounds, small impoundments. Throughout. Farm ponds, Hornsby Bend Ponds, Mitchell Lake.   *Austin, Bastrop, Bell, Bexar, Burnet, Guadalupe River, Lake Somerville, Lee, McKinney Falls, Palmetto, Pedernales Falls*

Willet, *Catoptrophorus semipalmatus:* Rare spring and fall migrant. Perennial waterways, riparian baregrounds, wastewater ponds. Hornsby Bend Ponds and Bexar and Burnet counties.   *Austin, Bexar, Burnet*

Spotted Sandpiper, *Actitis macularia:* Common except in June. Riparian baregrounds, perennial waterways, wastewater ponds. Throughout. Hornsby Bend Ponds, all area lakes. Does not nest.   *Austin, Bastrop, Bell, Bexar, Burnet, Enchanted Rock, Guadalupe River, Lake Somerville, Lee, McKinney Falls, Palmetto, Pedernales Falls*

Tribe NUMENIINI: Curlews

Upland Sandpiper, *Bartramia longicauda:* Common spring and fall migrant; occasional in summer. Croplands, range and pastures. Throughout. Often heard calling overhead at night during migration. Nesting suspected in Williamson County.   *Austin, Bastrop, Bell, Bexar, Lake Somerville, Lee, McKinney Falls, Palmetto*

Eskimo Curlew, *Numenius borealis:* Hypothetical in Bexar County.   *Bexar*

Whimbrel, *Numenius phaeopus:* Accidental in spring, summer, and fall. Wastewater ponds. Lake Somerville, Hornsby Bend Ponds, Bexar County.   *Austin, Bexar, Lake Somerville*

Long-billed Curlew, *Numenius americanus:* Rare spring and fall migrant; occasional in winter. Wastewater ponds, range and pastures. Throughout. Hornsby Bend Ponds.   *Austin, Bell, Bexar, Burnet, Lake Somerville, Palmetto*

Tribe LIMOSINI: Godwits

Hudsonian Godwit, *Limosa haemastica:* Rare spring migrant; accidental in fall. Wastewater ponds. Hornsby Bend Ponds, Lake Somerville, Bexar County.   *Austin, Bexar, Lake Somerville*

Bar-tailed Godwit, *Limosa lapponica:* Hypothetical in Gonzales County.   *Palmetto*

Marbled Godwit, *Limosa fedoa:* Occasional spring and fall migrant; accidental in summer. Wastewater ponds. Hornsby Bend Ponds, Lake Somerville, Bexar County.   *Austin, Bexar, Lake Somerville*

Tribe ARENARIINI: Turnstones

Ruddy Turnstone, *Arenaria interpres:* Rare spring and fall migrant. Riparian baregrounds, wastewater ponds. Hornsby Bend Ponds, Lake Somerville, Bexar County.   *Austin, Bexar, Lake Somerville*

Tribe CALIDRIDINI: Calidridine Sandpipers

Red Knot, *Calidris canutus:* Occasional fall migrant. Wastewater ponds. Hornsby Bend Ponds.   *Austin*

Sanderling, *Calidris alba:* Rare fall migrant; occasional in spring. Riparian baregrounds, wastewater ponds. Hornsby Bend Ponds, Mitchell Lake, Bell County.   *Austin, Bell, Bexar*

Semipalmated Sandpiper, *Calidris pusilla:* Uncommon spring and fall migrant. Riparian baregrounds, wastewater ponds. Hornsby Bend Ponds, Lake Somerville, Bell and Bexar counties.   *Austin, Bell, Bexar, Lake Somerville*

Western Sandpiper, *Calidris mauri:* Common spring and fall migrant; rare in winter. Riparian baregrounds, wastewater ponds. Throughout. All area lakes.   *Austin, Bell, Bexar, Lake Somerville, Lee, McKinney Falls, Palmetto*

Least Sandpiper, *Calidris minutilla:* Abundant resident except in June. Riparian baregrounds, wastewater ponds. All area lakes, Hornsby Bend Ponds. Does not nest.   *Austin, Bastrop, Bell, Bexar, Burnet, Enchanted Rock, Lake Somerville, Lee, McKinney Falls, Palmetto, Pedernales Falls*

White-rumped Sandpiper, *Calidris fuscicollis:* Uncommon late spring migrant; occasional fall migrant. Riparian baregrounds, wastewater ponds. Hornsby Bend Ponds.   *Austin, Bell, Bexar, Lake Somerville*

Baird's Sandpiper, *Calidris bairdii:* Uncommon spring and fall migrant. Riparian baregrounds, wastewater ponds. Hornsby Bend Ponds; Lake Somerville; Bell and Bexar counties.   *Austin, Bell, Bexar, Lake Somerville*

Pectoral Sandpiper, *Calidris melanotos:* Common spring and fall migrant; rare in winter. Riparian baregrounds, wastewater ponds. Throughout. Hornsby Bend Ponds.   *Austin, Bell, Bexar, Enchanted Rock, Lake Somerville, Lee, McKinney Falls, Palmetto, Pedernales Falls*

Purple Sandpiper, *Calidris maritima:* Accidental in spring. Wastewater ponds. Hornsby Bend Ponds.   *Austin*

Dunlin, *Calidris alpina:* Occasional, all seasons. Wastewater ponds. Hornsby Bend Ponds; Lake Somerville; Bexar and Gonzales counties. Does not nest.   *Austin, Bexar, Lake Somerville, Palmetto*

Curlew Sandpiper, *Calidris ferruginea:* Accidental in spring and fall. Wastewater ponds. Travis and Bexar counties.   *Austin, Bexar*

Stilt Sandpiper, *Calidris himantopus:* Uncommon spring and fall migrant. Riparian baregrounds, wastewater ponds. Hornsby Bend Ponds; Lake Somerville; Bell and Bexar counties.   *Austin, Bell, Bexar, Lake Somerville*

Buff-breasted Sandpiper, *Tryngites subruficollis:* Uncommon fall and rare spring migrant. Croplands, range and pastures, riparian baregrounds, wastewater ponds. Golf courses; Hornsby Bend Ponds; Lake Somerville; Bell and Bexar counties.   *Austin, Bell, Bexar, Lake Somerville*

Ruff (male), Reeve (female), *Philomachus pugnax:* Occasional, all seasons. Wastewater ponds. Hornsby Bend Ponds, Bexar County.   *Austin, Bexar*

Tribe LIMNODROMINI: Dowitchers

Short-billed Dowitcher, *Limnodromus griseus:* Rare to uncommon spring and fall migrant. Wastewater ponds. Hornsby Bend Ponds, Bexar County.   *Austin, Bexar*

Long-billed Dowitcher, *Limnodromus scolopaceus:* Uncommon spring and fall migrant; rare in winter. Riparian baregrounds, wastewater ponds. Mostly east of Balcones Escarpment. Hornsby Bend Ponds.   *Austin, Bell, Bexar, Lake Somerville, Lee, Palmetto, Pedernales Falls*

Tribe GALLINAGININI: Snipe

Common Snipe, *Gallinago gallinago:* Uncommon spring, fall, and winter resident. Marshes, riparian baregrounds, wastewater ponds.

Throughout. Farm ponds. *Austin, Bastrop, Bell, Bexar, Burnet, En-*
chanted Rock, Lake Somerville, Lee, McKinney Falls, Palmetto, Pedernales Falls

Tribe SCOLOPACINI: Woodcocks

American Woodcock, *Scolopax minor*[†]: Rare winter resident. Riparian
woodlands, especially with thick leaf mold. Throughout. McKinney Falls State Park, Hornsby Bend Ponds. *Austin, Bastrop, Bell,*
Bexar, Burnet, Lake Somerville, Lee, McKinney Falls, Palmetto

Subfamily PHALAROPODINAE: Phalaropes

Wilson's Phalarope, *Phalaropus tricolor:* Common spring and fall
migrant; accidental in winter. Wastewater ponds. Throughout.
Hornsby Bend Ponds. Most numerous phalarope in the area.
Austin, Bell, Bexar, Burnet, Lake Somerville, Lee, McKinney Falls, Palmetto,
Pedernales Falls
Red-necked Phalarope (Northern Phalarope), *Phalaropus lobatus:* Rare
spring and fall migrant. Wastewater ponds. Hornsby Bend Ponds,
Bexar County. *Austin, Bexar*
Red Phalarope, *Phalaropus fulicaria:* Accidental in spring, summer, and
fall. Wastewater ponds. Hornsby Bend Ponds, Bexar County.
Austin, Bexar

Suborder LARI: Skuas, Gulls, Terns, and Skimmers

Family LARIDAE: Skuas, Gulls, Terns, and Skimmers

Subfamily STERCORARIINAE: Skuas and Jaegers

Pomarine Jaeger, *Stercorarius pomarinus:* Accidental in winter. Travis
County. Lake Travis. *Austin*
Parasitic Jaeger, *Stercorarius parasiticus:* Accidental in summer. Mitch-
ell Lake. *Bexar*
Long-tailed Jaeger, *Stercorarius longicaudus:* Accidental in summer.
Wastewater ponds. Travis County. *Austin, Bexar*

Subfamily LARINAE: Gulls

Laughing Gull, *Larus atricilla:* Rare in Bexar County in summer and
fall; occasional elsewhere; all seasons. Wastewater ponds. Usually
blown in by gulf storms. Lake Somerville, Bexar and Travis
counties. *Austin, Bexar, Lake Somerville*
Franklin's Gull, *Larus pipixcan:* Common spring migrant and rare fall
migrant; occasional in winter. Croplands, perennial waterways.
Throughout. Often migrates in large numbers. *Austin, Bastrop,*

Bell, Bexar, Burnet, Lake Somerville, Lee, McKinney Falls, Palmetto, Pedernales Falls

Little Gull, *Larus minutus:* Accidental in spring and winter. Perennial waterways. Granger Lake.   *Austin*

Bonaparte's Gull, *Larus philadelphia:* Uncommon fall and winter resident. Perennial waterways, wastewater ponds. Lake Buchanan, Lake Somerville.   *Austin, Bell, Bexar, Burnet, Lake Somerville, Palmetto*

Mew Gull, *Larus canus:* Accidental in winter. Calaveras Lake, Bexar County.

Ring-billed Gull, *Larus delawarensis:* Abundant spring, fall, and winter resident; rare in summer. Perennial waterways, wastewater ponds, landfill sites. Throughout.   *Austin, Bastrop, Bell, Bexar, Burnet, Lake Somerville, Lee, McKinney Falls, Pedernales Falls, Palmetto*

California Gull, *Larus californicus:* Accidental in spring. Bexar County (Calaveras Lake).

Herring Gull, *Larus argentatus:* Uncommon winter resident; rare in spring and fall. Perennial waterways, wastewater ponds. Lake Buchanan, Lake Somerville.   *Austin, Bastrop, Bell, Bexar, Burnet, Lake Somerville, Palmetto*

Thayer's Gull, *Larus thayeri:* Hypothetical. Braunig Lake.   *Bexar*

Glaucous Gull, *Larus hyperboreus:* Accidental in winter. Wastewater ponds. Hornsby Bend Ponds.   *Austin*

Black-legged Kittiwake, *Rissa tridactyla:* Accidental in fall and winter. Perennial waterways. Lake Buchanan, Bexar County.   *Austin, Bexar, Burnet*

Sabine's Gull, *Xema sabini:* Accidental in fall. Perennial waterways, wastewater ponds. Granger Lake, Hornsby Bend Ponds, Mitchell Lake.   *Austin*

Subfamily STERNINAE: Terns

Gull-billed Tern, *Sterna nilotica:* Formerly recorded. Bexar County (September 1961), Travis County (February 1963).   *Austin, Bexar*

Caspian Tern, *Sterna caspia:* Occasional spring visitor; accidental in fall. Wastewater ponds. Hornsby Bend Ponds, Lake Somerville, Bexar and Gonzales counties.   *Austin, Bexar, Lake Somerville, Palmetto*

Royal Tern, *Sterna maxima:* Accidental in summer and fall. Lake Somerville, Bexar County.   *Austin, Bexar, Lake Somerville*

Sandwich Tern, *Sterna sandvicensis:* Formerly recorded. Travis County (September 1961).   *Austin*

Common Tern, *Sterna hirundo:* Occasional spring and summer visitor. Perennial waterways, wastewater ponds. Hornsby Bend Ponds, Lake Somerville, Bexar County.   *Austin, Bexar, Lake Somerville*

Forster's Tern, *Sterna forsteri:* Uncommon spring, fall, and winter resident. Perennial waterways, wastewater ponds. Throughout. Lake Buchanan, Lake Somerville. Most likely white tern in the area.
Austin, Bell, Bexar, Burnet, Lake Somerville, Palmetto

Least Tern, *Sterna antillarum:* Occasional spring, summer, and winter visitor. Wastewater ponds. Hornsby Bend Ponds, Bell, Bexar, Burnet, and Gonzales counties. *Austin, Bell, Bexar, Burnet, Palmetto*

Sooty Tern, *Sterna fuscata:* Accidental in summer and fall. Bexar County. *Austin, Bexar*

Black Tern, *Chlidonias niger:* Uncommon spring and fall migrant. Perennial waterways, wastewater ponds. Throughout. All area lakes.
Austin, Bastrop, Bell, Bexar, Burnet, Lake Somerville, Lee, Palmetto

Subfamily RYNCHOPINAE: Skimmers

Black Skimmer, *Rynchops niger:* Rare spring, summer, and fall visitor. Wastewater ponds, perennial waterways. Lake Somerville, Bexar County. *Austin, Bexar, Lake Somerville*

Order COLUMBIFORMES: Sandgrouse, Pigeons, and Doves

Suborder COLUMBAE: Pigeons and Doves

Family COLUMBIDAE: Pigeons and Doves

Rock Dove, *Columba livia*[‡][*]: Abundant permanent resident. Cultural areas. Throughout. Introduced from Eurasia. *Austin, Bastrop, Bell, Bexar, Burnet, Enchanted Rock, Guadalupe River, Lake Somerville, Lee, McKinney Falls, Palmetto*

White-winged Dove, *Zenaida asiatica*[‡]: Uncommon permanent resident. Cultural areas. Towns and cities. Now nests in Austin. Apparently extending its range northward and increasing. *Austin, Bell, Bexar, McKinney Falls, Palmetto*

Mourning Dove, *Zenaida macroura*[‡]: Abundant permanent resident. All habitats. Throughout. *Austin, Bastrop, Bell, Bexar, Burnet, Enchanted Rock, Guadalupe River, Lake Somerville, Lee, McKinney Falls, Palmetto, Pedernales Falls*

Passenger Pigeon, *Ectopistes migratorius:* Extinct. Travis County (1878) and Lee County (1886). *Austin*

Inca Dove, *Columbina inca*[‡]: Common permanent resident. Cultural areas. Throughout. *Austin, Bastrop, Bell, Bexar, Burnet, Enchanted Rock, Guadalupe River, Lake Somerville, Lee, McKinney Falls, Palmetto, Pedernales Falls*

Common Ground-Dove (Ground Dove), *Columbina passerina*‡: Uncommon permanent resident. Range and pastures. Throughout. Bexar and Gonzales counties; rare northward.   *Austin, Bastrop, Bell, Bexar, Guadalupe River, Lake Somerville, Lee, McKinney Falls, Palmetto, Pedernales Falls*

Order PSITTACIFORMES: Parrots and Allies

Family PSITTACIDAE: Lories, Parakeets, Macaws, and Parrots

Subfamily ARINAE: New World Parakeets, Macaws, and Parrots

Monk Parakeet, *Myiopsitta monachus*‡*: Rare permanent resident. Cultural areas. Nests locally in Austin near Lamar Boulevard and Town Lake. Introduced from southern South America.   *Austin*

Order CUCULIFORMES: Cuckoos and Allies

Family CUCULIDAE: Cuckoos, Roadrunners, and Anis

Subfamily COCCYZINAE: New World Cuckoos

Black-billed Cuckoo, *Coccyzus erythropthalmus:* Rare spring and fall migrant. Riparian woodlands, wooded uplands. Throughout. Capitol grounds.   *Austin, Bell, Bexar, Guadalupe River, Lake Somerville, Lee, McKinney Falls, Palmetto*

Yellow-billed Cuckoo, *Coccyzus americanus*‡: Common spring and summer resident; uncommon in fall. Cultural areas, riparian woodlands, wooded uplands. Throughout.   *Austin, Bastrop, Bell, Bexar, Burnet, Enchanted Rock, Guadalupe River, Lake Somerville, Lee, McKinney Falls, Palmetto, Pedernales Falls*

Subfamily NEOMORPHINAE: Ground-Cuckoos and Roadrunners

Greater Roadrunner (Roadrunner), *Geococcyx californianus*‡: Uncommon permanent resident. Range and pastures. Throughout.   *Austin, Bastrop, Bell, Bexar, Burnet, Enchanted Rock, Guadalupe River, Lake Somerville, Lee, McKinney Falls, Palmetto, Pedernales Falls*

Subfamily CROTOPHAGINAE: Anis

Groove-billed Ani, *Crotophaga sulcirostris*‡: Occasional spring, summer, and fall visitor. Intermittent streams. McKinney Falls State Park. Nested at Mitchell Lake in 1990.   *Austin, Bexar, McKinney Falls*

Order STRIGIFORMES: Owls

Family TYTONIDAE: Barn Owls

Barn Owl (Common Barn-Owl), *Tyto alba*[‡]: Rare permanent resident. Throughout, but rarely seen. *Austin, Bell, Bexar, Lake Somerville, Lee, McKinney Falls, Palmetto*

Family STRIGIDAE: Typical Owls

Eastern Screech-Owl (Screech Owl), *Otus asio*[‡]: Common permanent resident. Cultural areas, riparian woodlands, wooded uplands. Throughout. *Austin, Bastrop, Bell, Bexar, Burnet, Enchanted Rock, Guadalupe River, Lake Somerville, Lee, McKinney Falls, Palmetto, Pedernales Falls*

Western Screech-Owl, *Otus kennicottii:* Accidental in winter. Bexar County. *Bexar*

Great Horned Owl, *Bubo virginianus*[‡]: Uncommon permanent resident. Riparian woodlands, wooded uplands. Throughout. *Austin, Bastrop, Bell, Bexar, Burnet, Enchanted Rock, Guadalupe River, Lake Somerville, Lee, McKinney Falls, Palmetto, Pedernales Falls*

Snowy Owl, *Nyctea scandiaca:* Formerly recorded. Bexar County (1857) and Travis County (1876). *Austin, Bexar*

Burrowing Owl, *Speotyto cunicularia:* Rare fall and winter resident; occasional in spring. Range and pastures, especially along fence rows. Blackland prairies. Bell, Bexar, Comal, and Travis counties. *Austin, Bell, Bexar*

Barred Owl, *Strix varia*[‡]: Uncommon permanent resident. Riparian woodlands. Throughout. Buescher State Park, Palmetto State Park. *Austin, Bastrop, Bell, Bexar, Burnet, Enchanted Rock, Guadalupe River, Lake Somerville, Lee, McKinney Falls, Palmetto, Pedernales Falls*

Long-eared Owl, *Asio otus:* Accidental in spring, fall, and winter. Wooded uplands. Lake Somerville, Bell, Bexar, and Travis counties. *Austin, Bell, Bexar, Lake Somerville*

Short-eared Owl, *Asio flammeus:* Rare winter resident; occasional in spring and fall. Range and pastures, especially where Northern Harriers hunt regularly. Throughout. *Austin, Bell, Bexar, Burnet, Enchanted Rock, Lake Somerville, McKinney Falls*

Northern Saw-whet Owl, *Aegolius acadicus:* Accidental in winter. Travis County. *Austin*

Order CAPRIMULGIFORMES: Goatsuckers, Oilbirds, and Allies

Family CAPRIMULGIDAE: Goatsuckers

Subfamily CHORDEILINAE: Nighthawks

Lesser Nighthawk, *Chordeiles acutipennis*‡: Uncommon spring and summer resident. Has nested at Mitchell Lake. Enchanted Rock State Natural Area, Bexar and Burnet counties.   *Bexar, Burnet, Enchanted Rock*

Common Nighthawk, *Chordeiles minor*‡: Abundant spring and summer resident; rare in fall and winter. Range and pastures, cultural areas. Throughout.   *Austin, Bastrop, Bell, Bexar, Burnet, Enchanted Rock, Guadalupe River, Lake Somerville, Lee, McKinney Falls, Palmetto, Pedernales Falls*

Subfamily CAPRIMULGINAE: Nightjars

Pauraque (Common Pauraque), *Nyctidromus albicollis*: Accidental in spring and fall. Bastrop, Bexar, and Gonzales counties.   *Austin, Bexar, Palmetto*

Common Poorwill (Poorwill), *Phalaenoptilus nuttallii*‡: Uncommon spring, summer, and fall resident; occasional in winter. Wooded uplands, range and pastures. Edwards Plateau. Enchanted Rock State Natural Area.   *Austin, Bell, Bexar, Burnet, Enchanted Rock, Guadalupe River, Palmetto, Pedernales Falls*

Chuck-will's-widow, *Caprimulgus carolinensis*‡: Common spring and summer resident; rare in fall. Riparian woodlands, wooded uplands. Throughout.   *Austin, Bastrop, Bell, Bexar, Burnet, Enchanted Rock, Guadalupe River, Lake Somerville, Lee, McKinney Falls, Palmetto, Pedernales Falls*

Whip-poor-will, *Caprimulgus vociferus*: Rare spring and fall migrant; accidental in winter and summer. Wooded uplands, riparian woodlands. Throughout.   *Austin, Bexar, Guadalupe River, Lake Somerville, Lee, McKinney Falls, Palmetto*

Order APODIFORMES: Swifts and Hummingbirds

Family APODIDAE: Swifts

Subfamily CHAETURINAE: Chaeturine Swifts

Chimney Swift, *Chaetura pelagica*‡: Abundant spring, summer, and fall resident; accidental in winter. Cultural areas. Throughout.

Austin, Bastrop, Bell, Bexar, Burnet, Enchanted Rock, Guadalupe River, Lake Somerville, Lee, McKinney Falls, Palmetto, Pedernales Falls

Subfamily APODINAE: Apodine Swifts

White-throated Swift, *Aeronautes saxatalis:* Accidental in fall and winter. Bexar and Travis counties.   *Austin, Bexar*

Family TROCHILIDAE: Hummingbirds

Green Violet-ear, *Colibri thalassinus:* Accidental in spring and summer. Hays County.   *Austin*

Broad-billed Hummingbird, *Cynanthus latirostris:* Accidental in spring. Bexar County.   *Bexar*

Buff-bellied Hummingbird, *Amazilia yucatanensis:* Accidental, all seasons. Bastrop, Bexar, and Travis counties.   *Austin, Bexar*

Magnificent Hummingbird, *Eugenes fulgens:* Formerly recorded. Bexar County.   *Bexar*

Ruby-throated Hummingbird, *Archilochus colubris*[‡]: Uncommon summer resident; common spring and fall migrant. Throughout. The common nesting hummingbird east of the Balcones Escarpment.
Austin, Bastrop, Bell, Bexar, Burnet, Enchanted Rock, Guadalupe River, Lake Somerville, Lee, McKinney Falls, Palmetto, Pedernales Falls

Black-chinned Hummingbird, *Archilochus alexandri*[‡]: Abundant spring and summer resident; uncommon in fall. Throughout. The common nesting hummingbird west of the Balcones Escarpment.
Austin, Bastrop, Bell, Bexar, Burnet, Enchanted Rock, Guadalupe River, McKinney Falls, Palmetto, Pedernales Falls

Anna's Hummingbird, *Calypte anna:* Occasional fall and winter visitor. Cultural areas. Most records at feeders.   *Austin, Bexar*

Costa's Hummingbird, *Calypte costae:* Accidental in winter. Hays County.   *Austin*

Calliope Hummingbird, *Stellula calliope:* Accidental in summer. Bexar, Burnet, and Hays counties.   *Austin, Bexar*

Broad-tailed Hummingbird, *Selasphorus platycercus:* Occasional, all seasons. Cultural areas. Most records at feeders.   *Austin, Bexar*

Rufous Hummingbird, *Selasphorus rufus:* Rare fall and winter resident; occasional in spring and summer. Cultural areas. Mostly west of Balcones Escarpment. Usually seen at feeders.   *Austin, Bell, Bexar, Burnet, Enchanted Rock, Guadalupe River, Palmetto*

Allen's Hummingbird, *Selasphorus sasin:* Accidental in winter. Bexar and Travis counties.   *Austin, Bexar*

Order CORACIIFORMES: Kingfishers, Rollers, Hornbills, and Allies

Suborder ALCEDINES: Todies, Motmots, and Kingfishers

Superfamily ALCEDINOIDEA: Kingfishers

Family ALCEDINIDAE: Kingfishers

Subfamily CERYLINAE: Typical Kingfishers

Ringed Kingfisher, *Ceryle torquata:* Occasional fall, winter, and spring visitor. Perennial waterways. Town Lake, Inks Lake State Park. *Austin*

Belted Kingfisher, *Ceryle alcyon*[‡]: Common permanent resident. Intermittent waterways, perennial waterways. Throughout. All area streams and lakes.   *Austin, Bastrop, Bell, Bexar, Burnet, Enchanted Rock, Guadalupe River, Lake Somerville, Lee, McKinney Falls, Palmetto, Pedernales Falls*

Green Kingfisher, *Chloroceryle americana:* Rare permanent resident. Intermittent waterways in undisturbed portions of the Edwards Plateau, especially clear unpolluted streams. Onion Creek, Pedernales River.   *Austin, Bell, Bexar, Guadalupe River, McKinney Falls, Palmetto, Pedernales Falls*

Order PICIFORMES: Puffbirds, Toucans, Woodpeckers, and Allies

Suborder PICI: Barbets, Woodpeckers, and Allies

Family PICIDAE: Woodpeckers and Allies

Subfamily PICINAE: Woodpeckers

Lewis' Woodpecker, *Melanerpes lewis:* Accidental in winter. Wooded uplands. Travis County.   *Austin*

Red-headed Woodpecker, *Melanerpes erythrocephalus*[‡]: Uncommon permanent resident. Riparian woodlands. Mostly east of Balcones Escarpment. Colorado River, Bastrop County, Palmetto State Park. *Austin, Bastrop, Bell, Bexar, Burnet, Enchanted Rock, Lake Somerville, Lee, Palmetto*

Acorn Woodpecker, *Melanerpes formicivorus:* Accidental in spring. Wooded uplands. Bastrop and Hays counties.   *Austin, Bastrop*

Golden-fronted Woodpecker, *Melanerpes aurifrons*[‡]: Uncommon permanent resident. Wooded uplands. Edwards Plateau. Enchanted

Rock State Natural Area, Inks Lake State Park, Pedernales Falls State Park. Most common woodpecker in San Antonio. *Austin, Bastrop, Bell, Bexar, Burnet, Enchanted Rock, Guadalupe River, McKinney Falls, Palmetto, Pedernales Falls*

Red-bellied Woodpecker, *Melanerpes carolinus*[‡]: Common permanent resident. Riparian woodlands, wooded uplands, cultural areas. Mostly east of Balcones Escarpment. Bastrop State Park. Most common woodpecker in Austin. *Austin, Bastrop, Bell, Bexar, Guadalupe River, Lake Somerville, Lee, McKinney Falls, Palmetto, Pedernales Falls*

Yellow-bellied Sapsucker, *Sphyrapicus varius:* Common spring, fall, and winter resident. Riparian woodlands, wooded uplands. Throughout. *Austin, Bastrop, Bell, Bexar, Burnet, Enchanted Rock, Guadalupe River, Lake Somerville, Lee, McKinney Falls, Palmetto, Pedernales Falls*

Red-naped Sapsucker, *Sphyrapicus nuchalis:* Accidental in fall and winter. Barton Creek Greenbelt and McKinney Falls State Park in Travis County. *Austin*

Williamson's Sapsucker, *Sphyrapicus thyroideus:* Accidental in spring, fall, and winter. Riparian woodlands, wooded uplands. McKinney Falls State Park. *Austin, McKinney Falls*

Ladder-backed Woodpecker, *Picoides scalaris*[‡]: Common permanent resident. Wooded uplands, range and pastures. Throughout. *Austin, Bastrop, Bell, Bexar, Burnet, Enchanted Rock, Guadalupe River, Lake Somerville, Lee, McKinney Falls, Palmetto, Pedernales Falls*

Downy Woodpecker, *Picoides pubescens*[‡]: Common permanent resident. Riparian woodlands, wooded uplands. Throughout. Bastrop State Park, Palmetto State Park, McKinney Falls State Park. *Austin, Bastrop, Bell, Bexar, Burnet, Enchanted Rock, Guadalupe River, Lake Somerville, Lee, McKinney Falls, Palmetto*

Hairy Woodpecker, *Picoides villosus:* Rare winter resident; occasional in spring and summer. Riparian woodlands, wooded uplands. Bastrop State Park, Palmetto State Park. *Austin, Bastrop, Bell, Bexar, Burnet, Lake Somerville, Lee, Palmetto*

Northern Flicker (Common Flicker), *Colaptes auratus:* Common spring, fall, and winter resident. Riparian woodlands, wooded uplands. Throughout. *Austin, Bastrop, Bell, Bexar, Burnet, Enchanted Rock, Guadalupe River, Lake Somerville, Lee, McKinney Falls, Palmetto, Pedernales Falls*

Pileated Woodpecker, *Dryocopus pileatus*[‡]: Rare permanent resident. Riparian woodlands, wooded uplands. Bastrop and Lee counties, Palmetto State Park. *Austin, Bastrop, Bexar, Lake Somerville, Lee, Palmetto*

Order PASSERIFORMES: Passerine Birds
Suborder TYRANNI: Suboscines
Superfamily TYRANNOIDEA: Tyrant Flycatchers and Allies
Family TYRANNIDAE: Tyrant Flycatchers
Subfamily FLUVICOLINAE: Fluvicoline Flycatchers

Olive-sided Flycatcher, *Contopus borealis:* Uncommon spring and fall migrant. Wooded uplands, riparian woodlands. Throughout. Often seen perched at top of a dead snag. *Austin, Bastrop, Bexar, Burnet, Enchanted Rock, Guadalupe River, Lake Somerville, Lee, McKinney Falls, Palmetto, Pedernales Falls*

Western Wood-Pewee, *Contopus sordidulus:* Rare spring and fall visitor. Wooded uplands. Bexar and Travis counties. *Austin, Bexar*

Eastern Wood-Pewee, *Contopus virens*[‡]: Uncommon spring and fall migrant; rare summer resident. Riparian woodlands, wooded uplands. Bastrop State Park, Pace Bend Park. *Austin, Bastrop, Bell, Bexar, Burnet, Enchanted Rock, Guadalupe River, Lake Somerville, Lee, McKinney Falls, Palmetto, Pedernales Falls*

Yellow-bellied Flycatcher, *Empidonax flaviventris:* Uncommon spring and fall migrant. Riparian woodlands, wooded uplands. Throughout. *Austin, Bastrop, Bexar, Burnet, Lake Somerville, Lee, McKinney Falls, Palmetto*

Acadian Flycatcher, *Empidonax virescens*[‡]: Uncommon spring and summer resident. Riparian woodlands, wooded uplands. Throughout. Guadalupe River State Park, Hamilton Pool Park, Bastrop State Park. *Austin, Bastrop, Bexar, Enchanted Rock, Guadalupe River, Lake Somerville, Lee, McKinney Falls, Palmetto, Pedernales Falls*

"Traill's-type" Flycatcher: Uncommon spring and fall migrant. Riparian woodlands, wooded uplands. Bexar, Hays, Lee, and Travis counties. The Alder and Willow flycatchers can be identified during migration by voice only, even in the hand; therefore, they are referred to as "Traill's-type." Among the *empidonax* flycatchers, second in abundance only to the Least Flycatcher in migration. *Austin*

Alder Flycatcher, *Empidonax alnorum:* Uncommon spring and fall migrant. Riparian woodlands, wooded uplands. Bexar, Hays, Lee, and Travis counties. Very likely most migrants are recorded as "Empidonax Flycatcher." *Austin, Bexar, Lee, McKinney Falls*

Willow Flycatcher, *Empidonax trailii:* Occasional spring migrant; accidental in fall. Riparian woodlands, wooded uplands. Bexar, Hays, Lee, and Travis counties. *Austin, Bexar, Lee, McKinney Falls*

Least Flycatcher, *Empidonax minimus:* Uncommon spring and fall migrant. Riparian woodlands, wooded uplands. Throughout. *Austin, Bastrop, Bell, Bexar, Guadalupe River, Lake Somerville, Lee, McKinney Falls, Palmetto*

Hammond's Flycatcher, *Empidonax hammondii:* Accidental in winter. Bastrop County. *Austin*

Cordilleran Flycatcher (Western Flycatcher), *Empidonax occidentalis:* Accidental in summer. Bexar County. *Bexar*

Black Phoebe, *Sayornis nigricans:* Accidental in spring, fall, and winter. Riparian baregrounds. Bexar, Burnet, and Travis counties. *Austin, Bexar, Burnet, Pedernales Falls*

Eastern Phoebe, *Sayornis phoebe*[‡]: Common fall and winter resident; uncommon spring and summer resident. Riparian woodlands, riparian baregrounds. Throughout. *Austin, Bastrop, Bell, Bexar, Burnet, Enchanted Rock, Guadalupe River, Lake Somerville, Lee, McKinney Falls, Palmetto, Pedernales Falls*

Say's Phoebe, *Sayornis saya:* Rare spring and winter resident. Invaded fields, riparian baregrounds. Throughout. Often near cattle corrals. *Austin, Bell, Bexar, Burnet, Guadalupe River, McKinney Falls, Palmetto*

Vermilion Flycatcher, *Pyrocephalus rubinus*[‡]: Uncommon spring and summer resident; accidental in winter. Riparian woodlands, wooded uplands, range and pastures. Mostly west of Balcones Escarpment. Often near ranch water troughs. *Austin, Bastrop, Bexar, Burnet, Enchanted Rock, Guadalupe River, Palmetto, Pedernales Falls*

Subfamily TYRANNINAE: Tyrannine Flycatchers

Ash-throated Flycatcher, *Myiarchus cinerascens*[‡]: Uncommon spring and summer resident; rare in winter. Wooded uplands, range and pastures. Edwards Plateau; less frequently in mesquite thickets east of Austin. *Austin, Bell, Bexar, Burnet, Enchanted Rock, Guadalupe River, Palmetto, Pedernales Falls*

Great Crested Flycatcher, *Myiarchus crinitus*[‡]: Common spring and summer resident. Riparian woodlands, wooded uplands. Throughout. *Austin, Bastrop, Bell, Bexar, Burnet, Enchanted Rock, Guadalupe River, Lake Somerville, Lee, McKinney Falls, Palmetto, Pedernales Falls*

Brown-crested Flycatcher, *Myiarchus tyrannulus*[‡]: Uncommon spring and summer resident; occasional in fall. Riparian woodlands, wooded uplands. Bexar and Guadalupe counties. *Austin, Bexar*

Great Kiskadee, *Pitangus sulphuratus:* Accidental in spring and winter.

Mitchell Lake and wastewater treatment plant on San Marcos River east of San Marcos. *Austin*

Couch's Kingbird, *Tyrannus couchii*: Accidental in spring and winter. Mitchell Lake and Travis County. Winter sight records may be Tropical Kingbird. *Austin*

Cassin's Kingbird, *Tyrannus vociferans*: Accidental in fall. Bexar and Lee counties. *Bexar, Lee*

Western Kingbird, *Tyrannus verticalis*[‡]: Common spring and summer resident. Cultural areas, wooded uplands. Throughout. Nests on utility poles in towns; often seen perched on utility lines. *Austin, Bastrop, Bell, Bexar, Burnet, Enchanted Rock, Guadalupe River, Lake Somerville, Lee, McKinney Falls, Palmetto, Pedernales Falls*

Eastern Kingbird, *Tyrannus tyrannus*[‡]: Common spring and fall migrant; uncommon summer resident; accidental in winter. Range and pastures. Throughout, but usually east of Balcones Escarpment. *Austin, Bastrop, Bell, Bexar, Burnet, Enchanted Rock, Guadalupe River, Lake Somerville, Lee, McKinney Falls, Palmetto, Pedernales Falls*

Scissor-tailed Flycatcher, *Tyrannus forficatus*[‡]: Abundant spring, summer, and fall resident. Cultural areas, range and pastures. Throughout. Often seen on fences and utility lines. *Austin, Bell, Bexar, Burnet, Enchanted Rock, Guadalupe River, Lake Somerville, Lee, McKinney Falls, Palmetto, Pedernales Falls*

Fork-tailed Flycatcher, *Tyrannus savana*: Accidental in spring. Travis County. *Austin*

Suborder PASSERES: Oscines

Family ALAUDIDAE: Larks

Horned Lark, *Eremophila alpestris*[†]: Uncommon winter resident; accidental in spring. Croplands, highway easements. Blackland Prairies. *Austin, Bell, Bexar, Burnet, Enchanted Rock, Lake Somerville, McKinney Falls, Palmetto*

Family HIRUNDINIDAE: Swallows

Subfamily HIRUNDININAE: Typical Swallows

Purple Martin, *Progne subis*[‡]: Abundant spring and summer resident. Cultural areas. Throughout where nesting houses provided. *Austin, Bastrop, Bell, Bexar, Burnet, Enchanted Rock, Guadalupe River, Lake Somerville, Lee, McKinney Falls, Palmetto, Pedernales Falls*

Tree Swallow, *Tachycineta bicolor*[†]: Uncommon spring and fall migrant; occasional in winter. Perennial waterways, wastewater

ponds. Throughout. Hornsby Bend Ponds.   *Austin, Bastrop, Bell,*
Bexar, Lake Somerville, Lee, McKinney Falls, Palmetto

Violet-green Swallow, *Tachycineta thalassina:* Occasional spring and
fall migrant. Perennial waterways, wastewater ponds. Hornsby
Bend Ponds.   *Austin, Bexar*

Northern Rough-winged Swallow (Rough-winged Swallow), *Stelgidop-*
teryx serripennis[‡]: Uncommon spring and summer resident; common fall migrant. Riparian baregrounds on steep slopes, highway
cuts. Throughout.   *Austin, Bastrop, Bell, Bexar, Burnet, Enchanted Rock,*
Guadalupe River, Lake Somerville, Lee, McKinney Falls, Palmetto, Pedernales
Falls

Bank Swallow, *Riparia riparia*[‡]: Uncommon spring and fall migrant;
rare summer resident. Perennial waterways, wastewater ponds,
sand and gravel pits. Has nested in Hays County.   *Austin, Bastrop,*
Bell, Bexar, Lake Somerville, Lee, McKinney Falls, Palmetto

Cliff Swallow, *Hirundo pyrrhonota*[‡]: Abundant spring and summer resident; common in fall. Cliffs and large highway bridges. Throughout.   *Austin, Bastrop, Bell, Bexar, Burnet, Enchanted Rock, Guadalupe River,*
Lake Somerville, Lee, McKinney Falls, Palmetto, Pedernales Falls

Cave Swallow, *Hirundo fulva*[‡]: Uncommon spring and summer resident; rare in fall and winter. Perennial waterways, large highway
bridges. Several nest sites in Bexar County. Nest found in Gonzales County, also. Apparently expanding its range northward and
may become a common spring and summer resident throughout
in the near future.   *Austin, Bexar, Palmetto*

Barn Swallow, *Hirundo rustica*[‡]: Abundant spring, summer, and fall
resident; occasional in winter. Cultural areas, culverts. Throughout. Ubiquitous in migration.   *Austin, Bastrop, Bell, Bexar, Burnet, En-*
chanted Rock, Guadalupe River, Lake Somerville, Lee, McKinney Falls, Pal-
metto, Pedernales Falls

Family CORVIDAE: Jays, Magpies, and Crows

Steller's Jay, *Cyanocitta stelleri:* Formerly recorded. Travis County (September 1961).   *Austin*

Blue Jay, *Cyanocitta cristata*[‡]: Common permanent resident. Cultural
areas, riparian woodlands, wooded uplands. Less common on the
Edwards Plateau but seems to be moving west.   *Austin, Bastrop,*
Bell, Bexar, Burnet, Enchanted Rock, Lake Somerville, Lee, McKinney Falls, Pal-
metto, Pedernales Falls

Green Jay, *Cyanocorax yncas*[†]: Accidental, all seasons. Riparian woodlands, wooded uplands. Bexar County.   *Bexar*

Scrub Jay, *Aphelocoma coerulescens*[‡]: Uncommon permanent resident.
Wooded uplands, riparian woodlands. Edwards Plateau.   *Austin,*
Bell, Bexar, Burnet, Enchanted Rock, Guadalupe River, Pedernales Falls

American Crow (Common Crow), *Corvus brachyrhynchos*[‡]: Common
permanent resident. Wooded uplands, riparian woodlands, range
and pastures. Throughout, but mostly east of US 281.   *Austin, Bas-*
trop, Bell, Bexar, Burnet, Enchanted Rock, Guadalupe River, Lake Somerville,
Lee, McKinney Falls, Palmetto, Pedernales Falls

Chihuahuan Raven (White-necked Raven), *Corvus cryptoleucus:* Occasional spring and winter visitor. Bell and Hays counties.   *Austin,*
Bell

Common Raven, *Corvus corax:* Uncommon permanent resident.
Wooded uplands, riparian woodlands, range and pastures. Mostly
west of US 281. Enchanted Rock State Natural Area, Burnet and
Hays counties.   *Austin, Bexar, Burnet, Enchanted Rock, Guadalupe River*

Family PARIDAE: Titmice

Carolina Chickadee, *Parus carolinensis*[‡]: Abundant permanent resident.
Riparian woodlands, wooded uplands. Throughout.   *Austin, Bas-*
trop, Bell, Bexar, Burnet, Enchanted Rock, Guadalupe River, Lake Somerville,
Lee, McKinney Falls, Palmetto, Pedernales Falls

Tufted Titmouse (Black-crested Titmouse), *Parus bicolor*[‡]: Abundant
permanent resident. Riparian woodlands, wooded uplands.
Throughout.   *Austin, Bastrop, Bell, Bexar, Burnet, Enchanted Rock, Gua-*
dalupe River, Lake Somerville, Lee, McKinney Falls, Palmetto, Pedernales Falls

Family REMIZIDAE: Penduline Tits and Verdins

Verdin, *Auriparus flaviceps*[‡]: Uncommon permanent resident. Wooded
uplands, range and pastures. Edwards Plateau.   *Austin, Bexar, Bur-*
net, Enchanted Rock, Palmetto, Pedernales Falls

Family AEGITHALIDAE: Long-tailed Tits and Bushtits

Bushtit, *Psaltriparus minimus*[‡]: Rare permanent resident. Riparian
woodlands, wooded uplands. Edwards Plateau. Pedernales Falls
State Park.   *Austin, Bexar, Enchanted Rock, Guadalupe River, Pedernales*
Falls

Family SITTIDAE: Nuthatches
Subfamily SITTINAE: Typical Nuthatches

Red-breasted Nuthatch, *Sitta canadensis:* Uncommon spring, fall, and
winter resident. Erratic. Riparian woodlands, wooded uplands.

Throughout. Bastrop State Park. *Austin, Bastrop, Bexar, Enchanted Rock, Lake Somerville, Lee, McKinney Falls, Palmetto*
White-breasted Nuthatch, *Sitta carolinensis:* Occasional spring, fall, and winter visitor. Riparian woodlands. Mostly east of Balcones Escarpment. Milam and Williamson counties along San Gabriel River. *Austin, Bexar, Burnet, Lake Somerville, Lee, Palmetto*

Family CERTHIIDAE: Creepers

Subfamily CERTHIINAE: Typical Creepers

Brown Creeper, *Certhia americana:* Uncommon spring, fall, and winter resident. Riparian woodlands, wooded uplands. Throughout. Bastrop State Park, McKinney Falls State Park, Inks Lake State Park. *Austin, Bastrop, Bell, Bexar, Burnet, Enchanted Rock, Guadalupe River, Lake Somerville, Lee, McKinney Falls, Palmetto, Pedernales Falls*

Family TROGLODYTIDAE: Wrens

Cactus Wren, *Campylorhynchus brunneicapillus*[‡]: Uncommon permanent resident. Wooded uplands, range and pastures. Edwards Plateau, Highlands Lakes area. *Austin, Bexar, Burnet, Palmetto, Pedernales Falls*
Rock Wren, *Salpinctes obsoletus*[‡]: Rare permanent resident. Upland baregrounds, along cliffs where rock talus has accumulated, rock quarries, rocky embankments (such as those around large earthen dams). Lake Georgetown, Mansfield Dam, Inks Lake State Park. *Austin, Bexar, Burnet, Enchanted Rock, Lee, McKinney Falls, Pedernales Falls*
Canyon Wren (Canon Wren), *Catherpes mexicanus*[‡]: Uncommon permanent resident. Riparian baregrounds, upland baregrounds, along cliffs where rock talus has accumulated. Edwards Plateau. Pedernales Falls State Park, Enchanted Rock State Natural Area, Guadalupe River State Park. *Austin, Bastrop, Bell, Bexar, Burnet, Enchanted Rock, Guadalupe River, Lee, McKinney Falls, Pedernales Falls*
Carolina Wren, *Thryothorus ludovicianus*[‡]: Abundant permanent resident. Riparian woodlands, cultural areas. Throughout. *Austin, Bell, Bexar, Burnet, Enchanted Rock, Guadalupe River, Lake Somerville, Lee, McKinney Falls, Palmetto, Pedernales Falls*
Bewick's Wren, *Thryomanes bewickii*[‡]: Abundant permanent resident. Wooded uplands, range and pastures. Throughout. Easier to find west of Balcones Escarpment. *Austin, Bastrop, Bell, Bexar, Burnet, Enchanted Rock, Guadalupe River, Lake Somerville, Lee, McKinney Falls, Palmetto, Pedernales Falls*

House Wren, *Troglodytes aedon:* Uncommon spring, fall, and winter resident; occasional in summer. Riparian woodlands, wooded uplands where understory vegetation is dense. Throughout.   *Austin, Bastrop, Bell, Bexar, Burnet, Enchanted Rock, Guadalupe River, Lake Somerville, Lee, McKinney Falls, Palmetto, Pedernales Falls*

Winter Wren, *Troglodytes troglodytes:* Rare spring, fall, and winter resident. Riparian woodlands where understory vegetation is dense. Throughout.   *Austin, Bastrop, Bell, Bexar, Burnet, Guadalupe River, McKinney Falls, Lake Somerville, Lee, Palmetto, Pedernales Falls*

Sedge Wren (Short-billed Marsh Wren), *Cistothorus platensis:* Rare spring, fall, and winter resident. Marshes, range and pastures. Mostly east of Balcones Escarpment. Erratic (or overlooked).   *Austin, Bexar, Lake Somerville, Lee, McKinney Falls, Palmetto*

Marsh Wren (Long-billed Marsh Wren), *Cistothorus palustris:* Rare spring, fall, and winter resident. Marshes. Throughout.   *Austin, Bastrop, Bexar, Burnet, Lake Somerville, Lee, Palmetto*

Family MUSCICAPIDAE: Muscicapids

Subfamily SYLVIINAE: Old World Warblers, Kinglets, and Gnatcatchers

Tribe SYLVIINI: Old World Warblers and Kinglets

Golden-crowned Kinglet, *Regulus satrapa:* Uncommon spring, fall, and winter resident. Riparian woodlands, wooded uplands. Throughout. McKinney Falls State Park, Bastrop State Park, Palmetto State Park.   *Austin, Bastrop, Bell, Bexar, Burnet, Enchanted Rock, Guadalupe River, Lake Somerville, Lee, McKinney Falls, Palmetto, Pedernales Falls*

Ruby-crowned Kinglet, *Regulus calendula:* Common spring, fall, and winter resident. Riparian woodlands, wooded uplands. Throughout.   *Austin, Bastrop, Bell, Bexar, Burnet, Enchanted Rock, Guadalupe River, Lake Somerville, Lee, McKinney Falls, Palmetto, Pedernales Falls*

Tribe POLIOPTILINI: Gnatcatchers

Blue-gray Gnatcatcher, *Polioptila caerulea*[‡]: Uncommon summer resident; common spring and fall migrant; rare in winter. Riparian woodlands, wooded uplands. Throughout. Bastrop State Park, Enchanted Rock State Natural Area.   *Austin, Bastrop, Bell, Bexar, Burnet, Enchanted Rock, Guadalupe River, Lake Somerville, Lee, McKinney Falls, Palmetto, Pedernales Falls*

Black-tailed Gnatcatcher, *Polioptila melanura:* Accidental in spring, fall, and winter. Bexar County. *Bexar*

Subfamily TURDINAE: Solitaires, Thrushes, and Allies

Eastern Bluebird, *Sialia sialis*[‡]: Common permanent resident. Range and pastures adjacent to wooded uplands. Throughout. More numerous in winter. *Austin, Bastrop, Bell, Bexar, Burnet, Enchanted Rock, Guadalupe River, Lake Somerville, Lee, McKinney Falls, Palmetto, Pedernales Falls*

Western Bluebird, *Sialia mexicana:* Formerly recorded. Bexar County (November 1956). *Bastrop, Bexar*

Mountain Bluebird, *Sialia currucoides:* Accidental in winter. Gillespie County. *Austin, Bexar, Pedernales Falls*

Townsend's Solitaire, *Myadestes townsendi:* Accidental in spring, fall, and winter. Wooded uplands, riparian woodlands. Edwards Plateau. Bastrop, Bexar, and Hays counties. *Austin, Bastrop, Bexar*

Veery, *Catharus fuscescens:* Rare spring migrant; accidental in fall and winter. Riparian woodlands, wooded uplands. Throughout. *Austin, Bastrop, Bell, Bexar, Burnet, Lake Somerville, Lee, McKinney Falls, Palmetto, Pedernales Falls*

Gray-cheeked Thrush, *Catharus minimus:* Rare spring migrant; accidental in fall and winter. Riparian woodlands, wooded uplands. Throughout. Capitol grounds. *Austin, Bastrop, Bell, Bexar, Guadalupe River, Lake Somerville, Lee, McKinney Falls, Palmetto*

Swainson's Thrush, *Catharus ustulatus:* Uncommon spring migrant; rare fall migrant. Riparian woodlands, particularly where mulberry trees are in fruit. Throughout. *Austin, Bell, Bexar, Enchanted Rock, Guadalupe River, Lake Somerville, Lee, McKinney Falls, Palmetto, Pedernales Falls*

Hermit Thrush, *Catharus guttatus:* Common spring, fall, and winter resident. Riparian woodlands, wooded uplands. Throughout. *Austin, Bastrop, Bell, Bexar, Burnet, Enchanted Rock, Guadalupe River, Lake Somerville, Lee, McKinney Falls, Palmetto, Pedernales Falls*

Wood Thrush, *Hylocichla mustelina*[‡]: Rare summer resident; accidental in fall and winter. Riparian woodlands. Mostly east of Balcones Escarpment. Bastrop County. *Austin, Bastrop, Bell, Bexar, Guadalupe River, Lake Somerville, Lee, McKinney Falls, Palmetto*

American Robin, *Turdus migratorius*[‡]: Abundant spring, fall, and winter resident; uncommon summer resident. Wooded uplands, riparian woodlands. Throughout in fall, winter, and spring; very localized nester.   *Austin, Bastrop, Bell, Bexar, Burnet, Enchanted Rock, Guadalupe River, Lake Somerville, Lee, McKinney Falls, Palmetto, Pedernales Falls*

Varied Thrush, *Ixoreus naevius:* Hypothetical. Williamson County (February 1985).   *Austin*

Family MIMIDAE: Mockingbirds, Thrashers, and Allies

Gray Catbird, *Dumetella carolinensis:* Uncommon spring migrant; rare in late summer and fall; occasional in winter. Riparian woodlands, wooded uplands. Throughout.   *Austin, Bastrop, Bell, Bexar, Burnet, Guadalupe River, Lake Somerville, Lee, McKinney Falls, Palmetto*

Northern Mockingbird (Mockingbird), *Mimus polyglottos*[‡]: Abundant permanent resident. Wooded uplands, range and pastures, cultural areas. Throughout. Easily found when driving on any road.   *Austin, Bastrop, Bell, Bexar, Burnet, Enchanted Rock, Guadalupe River, Lake Somerville, Lee, McKinney Falls, Palmetto, Pedernales Falls*

Sage Thrasher, *Oreoscoptes montanus:* Occasional winter visitor. Range and pastures. Edwards Plateau. Erratic.   *Austin, Bexar, Burnet, Enchanted Rock, Guadalupe River, McKinney Falls*

Brown Thrasher, *Toxostoma rufum*[†]: Uncommon spring, fall, and winter resident; occasional in summer. Riparian woodlands, wooded uplands where there is dense understory vegetation. Throughout. Palmetto State Park.   *Austin, Bastrop, Bell, Bexar, Burnet, Enchanted Rock, Guadalupe River, Lake Somerville, Lee, McKinney Falls, Palmetto*

Long-billed Thrasher, *Toxostoma longirostre*[‡]: Uncommon permanent resident. Range and pastures, wooded uplands, riparian woodlands. Bexar County. Accidental in Gonzales, Hays, and Travis counties.   *Austin, Bexar, Palmetto*

Curve-billed Thrasher, *Toxostoma curvirostre*[‡]: Rare permanent resident. Wooded uplands, range and pastures. Edwards Plateau. Highland Lakes area, Mitchell Lake.   *Austin, Bexar, Burnet, Palmetto*

Family MOTACILLIDAE: Wagtails and Pipits

American Pipit (Water Pipit), *Anthus rubescens:* Common spring, fall, and winter resident. Croplands, intermittent waterways, perennial waterways, wastewater ponds, highway easements. Throughout.   *Austin, Bastrop, Bell, Bexar, Burnet, Enchanted Rock, Lake Somerville, Lee, McKinney Falls, Palmetto, Pedernales Falls*

Sprague's Pipit, *Anthus spragueii:* Rare spring, fall, and winter resident. Range and pastures, especially in tall grass. Blackland Prairies.   *Austin, Bell, Bexar, Burnet, Lake Somerville, Palmetto*

Family BOMBYCILLIDAE: Waxwings

Bohemian Waxwing, *Bombycilla garrulus:* Accidental in spring and
winter. Wooded uplands. Bastrop, Bexar, and Travis counties.
Austin, Bexar

Cedar Waxwing, *Bombycilla cedrorum:* Abundant spring and winter
resident; accidental in summer. Cultural areas, riparian woodlands, wooded uplands. Throughout.   *Austin, Bastrop, Bell, Bexar,
Burnet, Enchanted Rock, Guadalupe River, Lake Somerville, Lee, McKinney
Falls, Palmetto, Pedernales Falls*

Family LANIIDAE: Shrikes

Subfamily LANIINAE: Typical Shrikes

Loggerhead Shrike, *Lanius ludovicianus*[‡]: Common spring, fall, and
winter resident; uncommon summer resident. Invaded fields,
range and pastures. Often seen perched on utility wires. Throughout.   *Austin, Bastrop, Bell, Bexar, Burnet, Enchanted Rock, Guadalupe River,
Lake Somerville, Lee, McKinney Falls, Palmetto, Pedernales Falls*

Family STURNIDAE: Starlings and Allies

Subfamily STURNINAE: Starlings

European Starling (Starling), *Sturnus vulgaris*[‡*]: Abundant permanent
resident. Cultural areas, feedlots. Throughout. Introduced from
Eurasia.   *Austin, Bastrop, Bell, Bexar, Burnet, Enchanted Rock, Guadalupe
River, Lake Somerville, Lee, McKinney Falls, Palmetto*

Family VIREONIDAE: Vireos

Subfamily VIREONINAE: Typical Vireos

White-eyed Vireo, *Vireo griseus*[‡]: Common spring, summer, and fall
resident; uncommon winter resident. Riparian woodlands,
wooded uplands. Throughout.   *Austin, Bastrop, Bell, Bexar, Burnet, Enchanted Rock, Guadalupe River, Lake Somerville, Lee, McKinney Falls, Palmetto, Pedernales Falls*

Bell's Vireo, *Vireo bellii*[‡]: Uncommon spring, summer, and fall resident.
Invaded fields, range and pastures, wooded uplands. Mostly west
of Balcones Escarpment. Highland Lakes area, Enchanted Rock
State Natural Area.   *Austin, Bastrop, Bell, Bexar, Burnet, Enchanted
Rock, Guadalupe River, Lake Somerville, McKinney Falls, Palmetto, Pedernales
Falls*

Black-capped Vireo, *Vireo atricapillus*[‡]: Uncommon spring and summer resident; rare fall resident. Wooded uplands, particularly where sumac, shin oak, and small Texas Oak thrive in dense undergrowth. An endangered species decreasing at an alarming rate. Edwards Plateau.   *Austin, Bastrop, Bell, Bexar, Burnet, Enchanted Rock, Lee, Pedernales Falls*

Solitary Vireo, *Vireo solitarius:* Uncommon fall and winter resident; common spring migrant. Wooded uplands, riparian woodlands. Throughout.   *Austin, Bastrop, Bell, Bexar, Guadalupe River, Lake Somerville, Lee, McKinney Falls, Palmetto, Pedernales Falls*

Yellow-throated Vireo, *Vireo flavifrons*[‡]: Uncommon summer resident; accidental in late winter. Riparian woodlands. Throughout. Enchanted Rock State Natural Area, Bastrop State Park.   *Austin, Bastrop, Bell, Bexar, Burnet, Enchanted Rock, Guadalupe River, Lake Somerville, Lee, McKinney Falls, Palmetto, Pedernales Falls*

Warbling Vireo, *Vireo gilvus:* Uncommon spring and rare fall migrant. Riparian woodlands, wooded uplands. Throughout. Capitol grounds.   *Austin, Bastrop, Bell, Bexar, Burnet, Lake Somerville, Lee, McKinney Falls, Palmetto, Pedernales Falls*

Philadelphia Vireo, *Vireo philadelphicus:* Uncommon spring and rare fall migrant. Riparian woodlands, wooded uplands. Throughout. Capitol grounds.   *Austin, Bastrop, Bell, Bexar, Burnet, Lake Somerville, Lee, McKinney Falls, Palmetto, Pedernales Falls*

Red-eyed Vireo, *Vireo olivaceus*[‡]: Uncommon spring and summer resident. Riparian woodlands. Throughout. Palmetto State Park, Enchanted Rock State Natural Area.   *Austin, Bastrop, Bell, Bexar, Burnet, Enchanted Rock, Guadalupe River, Lake Somerville, Lee, McKinney Falls, Palmetto, Pedernales Falls*

Yellow-green Vireo, *Vireo flavoviridis:* Accidental in spring and summer. Travis County (Webberville Park).

Family EMBERIZIDAE: Emberizids

Subfamily PARULINAE: Wood-Warblers

Blue-winged Warbler, *Vermivora pinus:* Rare spring and fall migrant. Wooded uplands, riparian woodlands. Mostly east of Balcones Escarpment. Capitol grounds.   *Austin, Bell, Bexar, Burnet, Lee, McKinney Falls*

Golden-winged Warbler, *Vermivora chrysoptera:* Rare spring migrant. Wooded uplands, riparian woodlands. Throughout. Capitol grounds.   *Austin, Bastrop, Bexar, Guadalupe River, Lee, McKinney Falls*

Tennessee Warbler, *Vermivora peregrina:* Uncommon spring and rare fall migrant. Riparian woodlands, wooded uplands. Throughout.

Capitol grounds. *Austin, Bastrop, Bell, Bexar, Burnet, Guadalupe River, Lake Somerville, Lee, McKinney Falls, Palmetto, Pedernales Falls*

Orange-crowned Warbler, *Vermivora celata:* Uncommon spring, fall, and winter resident; common spring migrant. Invaded fields, riparian woodlands, wooded uplands. Throughout. *Austin, Bastrop, Bell, Bexar, Burnet, Enchanted Rock, Guadalupe River, Lake Somerville, Lee, McKinney Falls, Palmetto, Pedernales Falls*

Nashville Warbler, *Vermivora ruficapilla:* Common spring and fall migrant; rare winter resident. Riparian woodlands, wooded uplands. Throughout. *Austin, Bastrop, Bell, Bexar, Burnet, Enchanted Rock, Guadalupe River, Lake Somerville, Lee, McKinney Falls, Palmetto, Pedernales Falls*

Northern Parula, *Parula americana*[‡]: Uncommon spring and summer resident. Riparian woodlands. Palmetto State Park, Buescher State Park. Nests in trees with thick Spanish moss. *Austin, Bastrop, Bell, Bexar, Guadalupe River, Lake Somerville, Lee, McKinney Falls, Palmetto*

Tropical Parula, *Parula pitiayumi:* Accidental in spring. Travis County. *Austin*

Yellow Warbler, *Dendroica petechia*[†]: Common spring and uncommon fall migrant; occasional in winter. Riparian woodlands, wooded uplands. Throughout. *Austin, Bastrop, Bell, Bexar, Burnet, Enchanted Rock, Guadalupe River, Lake Somerville, Lee, McKinney Falls, Palmetto, Pedernales Falls*

Chestnut-sided Warbler, *Dendroica pensylvanica:* Uncommon spring and rare fall migrant; occasional winter visitor. Riparian woodlands, wooded uplands. Throughout. Capitol grounds. *Austin, Bastrop, Bell, Bexar, Guadalupe River, Lake Somerville, Lee, McKinney Falls, Palmetto, Pedernales Falls*

Magnolia Warbler, *Dendroica magnolia:* Common spring and rare fall migrant. Riparian woodlands, wooded uplands. Throughout. Capitol grounds. *Austin, Bell, Bexar, Guadalupe River, Lake Somerville, Lee, McKinney Falls, Palmetto, Pedernales Falls*

Cape May Warbler, *Dendroica tigrina:* Accidental in fall, winter, and spring. Palmetto State Park, Bexar and Travis counties. *Austin, Bexar, McKinney Falls, Palmetto*

Black-throated Blue Warbler, *Dendroica caerulescens:* Accidental in spring, fall, and winter. Riparian woodlands, wooded uplands. Bexar and Travis counties. *Austin, Bexar*

Yellow-rumped Warbler, *Dendroica coronata:* Abundant spring, fall, and winter resident. Invaded fields, riparian woodlands, wooded uplands. Throughout. The most common warbler in winter. *Austin, Bastrop, Bell, Bexar, Burnet, Enchanted Rock, Guadalupe River, Lake Somerville, Lee, McKinney Falls, Palmetto, Pedernales Falls*

Black-throated Gray Warbler, *Dendroica nigrescens:* Accidental in spring, fall, and winter. Wooded uplands. Palmetto State Park, Bastrop, Bexar, Travis counties.   *Austin, Bastrop, Bexar, Palmetto*

Townsend's Warbler, *Dendroica townsendi:* Accidental in spring and fall. Travis County.   *Austin, Bexar*

Black-throated Green Warbler, *Dendroica virens*[†]: Common spring and uncommon fall migrant; accidental in winter. Riparian woodlands, wooded uplands. Throughout.   *Austin, Bastrop, Bell, Bexar, Burnet, Guadalupe River, Lake Somerville, Lee, McKinney Falls, Palmetto, Pedernales Falls*

Golden-cheeked Warbler, *Dendroica chrysoparia*[‡]: Uncommon spring and summer resident. Wooded uplands dominated by stands of mature Ashe Juniper with oaks. An endangered species because of loss of habitat. The sole bird species that nests only in Texas. Edwards Plateau only. Pedernales Falls State Park, Guadalupe River State Park.   *Austin, Bell, Bexar, Burnet, Guadalupe River, Pedernales Falls*

Blackburnian Warbler, *Dendroica fusca:* Uncommon spring migrant, accidental in fall. Riparian woodlands, wooded uplands. Throughout. Capitol grounds.   *Austin, Bastrop, Bell, Bexar, Burnet, Guadalupe River, Lake Somerville, Lee, McKinney Falls, Palmetto, Pedernales Falls*

Yellow-throated Warbler, *Dendroica dominica*[‡]: Rare summer resident; rare spring and fall migrant; occasional in winter. Riparian woodlands, wooded uplands. Throughout.   *Austin, Bastrop, Bell, Bexar, Burnet, Guadalupe River, Lake Somerville, McKinney Falls, Palmetto*

Grace's Warbler, *Dendroica graciae:* Accidental in fall. Travis County.   *Austin*

Pine Warbler, *Dendroica pinus*[‡]: Uncommon permanent resident. Wooded uplands. Nests in Lost Pines of Bastrop County; wanders throughout in winter.   *Austin, Bastrop, Bexar, Lake Somerville, Lee, McKinney Falls, Palmetto*

Prairie Warbler, *Dendroica discolor:* Occasional, all seasons. Bell, Bexar, and Travis counties.   *Austin, Bell, Bexar*

Palm Warbler, *Dendroica palmarum:* Accidental in fall and winter. East of Balcones Escarpment. Palmetto State Park; Bexar, Lee, and Travis counties.   *Austin, Bexar, Lake Somerville, Palmetto*

Bay-breasted Warbler, *Dendroica castanea:* Uncommon spring migrant; occasional in fall. Riparian woodlands, wooded uplands. Throughout. Capitol grounds.   *Austin, Bastrop, Bell, Bexar, Burnet, Guadalupe River, Lake Somerville, Lee, McKinney Falls, Palmetto, Pedernales Falls*

Blackpoll Warbler, *Dendroica striata:* Occasional spring migrant. Wooded uplands, riparian woodlands. East of Balcones Escarpment. Bastrop, Bell, Bexar, and Travis counties.   *Austin, Bastrop, Bell, Bexar*

Cerulean Warbler, *Dendroica cerulea:* Rare spring migrant; accidental in fall. Riparian woodlands, wooded uplands. Throughout. Capitol grounds. *Austin, Bastrop, Bexar, Guadalupe River, Lee, McKinney Falls*

Black-and-white Warbler, *Mniotilta varia*‡: Common spring migrant; uncommon summer resident; rare in fall and winter. Riparian woodlands, wooded uplands. Migrant throughout; nests on Edwards Plateau and in Lost Pines of Bastrop County. *Austin, Bastrop, Bell, Bexar*‡*, Burnet, Enchanted Rock, Guadalupe River, Lake Somerville, Lee, McKinney Falls, Palmetto, Pedernales Falls*

American Redstart, *Setophaga ruticilla:* Uncommon spring and rare fall migrant. Riparian woodlands, wooded uplands. Throughout. Capitol grounds. *Austin, Bastrop, Bell, Bexar, Burnet, Enchanted Rock, Guadalupe River, Lake Somerville, Lee, McKinney Falls, Palmetto*

Prothonotary Warbler, *Protonotaria citrea*‡: Uncommon spring and summer resident. Intermittent waterways, perennial waterways. East of Balcones Escarpment. Lake Gonzales. *Austin, Bastrop, Bell, Bexar, Lake Somerville, Lee, Palmetto*

Worm-eating Warbler, *Helmitheros vermivorus:* Rare spring and occasional fall migrant. Riparian woodlands, wooded uplands. *Austin, Bastrop, Bexar, Lee, Palmetto, Pedernales Falls*

Swainson's Warbler, *Limnothlypis swainsonii*‡: Rare spring and summer resident. Riparian woodlands. Mostly east of Balcones Escarpment. Bastrop County, Lake Somerville. *Austin, Bastrop, Bell, Bexar, Lake Somerville, Lee, Palmetto*

Ovenbird, *Seiurus aurocapillus:* Uncommon spring and rare fall migrant; accidental in winter. Riparian woodlands, wooded uplands. Throughout. Capitol grounds. *Austin, Bastrop, Bell, Bexar, Guadalupe River, Lake Somerville, Lee, McKinney Falls, Palmetto, Pedernales Falls*

Northern Waterthrush, *Seiurus noveboracensis:* Uncommon spring and rare fall migrant; occasional in winter. Perennial waterways. Edge of flowing streams. *Austin, Bastrop, Bell, Bexar, Guadalupe River, Lake Somerville, Lee, McKinney Falls, Palmetto, Pedernales Falls*

Louisiana Waterthrush, *Seiurus motacilla*‡: Rare spring and summer resident; occasional in winter. Perennial waterways, intermittent waterways. Throughout. *Austin, Bastrop, Bell, Bexar, Enchanted Rock, Guadalupe River, Lake Somerville, McKinney Falls, Palmetto*

Kentucky Warbler, *Oporornis formosus*‡: Uncommon spring and summer resident. Riparian woodlands. Bastrop County. *Austin, Bastrop, Bell, Bexar, Lake Somerville, Lee, McKinney Falls, Palmetto, Pedernales Falls*

Connecticut Warbler, *Oporornis agilis:* Accidental in spring and fall. Wooded uplands, range and pastures. Bexar, Hays, and Lee counties. *Austin, Bexar, Lee*

Mourning Warbler, *Oporornis philadelphia:* Uncommon spring and fall

migrant. Riparian woodlands; wooded uplands where there is
dense understory vegetation. Throughout. Capitol grounds.
Austin, Bastrop, Bell, Bexar, Burnet, Lake Somerville, Lee, McKinney
Falls, Palmetto
MacGillivray's Warbler, *Oporornis tolmiei:* Rare spring and fall mi-
grant. Wooded uplands, riparian woodlands, range and pastures.
Bexar, Hays, Lee, and Travis counties. *Austin, Bexar, Lee*
Common Yellowthroat, *Geothlypis trichas*[†]: Uncommon spring and fall
migrant; uncommon winter resident. Riparian woodlands,
wooded uplands, marshes. Throughout. Capitol grounds. *Austin,*
Bastrop, Bell, Bexar, Burnet, Enchanted Rock, Guadalupe River, Lake Somer-
ville, Lee, McKinney Falls, Palmetto, Pedernales Falls
Hooded Warbler, *Wilsonia citrina*[‡]: Rare spring and summer resident;
occasional in fall and winter. Riparian woodlands, wooded uplands. Mostly east of Balcones Escarpment. Palmetto State Park,
Lost Pines in Bastrop County. *Austin, Bastrop, Bell, Bexar, Lake Som-*
erville, Lee, Palmetto
Wilson's Warbler, *Wilsonia pusilla:* Common spring and fall migrant;
occasional in winter. Riparian woodlands, wooded uplands.
Throughout. *Austin, Bastrop, Bell, Bexar, Burnet, Enchanted Rock, Gua-*
dalupe River, Lake Somerville, Lee, McKinney Falls, Palmetto, Pedernales Falls
Canada Warbler, *Wilsonia canadensis:* Uncommon spring and rare fall
migrant. Riparian woodlands, wooded uplands. Throughout.
Austin, Bastrop, Bell, Bexar, Guadalupe River, Lake Somerville, Lee, McKinney
Falls, Palmetto
Red-faced Warbler, *Cardellina rubrifrons:* Accidental in spring.
Buescher State Park. *Austin, Bastrop*
Yellow-breasted Chat, *Icteria virens*[‡]: Uncommon spring and summer
resident. Riparian woodlands, wooded uplands, range and pas-
tures. Throughout. *Austin, Bastrop, Bell, Bexar, Enchanted Rock, Guada-*
lupe River, Lake Somerville, Lee, McKinney Falls, Palmetto, Pedernales Falls

Subfamily THRAUPINAE: Tanagers

Tribe THRAUPINI: Typical Tanagers

Hepatic Tanager, *Piranga flava:* Occasional in spring, fall, and winter.
Wooded uplands. Mostly west of Balcones Escarpment. *Austin,*
Bastrop, Bexar, Burnet, Palmetto
Summer Tanager, *Piranga rubra*[‡]: Uncommon spring, summer, and fall
resident. Riparian woodlands, wooded uplands. Throughout.
Austin, Bastrop, Bell, Bexar, Burnet, Enchanted Rock, Guadalupe River, Lake
Somerville, Lee, McKinney Falls, Palmetto, Pedernales Falls

Scarlet Tanager, *Piranga olivacea:* Rare spring and occasional fall migrant. Riparian woodlands. Mostly east of Balcones Escarpment. *Austin, Bastrop, Bell, Bexar, Lake Somerville, McKinney Falls, Palmetto*

Western Tanager, *Piranga ludoviciana:* Accidental, all seasons. Wooded uplands, riparian woodlands. Bastrop, Bexar, Burnet, and Travis counties. *Austin, Bexar, Burnet*

Subfamily CARDINALINAE: Cardinals, Grosbeaks, and Allies

Northern Cardinal (Cardinal), *Cardinalis cardinalis*[‡]: Abundant permanent resident. Riparian woodlands, wooded uplands, range and pastures, cultural areas. Throughout. *Austin, Bastrop, Bell, Bexar, Burnet, Enchanted Rock, Guadalupe River, Lake Somerville, Lee, McKinney Falls, Palmetto, Pedernales Falls*

Pyrrhuloxia, *Cardinalis sinuatus:* Uncommon fall, winter, and early spring resident; occasional in late spring and summer. Range and pastures. Throughout. *Austin, Bastrop, Bell, Bexar, Burnet, Enchanted Rock, Guadalupe River, McKinney Falls, Palmetto*

Rose-breasted Grosbeak, *Pheucticus ludovicianus:* Uncommon spring and rare fall migrant. Riparian woodlands, particularly where mulberry trees are in fruit. Capitol grounds. *Austin, Bastrop, Bell, Bexar, Burnet, Guadalupe River, Lake Somerville, Lee, McKinney Falls, Palmetto*

Black-headed Grosbeak, *Pheucticus melanocephalus:* Rare spring, fall, and winter visitor. Wooded uplands. Often seen at feeders. *Austin, Bastrop, Bell, Bexar, Burnet, Lee, Palmetto*

Blue Grosbeak, *Guiraca caerulea*[‡]: Uncommon spring and summer resident; rare in fall. Wooded uplands, range and pastures. Throughout. Pedernales Falls State Park. *Austin, Bastrop, Bell, Bexar, Burnet, Enchanted Rock, Guadalupe River, Lake Somerville, Lee, McKinney Falls, Palmetto, Pedernales Falls*

Lazuli Bunting, *Passerina amoena:* Rare spring migrant; accidental in fall and winter. Range and pastures, riparian woodlands, wooded uplands. Bexar, Burnet, Lee, and Travis counties. Erratic. *Austin, Bexar, Burnet, Lee*

Indigo Bunting, *Passerina cyanea*[‡]: Uncommon spring migrant; rare summer and fall resident. Wooded uplands, riparian woodlands, range and pastures. Throughout. Palmetto State Park. *Austin, Bastrop, Bell, Bexar, Burnet, Guadalupe River, Lake Somerville, Lee, McKinney Falls, Palmetto, Pedernales Falls*

Varied Bunting, *Passerina versicolor:* Formerly recorded. Bexar County (May 1962). *Bexar*

Painted Bunting, *Passerina ciris*[‡]: Common spring and summer resident; uncommon in fall. Wooded uplands, range and pastures. Throughout. Palmetto State Park, Pedernales Falls State Park, Enchanted Rock State Natural Area.   *Austin, Bastrop, Bell, Bexar, Burnet, Enchanted Rock, Guadalupe River, Lake Somerville, Lee, McKinney Falls, Palmetto, Pedernales Falls*

Dickcissel, *Spiza americana*[‡]: Abundant spring and uncommon fall migrant; uncommon summer resident. Range and pastures, cultivated fields. Blackland Prairies.   *Austin, Bastrop, Bell, Bexar, Burnet, Enchanted Rock, Guadalupe River, Lake Somerville, Lee, McKinney Falls, Palmetto, Pedernales Falls*

Subfamily EMBERIZINAE: Emberizines

Olive Sparrow, *Arremonops rufivirgatus:* Rare, all seasons. Riparian woodlands, wooded uplands. Bexar County.   *Bexar*

Green-tailed Towhee, *Pipilo chlorurus*: Rare winter resident; occasional fall visitor. Wooded uplands, riparian woodlands, range and pastures. Throughout. Erratic.   *Austin, Bastrop, Bexar, Burnet, Enchanted Rock, Palmetto*

Rufous-sided Towhee, *Pipilo erythrophthalmus:* Common fall, winter, and spring resident. Riparian woodlands, wooded uplands, range and pastures. Throughout. Often found in dense understory vegetation.   *Austin, Bastrop, Bell, Bexar, Burnet, Enchanted Rock, Guadalupe River, Lake Somerville, Lee, McKinney Falls, Palmetto, Pedernales Falls*

Canyon Towhee (Brown Towhee), *Pipilo fuscus*[‡]: Uncommon permanent resident. Wooded uplands, range and pastures. Edwards Plateau. Enchanted Rock State Natural Area, Highland Lakes Area.   *Austin, Bell, Bexar, Burnet, Enchanted Rock, Pedernales Falls*

White-collared Seedeater, *Sporophila torqueola:* Formerly recorded. Bexar County (December 1966).   *Bexar*

Cassin's Sparrow, *Aimophila cassinii*[‡]: Rare summer resident; occasional in fall and winter. Invaded fields, range and pastures. Bexar, Burnet, and Gonzales counties.   *Austin, Bell, Bexar, Burnet, Palmetto*

Rufous-crowned Sparrow, *Aimophila ruficeps*[‡]: Uncommon permanent resident. Range and pastures, upland baregrounds, especially with rock outcrops. Edwards Plateau, Pedernales Falls State Park.   *Austin, Bell, Bexar, Burnet, Enchanted Rock, Guadalupe River, McKinney Falls, Pedernales Falls*

American Tree Sparrow, *Spizella arborea:* Accidental in winter. Wooded uplands. Guadalupe County.   *Austin*

Chipping Sparrow, *Spizella passerina*[‡]: Common spring, fall, and winter resident; uncommon summer resident. Wooded uplands, particu-

larly adjacent to range and pastures. Throughout. *Austin, Bastrop, Bell, Bexar, Burnet, Enchanted Rock, Guadalupe River, Lake Somerville, Lee, McKinney Falls, Palmetto, Pedernales Falls*
Clay-colored Sparrow, *Spizella pallida:* Common spring and uncommon fall migrant; rare in winter. Invaded fields, range and pastures. Throughout. Capitol grounds. *Austin, Bastrop, Bell, Bexar, Burnet, Guadalupe River, Lee, McKinney Falls, Palmetto, Pedernales Falls*
Brewer's Sparrow, *Spizella breweri:* Accidental in fall and winter. Burnet and Hays counties. *Austin, Burnet*
Field Sparrow, *Spizella pusilla*[‡]: Common spring, fall, and winter resident; uncommon summer resident. Wooded uplands, range and pastures. Throughout. *Austin, Bastrop, Bell, Bexar, Burnet, Enchanted Rock, Guadalupe River, Lake Somerville, Lee, McKinney Falls, Palmetto, Pedernales Falls*
Vesper Sparrow, *Pooecetes gramineus:* Abundant spring, fall, and winter resident. Range and pastures, brushy fence rows. Throughout. *Austin, Bastrop, Bell, Bexar, Burnet, Enchanted Rock, Guadalupe River, Lake Somerville, Lee, McKinney Falls, Palmetto, Pedernales Falls*
Lark Sparrow, *Chondestes grammacus*[‡]: Common permanent resident. Wooded uplands adjacent to range and pastures, fence rows. Throughout. *Austin, Bastrop, Bell, Bexar, Burnet, Enchanted Rock, Guadalupe River, Lake Somerville, Lee, McKinney Falls, Palmetto, Pedernales Falls*
Black-throated Sparrow, *Amphispiza bilineata*[‡]: Uncommon permanent resident. Range and pastures, invaded fields. Edwards Plateau. Highland Lakes area. *Austin, Bexar, Burnet, Enchanted Rock, McKinney Falls, Palmetto, Pedernales Falls*
Lark Bunting, *Calamospiza melanocorys:* Uncommon spring, fall, and winter resident. Erratic. Invaded fields, range and pastures. Edwards Plateau, less often on Blackland Prairies. *Austin, Bastrop, Bell, Bexar, Burnet, Lee, Palmetto*
Savannah Sparrow, *Passerculus sandwichensis:* Abundant spring, fall, and winter resident. Range and pastures, fence rows. Throughout. *Austin, Bastrop, Bell, Bexar, Burnet, Enchanted Rock, Guadalupe River, Lake Somerville, Lee, McKinney Falls, Palmetto, Pedernales Falls*
Baird's Sparrow, *Ammodramus bairdii:* Accidental in spring and winter. Bexar County. *Bexar*
Grasshopper Sparrow, *Ammodramus savannarum*[‡]: Rare permanent resident; uncommon spring migrant. Invaded fields, range and pastures. Throughout. Nests in Bastrop and Williamson counties. *Austin, Bastrop, Bell, Bexar, Enchanted Rock, Guadalupe River, Lake Somerville, Lee, McKinney Falls, Palmetto, Pedernales Falls*
Henslow's Sparrow, *Ammodramus henslowii:* Accidental in spring and

winter. Bell, Bexar, and Lee counties.   *Bell, Bexar, Lake Somerville, Lee*

LeConte's Sparrow, *Ammodramus leconteii:* Rare spring, fall, and winter resident. Range and pastures with tall grass. Mostly east of Balcones Escarpment. Hays and Travis counties.   *Austin, Bastrop, Bell, Bexar, Lake Somerville, Lee, Palmetto, Pedernales Falls*

Sharp-tailed Sparrow, *Ammodramus caudacutus:* Rare spring and fall migrant. Lake Somerville.   *Lake Somerville*

Fox Sparrow, *Passerella iliaca:* Uncommon fall and winter resident; rare spring resident. Riparian woodlands, wooded uplands. Throughout.   *Austin, Bastrop, Bell, Bexar, Burnet, Enchanted Rock, Lake Somerville, Lee, McKinney Falls, Palmetto, Pedernales Falls*

Song Sparrow, *Melospiza melodia:* Uncommon spring, fall, and winter resident. Riparian woodlands where there is dense understory vegetation, brush piles. Throughout. Lake Walter E. Long, Palmetto State Park.   *Austin, Bastrop, Bell, Bexar, Burnet, Enchanted Rock, Guadalupe River, Lake Somerville, Lee, McKinney Falls, Palmetto, Pedernales Falls*

Lincoln's Sparrow, *Melospiza lincolnii:* Uncommon spring, fall, and winter resident. Riparian woodlands, brush piles, wooded uplands with dense understory vegetation. Throughout.   *Austin, Bastrop, Bell, Bexar, Burnet, Enchanted Rock, Guadalupe River, Lake Somerville, Lee, McKinney Falls, Palmetto, Pedernales Falls*

Swamp Sparrow, *Melospiza georgiana:* Rare spring, fall, and winter resident. Riparian woodlands with dense understory vegetation, marshes. Granger Lake, Shipp Lake.   *Austin, Bastrop, Bell, Bexar, Burnet, Lake Somerville, Lee, McKinney Falls, Palmetto*

White-throated Sparrow, *Zonotrichia albicollis:* Common spring, fall, and winter resident. Wooded uplands, riparian woodlands where there is dense understory vegetation. Throughout.   *Austin, Bastrop, Bell, Bexar, Burnet, Enchanted Rock, Guadalupe River, Lake Somerville, Lee, McKinney Falls, Palmetto, Pedernales Falls*

White-crowned Sparrow, *Zonotrichia leucophrys:* Common spring, fall, and winter resident. Range and pastures, wooded uplands where there is dense understory vegetation, fence rows, brush piles. Throughout.   *Austin, Bastrop, Bell, Bexar, Burnet, Enchanted Rock, Guadalupe River, Lake Somerville, Lee, McKinney Falls, Palmetto, Pedernales Falls*

Harris' Sparrow, *Zonotrichia querula:* Common fall and winter resident; rare spring resident. Riparian woodlands, wooded uplands adjacent to range and pastures, brush piles. Throughout. Often seen with White-crowned Sparrow.   *Austin, Bastrop, Bell, Bexar, Burnet, Enchanted Rock, Guadalupe River, Lake Somerville, Lee, McKinney Falls, Palmetto, Pedernales Falls*

Dark-eyed Junco (Slate-colored Junco, Oregon Junco, Gray-headed Junco), *Junco hyemalis:* Common spring and winter resident; uncommon in fall. Riparian woodlands, wooded uplands in dense understory vegetation, brush piles. Throughout. *Austin, Bastrop, Bell, Bexar, Burnet, Enchanted Rock, Guadalupe River, Lake Somerville, Lee, McKinney Falls, Palmetto, Pedernales Falls*

McCown's Longspur, *Calcarius mccownii:* Uncommon winter resident. Croplands, range and pastures. Blackland Prairies. Bell, Williamson, and Guadalupe counties. *Austin, Bell, Bexar, Burnet*

Lapland Longspur, *Calcarius lapponicus:* Rare winter resident. Croplands, range and pastures. Blackland Prairies. *Austin, Bell, Bexar*

Smith's Longspur, *Calcarius pictus:* Accidental in winter. Croplands, range and pastures. Blackland Prairies. *Austin, Bexar*

Chestnut-collared Longspur, *Calcarius ornatus:* Uncommon winter resident. Croplands, range and pastures. Blackland Prairies. Bell, Williamson, and Guadalupe counties. *Austin, Bell, Bexar, Palmetto*

Subfamily ICTERINAE: Icterines

Tribe DOLICHONYCHINI: Bobolinks

Bobolink, *Dolichonyx oryzivorus:* Occasional in spring and fall. Croplands, range and pastures. Blackland Prairies. Usually found with migrating Dickcissels. *Austin, Bexar*

Tribe AGELAIINI: Blackbirds, Meadowlarks, Grackles, and Cowbirds

Red-winged Blackbird, *Agelaius phoeniceus*[‡]: Abundant permanent resident. Marshes, perennial waterways, riparian woodlands, small impoundments, wastewater ponds. Throughout. *Austin, Bastrop, Bell, Bexar, Burnet, Enchanted Rock, Lake Somerville, Lee, McKinney Falls, Palmetto, Pedernales Falls*

Eastern Meadowlark, *Sturnella magna*[‡]: Common permanent resident. Range and pastures. Throughout. *Austin, Bastrop, Bell, Bexar, Burnet, Enchanted Rock, Guadalupe River, Lake Somerville, Lee, McKinney Falls, Palmetto, Pedernales Falls*

Western Meadowlark, *Sturnella neglecta:* Common early spring, fall, and winter resident. Range and pastures, highway easements. Throughout. *Austin, Bastrop, Bell, Bexar, Burnet, Enchanted Rock, Lake Somerville, Lee, McKinney Falls, Palmetto, Pedernales Falls*

Yellow-headed Blackbird, *Xanthocephalus xanthocephalus:* Uncommon spring and fall migrant. Croplands, range and pastures, small impoundments. Blackland Prairies. Often seen at feedlots. *Austin, Bastrop, Bell, Bexar, Burnet, Lake Somerville, McKinney Falls, Palmetto*

Rusty Blackbird, *Euphagus carolinus:* Rare winter resident. Riparian woodlands, small impoundments, wastewater ponds. Hornsby Bend Ponds, Bastrop County.   *Austin, Bastrop, Bell, Bexar, Burnet, Guadalupe River, Lake Somerville, Palmetto*

Brewer's Blackbird, *Euphagus cyanocephalus:* Common fall and winter resident; uncommon to rare in spring. Croplands, range and pastures. Throughout. Often seen at livestock corrals.   *Austin, Bastrop, Bell, Bexar, Burnet, Enchanted Rock, Lake Somerville, Lee, McKinney Falls, Palmetto*

Great-tailed Grackle, *Quiscalus mexicanus*[‡]: Abundant permanent resident. Croplands, cultural areas. Throughout. Perhaps the most abundant bird in Austin.   *Austin, Bastrop, Bell, Bexar, Burnet, Guadalupe River, Lake Somerville, Lee, McKinney Falls, Palmetto*

Common Grackle, *Quiscalus quiscula*[‡]: Common permanent resident. Croplands, range and pastures, riparian woodlands, wooded uplands. Throughout, but mostly east of Balcones Escarpment.   *Austin, Bastrop, Bell, Bexar, Burnet, Lake Somerville, Lee, McKinney Falls, Palmetto*

Shiny Cowbird, *Molothrus bonariensis:* Accidental in Bell County. Collected at Fort Hood, May 23, 1990.

Bronzed Cowbird, *Molothrus aeneus*[‡]: Uncommon spring, summer, and fall resident. Cultural areas, wooded uplands. Edwards Plateau. Highland Lakes area, Lake Somerville, Bexar and Travis counties. Erratic.   *Austin, Bell, Bexar, Burnet, Guadalupe River, Lake Somerville*

Brown-headed Cowbird, *Molothrus ater*[‡]: Abundant permanent resident. Range and pastures, wooded uplands, cultural areas. Throughout.   *Austin, Bastrop, Bell, Bexar, Burnet, Enchanted Rock, Guadalupe River, Lake Somerville, Lee, McKinney Falls, Palmetto, Pedernales Falls*

Tribe ICTERINI: Oropendolas, Caciques, and American Orioles

Orchard Oriole, *Icterus spurius*[‡]: Uncommon spring and summer resident. Wooded uplands, particularly areas adjacent to range and pastures. Throughout. Inks Lake State Park, Enchanted Rock State Natural Area.   *Austin, Bastrop, Bell, Bexar, Burnet, Enchanted Rock, Guadalupe River, Lake Somerville, Lee, McKinney Falls, Palmetto, Pedernales Falls*

Hooded Oriole, *Icterus cucullatus:* Rare in spring, summer, and fall. Bexar and Hays counties.   *Austin, Bastrop, Bexar*

Altamira Oriole (Lichtenstein's Oriole), *Icterus gularis:* Formerly recorded. Bexar County (September 1963).   *Bexar*

Audubon's Oriole (Black-headed Oriole), *Icterus graduacauda:* Formerly recorded. Bexar and Travis (April 1964) counties.   *Austin, Bexar*

Northern Oriole (Baltimore Oriole, Bullock's Oriole), *Icterus galbula*[‡]: Both subspecies are uncommon spring and fall migrants; Bullock's is rare summer resident. Riparian woodlands, wooded uplands, range and pastures. Baltimore migrates throughout; Bullock's nests on Edwards Plateau. *Austin, Bastrop, Bell, Bexar, Burnet, Guadalupe River, Lake Somerville, Lee, McKinney Falls, Palmetto, Pedernales Falls*

Scott's Oriole, *Icterus parisorum*[‡]: Rare spring, summer, and fall resident. Range and pastures, wooded uplands. Edwards Plateau. Nests in Bexar County. *Austin, Bexar*

Family FRINGILLIDAE: Fringilline and Cardueline Finches and Allies

Subfamily CARDUELINAE: Cardueline Finches

Purple Finch, *Carpodacus purpureus:* Uncommon winter resident; rare in spring. Riparian woodlands, wooded uplands. Throughout. Erratic. *Austin, Bastrop, Bell, Bexar, Burnet, Enchanted Rock, Guadalupe River, Lake Somerville, Lee, McKinney Falls, Palmetto, Pedernales Falls*

Cassin's Finch, *Carpodacus cassinii:* Accidental in winter. Travis County. *Austin*

House Finch, *Carpodacus mexicanus*[‡]: Common permanent resident. Wooded uplands, cultural areas. More common west of Balcones Escarpment. *Austin, Bastrop, Bell, Bexar, Burnet, Enchanted Rock, Guadalupe River, McKinney Falls, Palmetto, Pedernales Falls*

Red Crossbill, *Loxia curvirostra:* Accidental in spring, fall, and winter. Bastrop, Bexar, and Travis counties. *Austin, Bastrop, Bexar*

Pine Siskin, *Carduelis pinus:* Uncommon (some years abundant) spring and winter resident; rare in fall. Cultural areas, wooded uplands. Throughout. Often seen with American Goldfinches and at feeders. *Austin, Bastrop, Bell, Bexar, Burnet, Enchanted Rock, Guadalupe River, Lake Somerville, Lee, McKinney Falls, Palmetto, Pedernales Falls*

Lesser Goldfinch, *Carduelis psaltria*[‡]: Uncommon permanent resident. Range and pastures, wooded uplands. Edwards Plateau. Pedernales Falls State Park, Highland Lakes area. *Austin, Bastrop, Bell, Bexar, Burnet, Enchanted Rock, Guadalupe River, Lee, McKinney Falls, Palmetto, Pedernales Falls*

American Goldfinch, *Carduelis tristis:* Common spring and winter resident; uncommon in fall; occasional in summer. Cultural areas, wooded uplands. Throughout. Often seen at feeders. *Austin, Bastrop, Bell, Bexar, Burnet, Enchanted Rock, Guadalupe River, Lake Somerville, Lee, McKinney Falls, Palmetto, Pedernales Falls*

Evening Grosbeak, *Coccothraustes vespertinus:* Occasional in winter.

Bastrop, Burnet, and Travis counties. Erratic.   *Austin, Bastrop, Bexar, Burnet*

Family PASSERIDAE: Old World Sparrows

House Sparrow, *Passer domesticus*‡*: Abundant permanent resident. Cultural areas. Throughout. Introduced from the Old World. *Austin, Bastrop, Bell, Bexar, Burnet, Enchanted Rock, Guadalupe River, Lake Somerville, Lee, McKinney Falls, Palmetto, Pedernales Falls*

Addenda

Order PELECANIFORMES: Totipalmate Swimmers

Suborder PELECANI: Boobies, Pelicans, Cormorants, and Darters

Family SULIDAE: Boobies and Gannets

Blue-footed Booby, *Sula nebouxii:* Accidental summer and fall, June 2 to October 9, 1993 (perhaps longer). Burnet County, Lake Lyndon B. Johnson. The second record for Texas; first was for one day only in Cameron County, Port Isabel (1976).

Order APODIFORMES: Swifts and Hummingbirds

Family TROCHILIDAE: Hummingbirds

Lucifer Hummingbird, *Calothorax lucifer:* Accidental. September 5–12, 1993. Hays County, Mountain City Oaks. First documented record for the nineteen county area.

CHAPTER 4

Mammals

RICKARD S. TOOMEY III AND S. CHRISTOPHER CARAN

THE LIST OF MAMMALS which follows includes eighty-two species, all of which have, may have, or formerly had free-living, reproducing populations in South Central Texas. Six of these species (five bats and one rodent) are known to occur in counties adjacent to the area and therefore may be part of the South Central Texas fauna, although their presence is not confirmed. Eight to eleven of the eighty-two species are known from the area historically but have been eliminated from the regional fauna by human activity. Nine or ten of the species listed are introduced. The introduced species are marked with an asterisk (*). There is debate about whether the red fox, *Vulpes vulpes*, was native and later pen-raised for release for hunting or whether it was introduced and became naturalized. This species is, therefore, marked *?. Important domestic mammals that have not established reproducing feral populations in the area are as follows: Order *Artiodactyla*, Family *Suidae*, hog, *Sus scrofa*; Family *Bovidae*, domestic cow, *Bos tasurus*; domestic sheep, *Ovis aries*; domestic goat, *Capra hircus*; also, Order *Perissodactyla*, Family *Equidae*, horse, *Equus caballus*; ass, *Equus hemionus*. In addition, many other exotic and domesticated species can be found in captivity; no attempt has been made to list these species.

The scientific and English names of most species, as well as the sequence in which they are listed, follow J. K. Jones et al., *Revised Checklist of North American Mammals North of Mexico, 1991:* Occasional papers of the Museum, no. 146, Texas Tech University (1992). The English names of domestic animals follow *Texas Mammals East of the Balcones Fault Zone* (D. J. Schmidly, 1983). For each species, the following information is provided: (1) current English name; (2) current scientific name; (3) relative abundance in the nineteen-county area; (4) habitat; (5) general distribution within the area; (6) other comments. There are no threatened or endangered mammals among the living fauna of South Central Texas, but five species known from the area in the past are endangered in their present range, and one extant species is considered threatened. All extant mammals are permanent residents except for the bats, most of which are migratory, emigrating in autumn or winter and returning in spring or summer. A few bat species overwinter in the area and several are year-round residents. Most bats hibernate in winter, and all roost during daylight hours. Habitat descriptions for bats refer to roosting and/ or hibernating sites. See the Selected References for complete list of sources.

Class MAMMALIA: Mammals
Order DIDELPHIMORPHIA: Opossums
Family DIDELPHIDAE: Opossums

Virginia Opossum, *Didelphis virginiana:* Abundant. All habitats. Throughout. Thrives in both rural and urban areas.

Order INSECTIVORA: Insectivores
Family SORICIDAE: Shrews

Least Shrew, *Cryptotis parva:* Uncommon. Abandoned fields, range and pastures. Difficult to capture; remains sometimes found in owl pellets.
Desert Shrew, *Notiosorex crawfordi:* Uncommon. Range and pastures. In South Central Texas, found only in Bexar County. Remains sometimes found in owl pellets.

Family TALPIDAE: Moles

Eastern Mole, *Scalopus aquaticus:* Uncommon. Cultivated fields; range and pastures; riparian woodlands, especially where soil is loose, well-drained, loamy, and moist. Throughout, more abundant east.

Order CHIROPTERA: Bats
Family MORMOOPIDAE: Mormoopid Bats

Ghost-faced Bat, *Mormoops megalophylla:* Locally common. Caves, cultural areas (tunnels, buildings). In South Central Texas, known only from Bexar County. Migratory, present in winter (November 1 to March 15) for hibernation. At northeastern limit of its range.

Family VESPERTILIONIDAE: Vespertilionid Bats

Cave Myotis, *Myotis velifer incautus:* Common. Caves, cultural areas (tunnels). Mostly west of the Balcones Escarpment. Year-round resident of area, although some males may emigrate in winter (November 1 to March 15). Hibernates in winter.

Eastern Red Bat, *Lasiurus borealis:* Common. Wooded uplands, riparian woodlands, cultural areas (urban trees), and rarely, caves. Throughout, but no records from Hays, Caldwell, Gonzales, or Burleson counties. Generally emigrates in winter, but some may overwinter, particularly in the eastern part of South Central Texas. Hibernates in winter.

Hoary Bat, *Lasiurus cinereus:* Rare. Wooded uplands, riparian woodlands. Probably throughout, but records from only a few counties scattered through area. Migratory, present in autumn and spring, but males may remain through summer, and some individuals may overwinter. Hibernates in winter.

Northern Yellow Bat, *Lasiurus intermedius floridanus:* Rare. Wooded uplands, riparian woodlands. Mostly east of the Balcones Escarpment; south and east of Williamson and Bell counties. In South Central Texas, known only from Travis, Milam, and Bexar counties. Distribution and abundance closely approximate that of Spanish moss, *Tillandsia usneoides,* on which this species typically roosts. Migratory; present in spring, summer, autumn, and perhaps late winter.

Seminole Bat, *Lasiurus seminolus:* Rare. Wooded uplands, riparian woodlands. In South Central Texas, known only from Burleson County, although there is an unverified record from McLennan County, just north of Bell County. Year-round resident, but there are few winter records. Probably does not hibernate.

Silver-Haired Bat, *Lasionycteris noctivagans:* Possible. Riparian woodlands, wooded uplands, cultural areas (urban trees and rarely, buildings). Could occur throughout, but there are no records from any of the counties of South Central Texas as here defined. Recorded in San Saba County immediately northwest of Burnet County and in Medina County just west of Bexar County. All of South Central Texas is within projected range. Within its known range in Texas, this species is migratory; present in autumn and spring.

Eastern Pipistrelle, *Pipistrellus subflavus:* Uncommon to locally abundant. Caves, wooded uplands, riparian woodlands, cultural areas (urban trees, tunnels, rarely buildings). Probably throughout; but in South Central Texas, not recorded east of counties bisected by Balcones Escarpment or north of Williamson County (species has been recorded east and north of area, however). Probably a year-round resident of area. Hibernates in winter.

Big Brown Bat, *Eptesicus fuscus* (probably *E. f. fuscus*): Possible (records uncertain). Caves, wooded uplands, cultural areas (urban trees, tunnels, buildings). Known from a single, unverified record in northern Bexar County; there is also a reported occurrence in McLennan County, just north of Bell County. Year-round resident of its known range in northwestern and northeastern Texas. Hibernates in winter.

Evening Bat, *Nycticeius humeralis:* Uncommon to common (abundance increases from west to east). Wooded uplands, riparian woodlands, cultural areas (urban trees, buildings). Throughout, although known in South Central Texas from only scattered records. Probably a year-round resident, but there are few winter records. Hibernates in winter.

Townsend's Big-eared Bat, *Plecotus townsendii pallescens:* Possible. Caves, cultural areas (tunnels; rarely, buildings). Known from Kimble County just west of Gillespie County; also, projected range (extrapolated from relatively recent records) includes the western part of Gillespie County. Year-round resident of its known range in western and southwestern Texas and the Panhandle. Hibernates in winter.

Pallid Bat, *Antrozous pallidus pallidus:* Possible. Caves, cultural areas (tunnels, buildings), possibly woodlands. Known from Kerr and Kimble counties, just west of Kendall and Gillespie counties; also, projected range (extrapolated from recent records) includes parts of Llano, Gillespie, Kendall, and Bexar counties. Migratory; present in spring, summer, and autumn in its known range in southwestern, western, and south Texas.

Family MOLOSSIDAE: Molossid Bats

Brazilian Free-tailed Bat, *Tadarida brasiliensis mexicanus:* Abundant. Caves, cultural areas (bridges, buildings). Throughout, but no records from Milam, Burleson, or Fayette counties. Colonial, with several very large colonies in the area. Migratory, present in spring, summer, and autumn.

Big Free-tailed Bat, *Nyctinomops macrotis:* Possible (low probability).
Caves, cultural areas (buildings). Known from Brazos County just
east of Burleson County; also, projected range (broadly interpolated from widely separated records) includes the entire South
Central Texas area with the possible exception of Burnet County.
Migratory, present in spring, summer, and autumn in its known
range in southwestern and southeastern Texas and the Panhandle.

Order XENARTHRA: Xenarthrans

Family DASYPODIDAE: Armadillos

Nine-banded Armadillo, *Dasypus novemcinctus:* Common. Range and
pastures, wooded uplands, riparian woodlands, cultural areas (occasionally). Throughout.

Order LAGOMORPHA: Lagomorphs

Family LEPORIDAE: Hares and Rabbits

Swamp Rabbit, *Sylvilagus aquaticus:* Uncommon or rare. Marshes, riparian woodlands. Mostly east of Balcones Escarpment.
Desert Cottontail, *Sylvilagus audubonii:* Rare. Range and pastures.
Llano, Gillespie, and Kendall counties represent the eastern limit
of its range.
Eastern Cottontail, *Sylvilagus floridanus:* Abundant. Cultivated fields,
range and pastures, riparian woodlands, cultural areas.
Throughout.
Black-tailed Jackrabbit, *Lepus californicus:* Common to abundant. Cultivated fields, range and pastures. Throughout. Most abundant in
western part of area.

Order RODENTIA: Rodents

Family SCIURIDAE: Squirrels

Mexican Ground Squirrel, *Spermophilus mexicanus:* Common to abundant. Riparian woodlands, range and pastures, cultural areas (open
parklands). Mostly in the western and southern parts of the area,
particularly where soils are sandy.
Thirteen-lined Ground Squirrel, *Spermophilus tridecemlineatus:* Possible. Range and pastures. Known from Colorado County just east
of Fayette County; also, projected range (interpolated from widely
separated records) includes parts of Fayette, Lee, Burleson, and
Milam counties.

Rock Squirrel, *Spermophilus variegatus:* Common. Wooded uplands, riparian woodlands. Edwards Plateau and westernmost edge of Gulf Coastal Plains in rocky habitats.

Black-tailed Prairie Dog, *Cynomys ludovicianus:* Historic. Range and pastures. Known from Bexar County, but this and all other populations (if any) in South Central Texas have been extirpated.

Eastern Gray Squirrel, *Sciurus carolinensis:* Rare. Wooded uplands. East of Balcones Escarpment, principally in the Post Oak Savannah. Range and abundance have decreased with clearing of hardwood forests.

Eastern Fox Squirrel, *Sciurus niger:* Abundant. Wooded uplands, riparian woodlands, cultural areas. Throughout. Highly adaptable; thrives in urban areas.

Southern Flying Squirrel, *Glaucomys volans:* Rare. Wooded uplands, riparian woodlands. In South Central Texas, known only from Bastrop County, but a record from McLennan County, just north of Bell County, extends the projected range to encompass the northeastern part of the area.

Family GEOMYIDAE: Pocket Gophers

Attwater's Pocket Gopher, *Geomys attwateri:* Common. Range and pastures (deep, sandy, well-drained soils). East of Balcones Escarpment.

Baird's Pocket Gopher, *Geomys breviceps:* Rare. Riparian areas. Generally ranges north and east of the Brazos River. In South Central Texas, known only from Lee and Milam counties in proximity to the Brazos River. Shifting river meanders isolated these populations thereby extending the species range.

Llano Pocket Gopher, *Geomys texensis:* Rare. Range and pastures. Llano and Gillespie counties in deep, sandy soils.

Family HETEROMYIDAE: Heteromyids

Merriam's Pocket Mouse, *Perognathus merriami:* Uncommon. Wooded uplands, range and pastures. Most common along and west of the Balcones Escarpment; possibly extending southeastward to Guadalupe and Gonzales counties and the western parts of Caldwell and Bastrop counties.

Hispid Pocket Mouse, *Chaetodipus hispidus:* Abundant. Range and pastures (sandy soils). Throughout.

Ord's Kangaroo Rat, *Dipodomys ordii:* Rare. Range and pastures (sandy soils). Known from Bexar and Gonzales counties.

Family CASTORIDAE: Beavers

American Beaver, *Castor canadensis:* Uncommon. Perennial waterways, small impoundments. Throughout. Almost extirpated, but
now increasing.

Family MURIDAE: Mice, Rats, and Voles

Fulvous Harvest Mouse, *Reithrodontomys fulvescens:* Abundant.
Range and pastures, riparian woodlands. Throughout, but most
common in eastern part of the area.

Plains Harvest Mouse, *Reithrodontomys montanus:* Common. Range
and pastures, cultural areas (highway rights-of-way). Throughout,
particularly in the western part of the area.

Texas Mouse, *Peromyscus attwateri:* Uncommon to locally common.
Wooded uplands. Edwards Plateau, especially in areas dominated
by juniper.

White-footed Mouse, *Peromyscus leucopus:* Common to abundant.
Wooded uplands, riparian woodlands. Throughout, but most common east of Balcones Escarpment.

Deer Mouse, *Peromyscus maniculatus:* Common. Range and pastures.
Throughout, but more common on Edwards Plateau.

White-ankled Mouse, *Peromyscus pectoralis:* Common. Range and pastures. Edwards Plateau.

Northern Pygmy Mouse, *Baiomys taylori:* Uncommon to common (dramatic seasonal changes in population). Wooded uplands, range and
pastures. Throughout; range has expanded greatly during historic
times.

Hispid Cotton Rat, *Sigmodon hispidus:* Abundant. Croplands, range
and pastures, grassy streamsides. Throughout. Populations fluctu-
ate drastically.

White-throated Woodrat, *Neotoma albigula:* Rare. Arid uplands. In
South Central Texas, known only from Llano County, but projected range encompasses Gillespie County and perhaps includes
northwestern Bexar County.

Eastern Woodrat, *Neotoma floridana:* Rare. Riparian woodlands,
wooded uplands. Throughout.

Southern Plains Woodrat, *Neotoma micropus:* Uncommon to common.
Range and pastures. In South Central Texas, known from Bexar,
Guadalupe, and Gonzales counties. Most often found in patches
of prickly pear cactus (*Opuntia* spp.).

Norway Rat, *Rattus norvegicus*:* Common. Cultural areas, marshes.
Throughout. Introduced.

Black Rat, *Rattus rattus*:* Abundant. Cultural areas. Throughout. Introduced.

House Mouse, *Mus musculus*:* Abundant. Cultural areas. Throughout. Introduced.

Family ERETHIZONTIDAE: New World Porcupines

Common Porcupine, *Erethizon dorsatum:* Rare. Wooded uplands, riparian woodlands. In South Central Texas, known from Gillespie, Kendall, and Bexar counties. Apparently becoming more common and extending its range eastward.

Family MYOCASTORIDAE: Myocastorids

Nutria, *Myocastor coypus*:* Uncommon to locally abundant. Permanent waterways, intermittent streams, small impoundments. Throughout. Introduced.

Order CARNIVORA: Carnivores

Family CANIDAE: Canids

Feral Dog, *Canis familiaris*:* Common. Cultural areas, range and pastures, wooded uplands. Throughout; free-living populations most common in the eastern part of the area. Introduced. Domestic and feral.

Coyote, *Canis latrans:* Uncommon. Range and pastures, wooded uplands. Throughout. Range and abundance reduced historically, but populations may be recovering.

Gray Wolf, *Canis lupus:* Historic. Range and pastures, wooded uplands. Extirpated in the early 1800's. Endangered throughout its current range.

Red Wolf, *Canis rufus:* Historic. Range and pastures, wooded uplands, riparian woodlands. Extirpated. Interbred with Coyote, *Canis latrans,* between 1890 and 1918. Endangered; total population may be limited to individuals currently maintained in captive breeding programs.

Red Fox, *Vulpes vulpes*?:* Rare. Wooded uplands, riparian woodlands. Probably introduced. If native, may have been extirpated locally and later reintroduced from populations outside the area, beginning about 1891.

Common Gray Fox, *Urocyon cinereoargenteus:* Common. Range and pastures, wooded uplands, riparian woodlands, cultural areas (occasionally). Throughout.

Family URSIDAE: Bears

Black Bear, *Ursus americanus:* Historic. Wooded uplands, riparian woodlands. Extirpated. Endangered in Texas.

Family PROCYONIDAE: Procyonids

Ringtail, *Bassariscus astutus:* Uncommon to common. Wooded uplands, riparian woodlands, cultural areas (occasionally). Throughout. Possibly increasing in abundance after virtual extirpation from its range.

Common Raccoon, *Procyon lotor:* Abundant. All habitats. Throughout.

Family MUSTELIDAE: Mustelids

Long-tailed Weasel, *Mustela frenata:* Rare. Riparian woodlands. Historically throughout, but now nearly extirpated.

Mink, *Mustela vison:* Rare. Marshes, riparian woodlands, permanent waterways. Historically throughout, primarily east of Balcones Escarpment, but now nearly extirpated.

American Badger, *Taxidea taxus:* Rare. Range and pastures, wooded uplands. In South Central Texas, known from Bexar, Guadalupe, Gonzales, and Travis counties. Nearly extirpated.

Western Spotted Skunk, *Spilogale gracilis:* Uncommon. Wooded uplands, riparian woodlands, range and pastures, cultural areas (occasionally). Southwestern part of the South Central Texas area; known from Bexar, Comal, Blanco, and Llano counties.

Eastern Spotted Skunk, *Spilogale putorius:* Rare. Wooded uplands, riparian woodlands, croplands, cultural areas (farmyards, rural parks). East of Balcones Escarpment; known from Bexar and Hays counties.

Striped Skunk, *Mephitis mephitis:* Abundant. All habitats. Throughout.

Common Hog-nosed Skunk, *Conepatus mesoleucus:* Uncommon. Wooded uplands, croplands, range and pastures. Mostly on Edwards Plateau.

Northern River Otter, *Lutra canadensis:* Probably historic. Permanent waterways, marshes, riparian woodlands. Possibly extant in Burleson County. Threatened in Texas.

Family FELIDAE: Cats

Feral Cat, *Felis catus*:* Abundant. Cultural areas; occasionally, range and pastures. Throughout. Introduced. Domestic and feral.

Mountain Lion, *Felis concolor:* Rare or historic. Wooded uplands, riparian woodlands, caves. Historically throughout, now possibly extirpated, although unconfirmed sightings are still reported from localities throughout South Central Texas.

Ocelot, *Felis pardalis:* Historic. Riparian woodlands, wooded uplands, caves. Extirpated. Endangered throughout its current range.

Bobcat, *Lynx rufus:* Uncommon. Riparian woodlands, wooded uplands, range and pastures. Throughout. Population density is low but appears stable.

Jaguar, *Panthera onca:* Historic. Wooded uplands, riparian woodlands, caves. Extirpated. Endangered in Texas.

Order ARTIODACTYLA: Even-toed Ungulates

Family DICOTYLIDAE: Peccaries

Collared Peccary, *Tayassu tajacu:* Probably historic. Wooded uplands. Possibly extant in southwestern part of South Central Texas.

Family CERVIDAE: Cervids

Axis Deer, *Cervus axis*:* Locally common. Wooded uplands, range and pastures. Mostly west of Balcones Escarpment. Introduced from India.

Fallow Deer, *Cervus dama*:* Locally common. Wooded uplands, range and pastures. Mostly west of Balcones Escarpment. Introduced from Eurasia.

Sika Deer, *Cervus nippon*:* Locally common. Wooded uplands, range and pastures. Mostly west of Balcones Escarpment. Introduced from the Orient.

White-tailed Deer, *Odocoileus virginianus:* Abundant. Wooded uplands, riparian woodlands, range and pastures, croplands. Throughout.

Family ANTILOCAPRIDAE: Pronghorn

Pronghorn, *Antilocapra americana:* Historic. Range. Mostly west of the Balcones Escarpment, but also known from Bastrop County. Extirpated in the late 1800's.

Family BOVIDAE: Bovids

American Bison, *Bos bison:* Historic. Range. Throughout, particularly in the western part of South Central Texas. Extirpated in the late 1800's.

CHAPTER 5

Amphibians and Reptiles

NAN HAMPTON

THE ANNOTATED CHECKLIST of the amphibians and reptiles for South Central Texas includes forty-one amphibians and ninety-four reptiles, encompassing all species known to have been recorded in the area. Of these species, four are introduced or possibly introduced. Because most amphibians and reptiles are secretive and have nocturnal habits, one of the most difficult questions to assess concerning amphibians and reptiles is their abundance. For those species that have been extensively studied within the area, e.g., the endangered and threatened species, a measure of the population size is relatively well established. For others, the "best estimate" of abundance within the nineteen-county area has been made using the sources below and personal observations. Habitats given for each species are the preferred habitats, i.e., the places in which they are most likely to be found. Introduced species are marked with an asterisk (*). Species that may have been introduced are denoted by (*?).

The order of presentation, for the most part, follows that of James Dixon's *Amphibians and Reptiles of Texas* (1987). Forms of both the English and scientific names follow that of *Standard Common and Current Scientific Names* (Joseph T. Collins, 1990), with the exception of family names which follow Conant and Collins' *Reptiles and Amphibians* (1991). The order of elements in each entry is as follows: (1) standard English name; (2) current scientific name; (3) abundance; (4) habitat preference; (5) general distribution in Texas; (6) recorded occurrences within the nineteen-county area; and (7) notes on unusual behavior or morphology, additional English names, and other comments.

This list is a revision and expansion of Nan Hampton's "Annotated Checklist of the Amphibians and Reptiles of Travis County, Texas" from Kutac and Caran's *A Bird Finding and Naturalist's Guide for the Austin, Texas, Area* (1975). The original checklist was reviewed by the late W. Frank Blair, Ph.D., in 1974 and 1975. This current list was reviewed by Michael Ryan, David Hillis, and James Bull, faculty members in the Department of Zoology at the University of Texas; and Paul Chippendale, graduate student in the Department of Zoology. The following publications were of invaluable assistance: (1) *The Snakes of Texas* (Alan Tenant, 1984); (2) *Snakes of South-Central Texas* (Thomas G. Vermesch and Robert E. Kuntz, 1986); (3) *A Field Guide to Reptiles and Amphibians of Texas* (Judith M. Garrett and David G. Barker, 1987); (4) *Amphibians and Reptiles of Texas* (James R. Dixon, 1987); (5) *Standard Common and Current Scientific Names for North American Amphibians and Reptiles* (Joseph T. Collins, 1990); and (6) *Reptiles and Amphibians: Eastern/Central North America* (Roger Conant and Joseph T. Collins, 1991). See the Selected References for complete list of sources.

Class AMPHIBIA: Amphibians
Order CAUDATA: Salamanders
Family SIRENIDAE: Sirens

Western Lesser Siren, *Siren intermedia nettingi:* Uncommon. Springs and seepage slopes, riparian woodlands. Scattered in eastern third of Texas. Burleson, Fayette, Gonzales, Guadalupe, and Lee counties.

Family AMBYSTOMATIDAE: Mole Salamanders

Smallmouth Salamander, *Ambystoma texanum:* Common. Springs and seepage slopes, riparian woodlands. Mostly east of Balcones Escarpment. Throughout, except Blanco, Gillespie, Kendall, and Llano counties.

Barred Tiger Salamander, *Ambystoma tigrinum mavortium**!: Uncommon or rare. Small impoundments. Scattered through western two-thirds of Texas. Burnet County. Probably introduced.

Eastern Tiger Salamander, *Ambystoma tigrinum tigrinum**!: Uncommon or rare. Small impoundments. Scattered through eastern third of Texas. Bexar and Milam counties. Probably introduced.

Family PLETHODONTIDAE: Lungless Salamanders

Cascade Caverns Salamander, *Eurycea latitans:* Rare. Caves. Found only in subterranean waters of Cascade Caverns in Kendall County. Neotenic, with external gills; completely aquatic and subterranean. May be a hybrid between Texas Salamander, *E. neotenes,* and Comal Blind Salamander, *E. tridentifera.* Threatened in Texas.

San Marcos Salamander, *Eurycea nana:* Generally rare, although abundant locally. Springs and spring pools. Found only in Spring Lake in Hays County. Neotenic, with external gills; completely aquatic. Threatened.

Texas Salamander, *Eurycea neotenes:* Common. Springs and seepage slopes, caves. Restricted to Balcones Escarpment. Bell, Bexar, Blanco, Comal, Gillespie, Hays, Kendall, Travis, and Williamson counties. Neotenic, with external gills; completely aquatic. Likely a species complex; many populations assigned to this species may soon be described as new species.

Dwarf Salamander, *Eurycea quadridigitata:* Uncommon. Springs and seepage slopes. Eastern third of Texas. Milam County.

Barton Springs Salamander, *Eurycea sosorum*: Rare. Known only from Barton Springs, Austin, Travis County. Neotenic, with external gills; completely aquatic. Specific name honors citizens' efforts in passing Save Our Springs (SOS) Ordinance in 1992. Under consideration by U.S. Fish and Wildlife Service to be listed as an endangered species.

Comal Blind Salamander, *Eurycea tridentifera:* Rare. Caves. Known only from Honey Creek Cave and nearby sinkholes in Comal County and from Elm Springs Cave in Bexar County, which extends into Kendall County. Neotenic, with external gills; completely aquatic. Threatened in Texas.

Western Slimy Salamander, *Plethodon albagula:* Common. Springs and seepage slopes, riparian woodlands. Balcones Escarpment and eastern portion of Edwards Plateau. Bell, Bexar, Blanco, Caldwell, Comal, Guadalupe, Hays, Kendall, Travis, and Williamson counties.

Texas Blind Salamander, *Typhlomolge rathbuni:* Rare. Caves. Known only from Hays County. Neotenic, with external gills; completely aquatic and subterranean. Endangered.

Blanco Blind Salamander, *Typhlomolge robusta:* Rare. Caves. Known only from Hays County but not same locale as Texas Blind Salamander. Neotenic, with external gills; completely aquatic and subterranean. Endangered in Texas.

Family SALAMANDRIDAE: Newts

Central Newt, *Notophthalmus viridescens louisianensis:* Rare. Marshes, small impoundments, intermittent streams, perennial waterways, riparian woodlands. Eastern third of Texas. Burleson and Milam counties.

Order SALIENTIA: Frogs and Toads

Family PELOBATIDAE: Spadefoot Toads

Couch's Spadefoot, *Scaphiopus couchii:* Common. Range and pastures, invaded fields. Western two-thirds of Texas. Throughout, except Blanco, Burleson, Fayette, Gonzales, Guadalupe, Lee, and Milam counties.

Hurter's Spadefoot, *Scaphiopus holbrookii hurterii:* Uncommon. Wooded uplands, riparian woodlands. Eastern half of Texas. Bastrop, Bexar, Burleson, Caldwell, Fayette, Gonzales, and Lee counties.

New Mexico Spadefoot, *Spea multiplicata:* Rare. Upland baregrounds, range and pastures. Scattered through western third of Texas. Isolated population in Gillespie County.

Family LEPTODACTYLIDAE: Tropical Frogs

Eastern Barking Frog, *Eleutherodactylus augusti latrans:* Rare. Wooded uplands, upland baregrounds, springs and seepage slopes, caves; occasionally, cultural areas. Primarily along Balcones Escarpment. Bexar, Comal, Hays, Kendall, Travis, and Williamson counties.

Rio Grande Chirping Frog, *Syrrhophus cystignathoides campi**: Rare to abundant locally. Small impoundments, cultural areas. Rio Grande Valley and scattered locations throughout southern Texas. Introduced into Bexar County via nursery plants.

Cliff Chirping Frog, *Syrrhophus marnockii:* Common. Springs and seepage slopes, wooded uplands, riparian woodlands (in canyons). Balcones Escarpment and southern Edwards Plateau. Bell, Bexar, Blanco, Burnet, Comal, Hays, Kendall, Travis, and Williamson counties.

Family HYLIDAE: Treefrogs and Allies

Blanchard's Cricket Frog, *Acris crepitans blanchardi:* Abundant. Small impoundments, intermittent streams, riparian baregrounds. Statewide. Throughout.

Cope's Gray Treefrog, *Hyla chrysocelis:* Common. Riparian woodlands. Primarily eastern half of Texas. Apparently throughout, except Bell, Blanco, and Lee counties. Distinguished from *H. versicolor* only on the basis of chromosome studies and voice. Ranges and habitats of these species apparently overlap.

Green Treefrog, *Hyla cinerea:* Common. Riparian woodlands, marshes.

Eastern and southern Texas. Throughout, except Bell, Blanco, Fayette, Gillespie, Kendall, Lee, and Milam counties.

Gray Treefrog, *Hyla versicolor:* Common. Riparian woodlands. Generally in eastern half of Texas. Apparently throughout, except Bell, Blanco, and Lee counties. Distinguished from *H. chrysocelis* only on the basis of chromosome studies and voice. Ranges and habitats of these species apparently overlap.

Northern Spring Peeper, *Pseudacris crucifer crucifer:* Uncommon. Riparian woodlands, marshes, intermittent streams. Eastern Texas. Burleson and Lee counties. Inconspicuous except during breeding season.

Spotted Chorus Frog, *Pseudacris clarkii:* Common. Small impoundments, marshes, intermittent streams. Central third of Texas. Throughout, except Blanco, Guadalupe, and Lee counties. Inconspicuous except during breeding season.

Stecker's Chorus Frog, *Pseudacris streckeri streckeri:* Common. All habitats. Eastern half of Texas. Throughout, except Blanco, Fayette, Guadalupe, and Kendall counties.

Upland Chorus Frog, *Pseudacris feriarum feriarum:* Uncommon. Small impoundments, marshes, intermittent streams. Eastern third of Texas. Bastrop, Burleson, Hays, Lee, Milam, and Travis counties.

Family BUFONIDAE: Toads

Eastern Green Toad, *Bufo debilis debilis:* Common. Upland baregrounds, range and pastures, invaded fields. Central third of Texas. Bell, Bexar, Burnet, Comal, Gillespie, Gonzales, Hays, Travis, and Williamson counties.

Houston Toad, *Bufo houstonensis:* Rare. Upland baregrounds, range and pastures, invaded fields. Populations known from only four counties statewide: Bastrop, Burleson, Colorado, and Harris. Endangered.

Red-spotted Toad, *Bufo punctatus:* Common. Upland baregrounds, range and pastures, springs and seepage slopes. Western half of Texas. Bell, Bexar, Blanco, Burnet, Comal, Gillespie, Hays, Kendall, Llano, Travis, and Williamson counties.

Texas Toad, *Bufo speciosus:* Common. Range and pastures, croplands, invaded fields. Western two-thirds of Texas. Bastrop, Bexar, Burnet, Caldwell, Comal, Fayette, Gonzales, Hays, Kendall, and Travis counties.

Gulf Coast Toad, *Bufo valliceps valliceps:* Abundant. All habitats.

Southeastern half of Texas. Throughout. The most commonly
encountered toad in the area.

Woodhouse's Toad, *Bufo woodhousii woodhousii:* Uncommon. All
habitats. Northeastern half of Texas. Throughout.

Family RANIDAE: True Frogs

Southern Crawfish Frog, *Rana areolata areolata:* Uncommon or rare.
Intermittent streams, small impoundments. Eastern third of
Texas. Burleson County. Often found in, but not restricted to,
abandoned crawfish holes.

Rio Grande Frog, *Rana berlandieri:* Abundant. Small impoundments,
intermittent streams, riparian woodlands, wooded uplands. Central and southwestern Texas. Throughout, except Burleson, Fayette, Lee, and Milam counties. This species and *R. utricularia* are
not separable on the basis of external morphology. Earlier records
may have referred one or both of these species to *R. pipiens,*
which is also inseparable, except by chromosome study, but
which does not occur in the area.

Bullfrog, *Rana catesbeiana:* Common. Permanent waterways, small impoundments. Statewide. Throughout, except Blanco County.

Bronze Frog, *Rana clamitans clamitans:* Uncommon or rare. Small impoundments, intermittent streams, riparian woodlands. Eastern
third of Texas. Bastrop, Burleson, and Williamson counties.

Pickerel Frog, *Rana palustris:* Uncommon or rare. Small impoundments, intermittent streams, riparian woodlands, wooded uplands. Eastern third of Texas. Burleson County.

Southern Leopard Frog, *Rana utricularia utricularia:* Abundant. Small
impoundments, intermittent streams, riparian woodlands,
wooded uplands. Eastern half of Texas. Bastrop, Bell, Bexar, Burleson, Fayette, Gonzales, Guadalupe, Kendall, Lee, Milam, and
Travis counties. See comments regarding Rio Grande Frog,
R. berlandieri.

Family MICROHYLIDAE: Narrowmouth Toads

Eastern Narrowmouth Toad, *Gastrophryne carolinensis:* Uncommon.
Marshes, range and pastures, upland baregrounds, riparian baregrounds. Eastern third of Texas. Bastrop, Burleson, Comal, Gonzales, Milam, Travis, and Williamson counties.

Great Plains Narrowmouth Toad, *Gastrophryne olivacea:* Common. Marshes, range and pastures, upland baregrounds, riparian baregrounds. Southern two-thirds of Texas. Throughout, except Blanco and Guadalupe counties.

Class REPTILIA: Reptiles
Order CROCODILIA: Crocodilians
Family ALLIGATORIDAE: Alligators

American Alligator, *Alligator mississippiensis:* Rare. Permanent waterways, small impoundments. Southeastern third of Texas. Recent records from Bastrop, Bexar, Burleson, Fayette, Hays, Lee, Milam, Travis, and Williamson counties, but throughout historically. Some recent records are possibly abandoned pets. Increasing in abundance and reoccupying part of its historic range. Resembles Spectacled Caiman, *Caiman crocodilus,* which was formerly introduced as a pet and may occasionally be encountered through escape or release. There are, however, no known free-living, reproducing populations of Spectacled Caiman in the area.

Order TESTUDINES: Turtles
Family CHELYDRIDAE: Snapping Turtles

Common Snapping Turtle, *Chelydra serpentina serpentina:* Common. Permanent waterways, small impoundments. Eastern half of Texas with isolated populations elsewhere. Bastrop, Bell, Bexar, Burleson, Burnet, Fayette, Hays, Kendall, Travis, and Williamson counties. Seldom basks.

Family KINOSTERNIDAE: Musk and Mud Turtles

Yellow Mud Turtle, *Kinosternon flavescens flavescens:* Common. Permanent waterways, small impoundments, intermittent streams. Primarily western two-thirds of Texas. Throughout, except for Burleson, Fayette, and Lee counties.

Mississippi Mud Turtle, *Kinosternon subrubrum hippocrepis:* Uncommon or rare. Permanent waterways, small impoundments. Eastern half of Texas. Throughout, except for Blanco, Burnet, Caldwell, Guadalupe, Kendall, and Llano counties. Seldom basks.

Razorback Musk Turtle, *Sternotherus carinatus:* Uncommon or rare. Permanent waterways, small impoundments. Scattered through northeastern Texas. Bell and Milam counties. Basks more frequently than do other musk turtles.

Common Musk Turtle, *Sternotherus odoratus:* Abundant or common. Permanent waterways (reservoirs), small impoundments, marshes. Central and eastern Texas. Throughout, except Bastrop, Bell, Burleson, Caldwell, and Fayette counties. Widely but informally known as "stinkpot turtle" because of its strong musky odor.

Family EMYDIDAE: Box and Water Turtles

Western Chicken Turtle, *Deirochelys reticularia miaria:* Uncommon or rare. Permanent waterways, small impoundments. Primarily eastern Texas. Lee and Williamson counties. Once sold in fish markets in the South for food. Often walks about on land.

Cagle's Map Turtle, *Graptemys caglei:* Uncommon or rare. Permanent waterways. Restricted to San Antonio–Guadalupe River basins. Bexar, Gonzales, Hays, and Kendall counties.

Texas Map Turtle, *Graptemys versa:* Uncommon. Permanent waterways. Restricted to central Colorado River basin in Texas. Bastrop, Blanco, Burnet, Hays, Llano, and Travis counties.

Texas River Cooter, *Pseudemys texana:* Common. Permanent waterways, small impoundments. Scattered statewide. Throughout except Bell, Burleson, Caldwell, Fayette, Guadalupe, Lee, and Milam counties.

Three-toed Box Turtle, *Terrapene carolina triunguis:* Uncommon. Wooded uplands, riparian woodlands. Eastern Texas. Throughout, except Blanco, Burnet, Caldwell, Gillespie, Kendall, and Williamson counties. Also called "eastern box turtle." Sometimes has four toes on each hind foot but typically has three.

Ornate Box Turtle, *Terrapene ornata ornata:* Common. Upland baregrounds, upland woodlands. Statewide. Throughout except Guadalupe and Kendall counties. Also called "western box turtle."

Red-eared Slider, *Trachemys scripta elegans:* Abundant. Permanent waterways. Statewide. Throughout, except Lee and Williamson counties. Often basks on logs or other objects in water. Young of this species commonly sold as pets.

Family TESTUDINIDAE: Gopher Tortoises

Texas Tortoise, *Gopherus berlandieri:* Rare. Upland baregrounds. Scattered through southern Texas. Bexar and Guadalupe counties. Threatened in Texas.

Family TRIONYCHAIDAE: Softshell Turtles

Midland Smooth Softshell, *Apalone mutica mutica:* Uncommon or rare. Permanent waterways. Discontinuous across eastern two-thirds of Texas. Milam County.

Guadalupe Spiny Softshell, *Apalone spinifera guadalupensis:* Common. Permanent waterways. Southern half of Texas. Throughout, except Bell, Burleson, Caldwell, Lee, Milam, and Williamson counties.

Pallid Spiny Softshell, *Apalone spinifera pallida:* Uncommon. Permanent waterways. Northern half of Texas. Bell, Burleson, Milam, and Williamson counties.

Order SQUAMATA: Lizards and Snakes
Suborder LACERTILIA: Lizards
Family GEKKONIDAE: Geckos

Texas Banded Gecko, *Coleonyx brevis:* Uncommon. Upland baregrounds. Southwestern Texas. Bexar County. Only native gecko with functional eyelids.

Mediterranean Gecko, *Hemidactylus turcicus*:* Uncommon to locally abundant. Cultural areas. Scattered localities throughout southern Texas. Bexar, Fayette, Gonzales, Hays, Lee, and Travis counties. Increasing in range and abundance. Only lizard in area with a voice. Introduced.

Family POLYCHRIDAE: Anoles

Green Anole, *Anolis carolinensis:* Abundant. Cultural areas, riparian woodlands, wooded uplands. Eastern half of Texas. Throughout except Bell, Burnet, Gillespie, and Llano counties. Commonly but improperly called "chameleon" because this species is capable of limited color changes. Males are particularly prone to change colors during territorial posturing and combat.

Family CROTAPHYTIDAE: Collared and Leopard Lizards

Eastern Collared Lizard, *Crotaphytus collaris collaris:* Common. Upland baregrounds. Northwestern two-thirds of Texas. Throughout except Caldwell, Fayette, Gonzales, Guadalupe, Lee, and Milam counties. Often runs on hind legs. Also called "mountain boomer," although voiceless.

Family PHRYNOSOMATIDAE: Earless, Spiny, Tree,
Side-blotched, and Horned Lizards

Texas Earless Lizard, *Cophosaurus texanus texanus:* Common. Upland baregrounds, riparian baregrounds. Most of the western half of Texas. Throughout, except Bastrop, Burleson, Caldwell, Guadalupe, Lee, and Milam counties.

Plateau Earless Lizard, *Holbrookia lacerata lacerata:* Uncommon. Upland baregrounds. Restricted to Edwards Plateau in Texas. Blanco, Comal, Gillespie, Hays, Kendall, and Travis counties.

Southern Earless Lizard, *Holbrookia lacerata subcaudalis:* Uncommon or rare. Croplands, range and pastures. Southern Texas. Bastrop and Bexar counties.

Eastern Earless Lizard, *Holbrookia maculata perspicua:* Uncommon. Croplands, range and pastures, upland baregrounds. North central Texas. Bell, Burnet, and Milam counties.

Keeled Earless Lizard, *Holbrookia propinqua propinqua:* Uncommon. Croplands, range and pastures. Southern Texas. Bexar, Gonzales, Guadalupe, and Hays counties.

Texas Horned Lizard, *Phrynosoma cornutum:* Uncommon or rare. Range and pastures, upland baregrounds. Statewide. Throughout except Caldwell County. Commonly but improperly called "horned toad." Formerly sold as pets, now protected in Texas. Threatened in Texas.

Texas Spiny Lizard, *Sceloporus olivaceus:* Abundant. Wooded uplands, riparian woodlands, cultural areas, invaded fields. Central third of Texas. Throughout except Burleson County. Also called "rusty lizard."

Crevice Spiny Lizard, *Sceloporus poinsettii poinsettii:* Uncommon. Upland baregrounds. Western and central Texas. Bexar, Blanco, Burnet, Comal, Gillespie, Kendall, and Llano counties.

Southern Prairie Lizard, *Sceloporus undulatus consobrinus:* Common. Upland baregrounds. Western two-thirds of Texas. Throughout, except Fayette and Gonzales counties.

Northern Fence Lizard, *Sceloporus undulatus hyacinthinus:* Uncommon. All habitats. Eastern third of Texas. Fayette and Gonzales counties.

Rosebelly Lizard, *Sceloporus variabilis marmoratus:* Uncommon. All habitats. Southern Texas. Bexar, Comal, Guadalupe, and Hays counties.

Eastern Tree Lizard, *Urosaurus ornatus ornatus:* Common. All habitats. Central and southwestern Texas. Throughout, except Bell, Burleson, Caldwell, Fayette, Gonzales, Lee, and Milam counties.

Family SCINCIDAE: Skinks

Five-lined Skink, *Eumeces fasciatus:* Rare. Range and pastures, wooded uplands, invaded fields. Eastern third of Texas. Burleson County. Across most of its range, this species is essentially ground-dwelling, but in Texas it is almost exclusively arboreal.

Broadhead Skink, *Eumeces laticeps:* Rare. Wooded uplands, riparian woodlands, invaded fields. Eastern Texas. Fayette and Williamson counties.

Great Plains Skink, *Eumeces obsoletus:* Uncommon. Range and pastures, upland baregrounds. Western two-thirds of Texas. Bexar, Blanco, Burnet, Gillespie, Milam, and Travis counties.

Southern Prairie Skink, *Eumeces septentrionalis obtusirostris:* Rare. Range and pastures, upland baregrounds, riparian baregrounds. Scattered through eastern Texas and central Texas Gulf Coast. Bexar, Burleson, Gonzales, Lee, and Milam counties.

Short-lined Skink, *Eumeces tetragrammus:* Common. Wooded uplands, riparian woodlands, upland baregrounds, range and pastures. Central and southwestern Texas. Bell, Bexar, Blanco, Burnet, Comal, Gillespie, Hays, Kendall, Llano, Travis, and Williamson counties.

Ground Skink, *Scincella lateralis:* Abundant. Wooded uplands, riparian woodlands. Eastern two-thirds of Texas. Throughout, except Caldwell County.

Family TEIIDAE: Whiptails

Texas Spotted Whiptail, *Cnemidophorus gularis gularis:* Common. Upland baregrounds, range and pastures. Western two-thirds of Texas. Throughout.

Six-lined Racerunner, *Cnemidophorus sexlineatus sexlineatus:* Common. Upland baregrounds, range and pastures, invaded fields, riparian baregrounds. Eastern two-thirds of Texas. Throughout, except Blanco, Burnet, Fayette, and Kendall counties.

Family ANGUIDAE: Glass and Alligator Lizards

Texas Alligator Lizard, *Gerrhonotus liocephalus infernales:* Uncommon. Upland baregrounds, wooded uplands. Principally Edwards Plateau and Big Bend area. Throughout, except Bastrop, Bell, Burleson, Caldwell, Gonzales, Guadalupe, Lee, and Milam counties.

Western Slender Glass Lizard, *Ophisaurus attenuatus attenuatus:* Uncommon or rare. Range and pastures, upland baregrounds, invaded fields. Eastern half of Texas. Bexar, Burleson, Burnet, Gonzales, ` Hays, Kendall, Lee, Travis, and Williamson counties. Legless. Commonly but improperly called "joint snake."

Suborder SERPENTES: Snakes

Family LEPTOTYPHLOPIDAE: Blind Snakes

Plains Blind Snake, *Leptotyphlops dulcis dulcis:* Common. Upland baregrounds, range and pastures, cultural areas, wooded uplands. Central third of Texas. Throughout, except Bastrop, Burleson, Caldwell, and Guadalupe counties. Generally subterranean.

Family COLUBRIDAE: Colubrids

Texas Glossy Snake, *Arizona elegans arenicola:* Uncommon. Croplands, wooded uplands, upland baregrounds, range and pastures. Southern third of Texas with scattered records in eastern Texas. Bastrop, Bexar, Burleson, Caldwell, Comal, Fayette, Gonzales, Hays, Lee, Milam, and Travis counties. Frequently, but not exclusively, subterranean.

Eastern Yellowbelly Racer, *Coluber constrictor flaviventris:* Common. Croplands, invaded fields, range and pastures, wooded uplands. Central and eastern Texas. Throughout, except Blanco, Gillespie, Lee, and Llano counties. Not a true constrictor, despite its specific name.

Prairie Ringneck Snake, *Diadophus punctatus arnyi:* Rare or uncommon. Wooded uplands, riparian woodlands, invaded fields, cultural areas. Scattered through northern two-thirds of Texas. Bexar, Blanco, Burnet, Gillespie, Hays, Kendall, Llano, Travis, and Williamson counties. Secretive, often subterranean.

Texas Indigo Snake, *Drymarchon corais erebennus:* Uncommon or rare. Riparian woodlands, range and pastures. Southern Texas. Bexar County. The largest snake found in the area. Prey includes poisonous snakes. Threatened in Texas.

Great Plains Rat Snake, *Elaphe guttata emoryi:* Common. Upland baregrounds, wooded uplands, croplands, invaded fields, range and pastures. Statewide. Throughout, except Fayette and Lee counties.

Texas Rat Snake, *Elaphe obsoleta lindheimerii:* Common. All habitats. Primarily eastern two-thirds of Texas with scattered records elsewhere. Throughout. Also called "chicken snake." Aggressive but nonpoisonous. Probably the most abundant large snake across most of its range.

Western Mud Snake, *Farancia abacura reinwardtii:* Rare. Marshes, small impoundments. Eastern third of Texas. Burleson County.

Western Hooknose Snake, *Gyalopion canum:* Rare. Upland baregrounds, range and pastures. Western and west-central Texas. Gillespie County. Rear-fanged and mildly venomous but not dangerous to humans.

Dusty Hognose Snake, *Heterodon nasicus gloydi:* Uncommon or rare. Upland baregrounds, range and pastures. Scattered through central third of Texas. Isolated populations in Bexar, Comal, and Hays counties. Rear-fanged and mildly venomous but not dangerous to humans.

Eastern Hognose Snake, *Heterodon platirhinos:* Common. All habitats. Eastern half of Texas. Throughout, except Caldwell County. Rear-fanged and mildly venomous but not harmful to humans. Commonly but improperly called "puff adder" or "spreading adder" because it hisses and spreads its neck in defense; plays dead.

Texas Night Snake, *Hypsiglena torquata jani:* Common, but secretive. Upland baregrounds, range and pastures. Western two-thirds of Texas. Bexar, Burnet, Caldwell, Comal, Hays, Kendall, and Llano counties. Rear-fanged and mildly venomous but not dangerous to humans. Vertically elliptical pupil.

Prairie Kingsnake, *Lampropeltis calligaster calligaster:* Uncommon. Wooded uplands, range and pastures, invaded fields. Scattered through eastern half of Texas. Bastrop, Bell, Bexar, Burleson, Comal, Fayette, Hays, Milam, Travis, and Williamson counties. A constrictor preying on snakes and lizards. Immune to venom of native poisonous snakes.

Speckled Kingsnake, *Lampropeltis getula holbrooki:* Uncommon or rare. All habitats. Eastern third of Texas. Intergrades with Desert Kingsnake, *L. g. splendida,* in the east-central portion of Texas; zone of intergradation includes Bastrop, Bell, Burleson, Burnet, Comal, Fayette, Gonzales, Guadalupe, Hays, Travis, and Williamson counties. Constrictor preying on snakes and lizards. Immune to venom of native poisonous snakes.

Desert Kingsnake, *Lampropeltis getula splendida:* Uncommon or rare.

All habitats. Western two-thirds of Texas. Bexar, Kendall, Guadalupe, and Gillespie counties. Constrictor preying on snakes and lizards. Immune to venom of native poisonous snakes. See comments regarding Speckled Kingsnake, *L. g. holbrooki.*

Louisiana Milk Snake, *Lampropeltis triangulum amaura:* Uncommon or rare. All habitats. Sparsely scattered through eastern Texas. Bell, Burleson, Comal, and Travis counties. Constrictor preying on snakes and lizards. Immune to venom of native poisonous snakes. Colors and pattern mimic Texas Coral Snake, *Micrurus fulvius tener.*

Mexican Milk Snake, *Lampropeltis triangulum annulata:* Uncommon. All habitats. Scattered throughout eastern Texas. Bexar, Comal, Gillespie, and Kendall counties. Constrictor preying on snakes and lizards. Immune to native poisonous snakes. Colors and pattern mimic Texas Coral Snake, *Micrurus fulvius tener.*

Western Coachwhip, *Masticophis flagellum testaceus:* Common. Range and pastures, upland baregrounds, invaded fields. Western two-thirds of Texas. Throughout.

Central Texas Whipsnake, *Masticophis taeniatus girardi:* Uncommon. Invaded fields, upland baregrounds, wooded uplands. Central and southwestern Texas. Bexar, Blanco, Burnet, Comal, Gillespie, Hays, Kendall, Llano, and Travis counties. Southern edge of range partly overlaps range of Schott's whipsnake, *M. t. schotti.*

Schott's Whipsnake, *Masticophis taeniatus schotti:* Uncommon or rare. Invaded fields, upland baregrounds, wooded uplands. Southern Texas. Bexar, Comal, Hays, and Travis counties. Northern edge of range partly overlaps range of Central Texas whipsnake, *M. t. girardi.*

Blotched Water Snake, *Nerodia erythrogaster transversa:* Uncommon. Permanent waterways, intermittent streams, small impoundments. Statewide. Throughout. Nonvenomous but often mistaken for the venomous Western Cottonmouth, *Agkistrodon piscirorus leucostoma.*

Broad-banded Water Snake, *Nerodia fasciata confluens:* Common. Marshes, small impoundments, permanent waterways, intermittent streams. Eastern Texas. Bastrop, Burleson, Caldwell, Gonzales, Lee, Travis, and Williamson counties. Nonvenomous but often mistaken for the venomous Western Cottonmouth, *Agkistrodon piscivorus leucostoma.*

Diamondback Water Snake, *Nerodia rhombifera rhombifera:* Common. Marshes, small impoundments, permanent waterways, intermittent streams. Eastern two-thirds of Texas. Throughout. Nonven-

omous but often mistaken for the venomous Western Cottonmouth, *Agkistrodon piscivorus leucostoma.*

Rough Green Snake, *Opheodrys aestivus:* Common. Wooded uplands,
riparian woodlands, range and pastures, invaded fields. Eastern
two-thirds of Texas. Throughout, except Bastrop, Lee, Milam, and
Williamson counties.

Bullsnake, *Pituophis catenifer sayi:* Common. Range and pastures, invaded fields, croplands. Scattered through western two-thirds of
Texas. Throughout, except Burleson, Fayette, Gillespie, Lee, and
Milam counties. Sometimes mistaken for a rattlesnake. Powerful
constrictor.

Graham's Crayfish Snake, *Regina grahamii:* Uncommon or rare. Permanent waterways, small impoundments. Scattered through eastern
half of Texas. Bexar, Burleson, and Fayette counties.

Texas Longnose Snake, *Rhinocheilus lecontei tessellatus:* Uncommon.
Upland baregrounds, range and pastures. Western two-thirds of
Texas. Throughout except Blanco, Fayette, and Kendall counties.

Texas Patchnose Snake, *Salvadora grahamiae lineata:* Uncommon to
common. Upland baregrounds, range and pastures, invaded fields.
Central Texas. Throughout, except Fayette and Guadalupe counties. Secretive, subterranean. Mildly venomous but not harmful to
humans.

Ground Snake, *Sonora semiannulata:* Common. Upland baregrounds,
range and pastures. North central Texas. Bell, Blanco, Burleson,
Gillespie, Kendall, and Llano counties. Intergrades with Taylor's
ground snake, *S. s. taylori* in Bexar, Comal, Hays, Travis, and Williamson counties.

Taylor's Ground Snake, *Sonora semiannulata taylori:* Common. Upland
baregrounds, range and pastures. Scattered through southern and
eastern Texas. Recognized as a separate subspecies by Dixon
(1987), but not by Collins (1990), Conant and Collins (1991), or
Vermersch and Kuntz (1986). See comments regarding Ground
Snake, *S. semiannulata.*

Texas Brown Snake, *Storeria dekayi texana:* Common. Riparian woodlands, wooded uplands, marshes, cultural areas. Eastern two-
thirds of Texas. Throughout, except Blanco, Caldwell, Guadalupe,
Lee, and Llano counties.

Flathead Snake, *Tantilla gracilis:* Uncommon to common. All habitats.
Eastern two-thirds of Texas. Throughout, except Fayette and Lee
counties. Rear-fanged and mildly venomous but not harmful to
humans.

Plains Blackhead Snake, *Tantilla nigriceps:* Uncommon. Upland baregrounds, wooded uplands. Central third of Texas. Bexar, Comal, Hays, Kendall, and Travis counties. Rear-fanged and mildly venomous but not harmful to humans.

Eastern Blackneck Garter Snake, *Thamnophis cyrtopsis ocellatus:* Common. Upland baregrounds, wooded uplands, riparian baregrounds, riparian woodlands. Restricted to Edwards Plateau and southwestern Texas. Bell, Bexar, Blanco, Comal, Hays, Kendall, Travis, and Williamson counties.

Checkered Garter Snake, *Thamnophis marcianus marcianus:* Common. Intermittent streams, riparian baregrounds, riparian woodlands. Western two-thirds of Texas. Throughout, except Burleson, Lee, and Milam counties.

Gulf Coast Ribbon Snake, *Thamnophis proximus orarius:* Uncommon. Intermittent streams, small impoundments, riparian woodlands, riparian baregrounds, marshes. Along Gulf Coast in Texas. Zone of intergradation with Redstripe Ribbon Snake, *T. p. rubrilineatus,* and/or Western Ribbon Snake, *T. p. proximus,* in Bastrop, Burleson, Caldwell, Fayette, Gonzales, Guadalupe, Lee, and Milam counties.

Western Ribbon Snake, *Thamnophis proximus proximus:* Uncommon. Intermittent streams, small impoundments, riparian woodlands, riparian baregrounds. Northeastern Texas. Zone of intergradation with Redstripe Ribbon Snake, *T. p. rubrilineatus,* and Gulf Coast Ribbon Snake, *T. p. orarius,* in Burleson, Lee, and Milam counties. Semiaquatic.

Redstripe Ribbon Snake, *Thamnophis proximus rubrilineatus:* Abundant. Intermittent streams, small impoundments, riparian woodlands, riparian baregrounds. Central Texas. Throughout, except Bastrop, Burleson, Caldwell, Fayette, Gonzales, Lee, and Milam counties. See comments regarding Gulf Coast Ribbon Snake, *T. p. orarius,* and Western Ribbon Snake, *T. p. proximus.*

Texas Garter Snake, *Thamnophis sirtalis annectens:* Generally uncommon but abundant locally. Intermittent streams, small impoundments, riparian woodlands, riparian baregrounds. Sparsely scattered through north central Texas. Bell, Bexar, Blanco, Burnet, Hays, Travis, and Williamson counties.

Eastern Garter Snake, *Thamnophis sirtalis sirtalis:* Uncommon or rare. Intermittent streams, small impoundments, riparian woodlands, riparian baregrounds, marshes. Sparsely scattered through eastern half of Texas. Fayette County.

Lined Snake, *Tropidoclonion lineatum:* Locally common. Range and pastures, invaded fields, cultural areas. Primarily eastern central

Texas. Throughout, except Bastrop, Blanco, Fayette, Gonzales, Kendall, Lee, Llano, and Milam counties.

Rough Earth Snake, *Virginia striatula:* Common. Wooded uplands, riparian woodlands, range and pastures. Eastern half of Texas. Throughout, except Blanco County.

Western Earth Snake, *Virginia valeriae elegans:* Generally uncommon but abundant locally. Wooded uplands, riparian woodlands, invaded fields. Sparsely scattered through central and eastern Texas. Bell, Bexar, Burnet, Comal, Kendall, Travis, and Williamson counties.

Family ELAPIDAE: Coral Snakes

Texas Coral Snake, *Micrurus fulvius tener:* Common. All habitats. Southern and southeastern Texas. Throughout. Venomous, but small mouth and short fangs make it difficult for Texas Coral Snake to bite humans.

Family VIPERIDAE: Vipers

Southern Copperhead, *Agkistrodon contortrix contortrix:* Uncommon. Wooded uplands, riparian woodlands, invaded fields. Eastern third of Texas. Intergrades with Broad-banded Copperhead, *A. c. laticinctus,* in Burleson, Fayette, Lee, and Milam counties. Venomous. Color and pattern variable.

Broad-banded Copperhead, *Agkistrodon contortrix laticinctus:* Common. Wooded uplands, riparian woodlands, invaded fields. Central third of Texas. Throughout. Venomous. See comments regarding Southern Copperhead, *A. c. contortrix.*

Western Cottonmouth, *Agkistrodon piscivorus leucostoma:* Uncommon to common locally. Riparian woodlands, permanent waterways, riparian baregrounds, marshes, small impoundments. Primarily in eastern half of Texas. Throughout except Caldwell, Gillespie, Lee, Milam, and Williamson counties. Venomous; can bite under water. Color variable.

Western Diamondback Rattlesnake, *Crotalus atrox:* Common. Wooded uplands, upland baregrounds, invaded fields, range and pastures. Western two-thirds of Texas. Throughout, except Burleson, Fayette, and Lee counties. Venomous. Responsible for more human deaths than any other North American snake.

Timber Rattlesnake, *Crotalus horridus:* Uncommon or rare. Wooded uplands, invaded fields. Scattered through eastern two-thirds of

Texas. Bexar, Burleson, Caldwell, Gonzales, Lee, and Williamson counties. Venomous. Threatened in Texas.

Blacktail Rattlesnake, *Crotalus molossus molossus:* Uncommon or rare. Wooded uplands, upland baregrounds. Scattered through Edwards Plateau and western Texas. Bexar, Burnet, Comal, Hays, Kendall, Llano, and Travis counties. Venomous.

Western Massasauga, *Sistrurus catenatus tergeminus:* Rare. Range and pastures, invaded fields, upland baregrounds. Eastern Panhandle and northern central Texas. Scattered through central Texas. Bell County. Venomous.

Addendum

Order TESTUDINES: Turtles

Family EMYDIDAE: Box and Water Turtles

Red-eared Slider, *Trachemys scripta elegans:* In addition to previously known records of its range in South Central Texas (see p. 120), this turtle was observed in Williamson County on October 8, 1993.

CHAPTER 6

Fishes

S. CHRISTOPHER CARAN AND CLARK HUBBS

THIS ANNOTATED CHECKLIST of the fishes of the South Central Texas area contains 130 species, including both extant and historic taxa. The modern fish fauna of the nineteen-county area consists of at least 93 species. The status of five other species is, however, uncertain so the number of species known or presumed to occur in the region at present may be as high as 98. Twenty-three additional species may occur here as well, although their presence is not confirmed by specimen records. If these additional species are present, the total modern fauna would include a maximum of 121 species. Three of these species are endangered, two are threatened (one may actually be extinct), and the status of three species is of special concern. An additional species warranting special concern throughout its modern range was formerly found in the area, but regional populations have been extirpated. One or two species that previously occupied this area may be extinct and 8 to 12 others appear to have been eliminated from the regional fauna, although they survive elsewhere. To sum up, the fish fauna of South Central Texas may have included 130 species in the recent past but has been reduced to as few as 93 species at present.

Human activities, both intentional and unintentional, have significantly affected the ichthyofauna (fish species) of South Central Texas, particularly during the late nineteenth and twentieth centuries. A total of twenty-five to twenty-eight species of fish have been artificially introduced to the waters of South Central Texas. In the checklist, introduced species are marked with an asterisk (*). Some of these probably were released or escaped bait fish. As early as 1875, however, American shad, coho salmon, and carp were deliberately brought into the area and released. These stocking attempts met with limited success, however, although the carp (now generally considered a detriment to the regional fishery) did survive and became a naturalized, reproducing species. Unsuccessful fish introductions have included the inadvertent stocking of nontarget species along with species intended for introduction. Marine fish such as Atlantic croaker, pinfish, southern flounder, blackcheeked tonguefish, and others, while not deliberately slated for naturalization, have from time to time been discharged into the region's lakes along with saltwater *transotics* (transplanted exotics) such as striped bass and red drum, which were brought in deliberately. Unadapted, most of these marine fish could not reproduce in their new environment and usually do not survive for long. Later experiments and modern stocking practices proved more successful, and many of the introduced species are well established, with self-sustaining, often large, populations. These naturalized species may compete for habitat and in some cases, interbreed with the native taxa, causing stress and genetic dilution.

Of great concern are "pet" species that may occasionally escape or be disposed of by disenchanted owners or "freed" by misguided humanitarians. The vast majority of these pets, most of which are tropical in their normal range, die from exposure to cold water during the winter months or at best take a forage fish's place in the food chain. Unregulated introductions could, however, result in serious damage to the native fauna through direct competition, unchecked breeding, and the spread of infectious diseases or parasites. Such factors may reduce the viability of local breeding groups and further diminish natural diversity.

Adverse effects on the fishes of South Central Texas are not confined to those resulting from introduction of exotic species. The most far-reaching, human-induced impact is the irreversible destruction of aquatic habitat. Many springs, underground aquatic ecosystems, and marshes have been completely destroyed by excessive withdrawal of groundwater, surface-water diversion, and filling. Channelization and dredging have eliminated streamside and channel-bottom habitats and permanently altered the flow regimes of entire water courses. Reservoir impoundment has inundated diverse riverine environments, to which many species were uniquely adapted, substituting deep, sterile reservoirs affording limited habitat potential. In addition, such reservoirs block inland migration routes of coastal species and discharge cold, oxygen-depleted bottom waters that are detrimental to native faunas downstream. Aquatic habitats may be affected for tens to hundreds of kilometers by: siltation caused by filling and gravel dredging along stream channels and by runoff from overgrazed and disturbed upland sites; improper sewage and waste disposal; and chemical pollution brought about by intensive agriculture, urbanization, and accidental spills. All of these factors serve to reduce the extent and vitality of environments supporting native fishes and other species.

Information regarding fish stocking is primarily drawn from unpublished records of the Texas Parks and Wildlife Department and its predecessor agencies. Fish names, both scientific and vernacular, and their sequence of presentation follow "An Annotated Checklist of the Freshwater Fishes of Texas, with Keys to the Identification of Species" (C. Hubbs et al., 1991) and *Common and Scientific Names of Fishes from the United States and Canada* (C. R. Robins et al., 1991). For definition of terms used to describe the status and habitat of species see the Appendix. A complete list of sources can be found in the Selected References.

Class CHONDRICHTHYES: Cartilaginous Fishes
Order SQUALIFORMES: Sharks
Family CARCHARHINIDAE: Requiem Sharks

Finetooth Shark, *Carcharhinus isodon:* Rare or uncommon. Perennial waterways (rivers). Generally a marine species. Occurred in rivers throughout the Gulf Coastal Plains prior to dam construction. Now restricted to the southeastern part of the area.
Bull Shark, *Carcharhinus leucas:* Possible. Perennial waterways (rivers). Generally a marine species. If present in South Central Texas, it is restricted to the southeasternmost part of the area.

Class OSTEICHTHYES: Bony Fishes
Order SEMIONOTIFORMES: Semionotiforms
Family LEPISOSTEIDAE: Gars

Spotted Gar, *Lepisosteus oculatus:* Uncommon. Perennial waterways. Throughout, particularly in the Gulf Coastal Plains.
Longnose Gar, *Lepisosteus osseus:* Abundant. Perennial waterways. Throughout.
Alligator Gar, *Lepisosteus spatula:* Uncommon. Perennial waterways. Throughout the Gulf Coastal Plains.

Order AMIIFORMES: Amiiforms
Family AMIIDAE: Bowfins

Bowfin, *Amia calva:* Possible. Perennial waterways. If present in South Central Texas, restricted to the southeasternmost part of the area.

Order ANGUILLIFORMES: Eels

Family ANGUILLIDAE: Freshwater Eels

American Eel, *Anguilla rostrata:* Formerly common, now probably uncommon. Perennial waterways (rivers) and spring-fed streams. Prior to dam construction, found throughout the Gulf Coastal Plains and along the Balcones Escarpment. Now essentially restricted to the southeastern part of the area. Catadromous; only females found inland, where they reach sexual maturity.

Order CLUPEIFORMES: Clupeiforms

Family CLUPEIDAE: Herrings

Skipjack Herring, *Alosa chrysochloris:* Uncommon. Perennial waterways. Generally a marine species. Occurred in most rivers of the Gulf Coastal Plains prior to dam construction. Now restricted to the southeastern part of the area.

American Shad, *Alosa sapidissima*:* Historic. Perennial waterways. Introduced, but stocking attempts failed.

Gizzard Shad, *Dorosoma cepedianum:* Abundant. Perennial waterways, particularly large reservoirs. Throughout.

Threadfin Shad, *Dorosoma petenense:* Common. Perennial waterways, particularly larger reservoirs. Native throughout the eastern half of the area but also widely stocked within its native range.

Order CYPRINIFORMES: Cypriniforms

Family CYPRINIDAE: Minnows and Carps

Central Stoneroller, *Campostoma anomalum:* Locally abundant. Spring-fed streams. Primarily in the Edwards Plateau.

Goldfish, *Carassius auratus*:* Locally common. Intermittent streams and small impoundments. Introduced. Scattered localities throughout the area. May assume an olive-gray color in the wild.

Plateau Shiner, *Cyprinella lepida:* Possible. Perennial waterways (rivers). If present in South Central Texas, restricted to the upper Guadalupe River drainage.

Red Shiner, *Cyprinella lutrensis:* Abundant. Perennial waterways and spring-fed streams. Throughout. Occasionally interbreeds with blacktail shiner, *C. venusta.*

Blacktail Shiner, *Cyprinella venusta:* Common to locally abundant. Perennial waterways (rivers), spring-fed streams, and intermittent streams. Throughout. Occasionally interbreeds with Red Shiner, *C. lutrensis.*

Common Carp, *Cyprinus carpio*:* Common to abundant. Perennial waterways, spring-fed streams, intermittent streams, and small im-.poundments. Introduced. Throughout. Scaleless and partially scaled individuals are occasionally seen.

Roundnose Minnow, *Dionda episcopa:* Uncommon to locally common. Spring-fed streams. Colorado and Guadalupe river drainages of the Edwards Plateau.

Mississippi Silvery Minnow, *Hybognathus nuchalis:* Uncommon to locally common. Perennial waterways (rivers) and intermittent streams. Brazos River drainage, particularly in the Gulf Coastal Plains.

Plains Minnow, *Hybognathus placitus:* Uncommon to locally common. Perennial waterways and intermittent streams. Colorado and Brazos river drainages, particularly in the Edwards Plateau and Lampasas Cut Plain.

Ribbon Shiner, *Lythrurus fumeus:* Uncommon to locally common. Perennial waterways and intermittent streams. Brazos, Colorado, and Lavaca river drainages of the Gulf Coastal Plains.

Speckled Chub, *Macrohybopsis aestivalis:* Locally common but declining in abundance. Perennial waterways (rivers). Throughout.

Silver Chub, *Macrohybopsis storeriana:* Possible. Perennial waterways (rivers). If present in South Central Texas, restricted to the southeastern part of the area in the Brazos River drainage.

Golden Shiner, *Notemigonus crysoleucas*:* Locally common. Perennial waterways and spring-fed streams. Introduced (released bait); probably throughout.

Texas Shiner, *Notropis amabilis:* Uncommon to locally abundant. Spring-fed streams. Throughout the Edwards Plateau as far north as the San Gabriel River (Brazos River drainage).

Pallid Shiner, *Notropis amnis:* Uncommon. Perennial waterways and intermittent streams. Throughout the Gulf Coastal Plains as far south as the Guadalupe River drainage.

Blackspot Shiner, *Notropis atrocaudalis:* Possible. Perennial waterways (rivers). If present in South Central Texas, restricted to the southeastern part of the area in the Brazos River drainage.

Smalleye Shiner, *Notropis buccula:* Threatened, probably extinct. Perennial waterways (rivers). Native to the middle and upper Brazos River drainage. A disjunct population in the Colorado River near Austin may have been introduced. No recent records of this species.

Ghost Shiner, *Notropis buchanani:* Uncommon. Perennial waterways
(rivers). Throughout.

Ironcolor Shiner, *Notropis chalybaeus:* Special concern. Perennial waterways (rivers) and spring-fed streams. In South Central Texas,
restricted to the headwaters of the San Marcos River in Hays
County.

Sharpnose Shiner, *Notropis oxyrhynchus:* Threatened. Perennial waterways (rivers), particularly silt-laden streams. Endemic to the
Brazos River drainage where it is declining in abundance. A disjunct population in the Colorado River above Lake Buchanan may
have been introduced.

Chub Shiner, *Notropis potteri:* Uncommon to locally abundant. Perennial waterways. Throughout the Brazos River drainage.

Silverband Shiner, *Notropis shumardi:* Locally common to abundant.
Perennial waterways (primarily rivers). Widespread in the Brazos
River drainage; found in most streams of the Gulf Coastal Plains
southward to the Lavaca River drainage.

Sand Shiner, *Notropis stramineus:* Locally common. Perennial waterways and intermittent streams. Scattered localities throughout
the Edwards Plateau.

Weed Shiner, *Notropis texanus:* Common to locally abundant. Perennial waterways and intermittent streams. Throughout, particularly in the Gulf Coastal Plains.

Mimic Shiner, *Notropis volucellus:* Common to locally abundant.
Perennial waterways and intermittent streams. Throughout.

Pugnose Minnow, *Opsopoeodus emiliae:* Common. Perennial waterways and intermittent streams. Throughout the Gulf Coastal
Plains.

Suckermouth Minnow, *Phenacobius mirabilis:* Rare to uncommon.
Perennial waterways. Scattered localities in the Colorado River
drainage of the Gulf Coastal Plains.

Fathead Minnow, *Pimephales promelas*:* Uncommon to locally common. Perennial waterways and intermittent streams. Introduced
(released bait). Throughout.

Bullhead Minnow, *Pimephales vigilax:* Locally common. Perennial waterways and intermittent streams. Throughout.

Rudd, *Scardinius erythrophthalmus*:* Possible. Perennial waterways.
Introduced at widely scattered localities throughout the state but
not definitely known from South Central Texas. Further introductions banned by state regulations.

Creek Chub, *Semotilus atromaculatus:* Possible. Perennial waterways
(rivers) and intermittent streams. If present in South Central

Texas, restricted to the southeasternmost part of the area in the Brazos River drainage.

Family CATOSTOMIDAE: Suckers

River Carpsucker, *Carpiodes carpio:* Abundant. Perennial waterways, spring-fed streams, intermittent streams, and small impoundments. Throughout.

Blue Sucker, *Cycleptus elongatus:* Special concern. Perennial waterways (rivers). Scattered localities throughout.

Lake Chubsucker, *Erimyzon sucetta:* Uncommon. Perennial waterways. Brazos and upper Guadalupe river drainages.

Smallmouth Buffalo, *Ictiobus bubalus:* Common to locally abundant. Perennial waterways. Throughout.

Black Buffalo, *Ictiobus niger*:* Rare. Perennial waterways. Possibly introduced; scattered localities throughout the Brazos and Colorado river drainages.

Spotted Sucker, *Minytrema melanops:* Uncommon. Perennial waterways (rivers). Brazos River drainage. A disjunct population may range into the extreme western edge of Llano County but is not known to occur east of central Mason County in Llano River drainage (outside of nineteen-county area).

Gray Redhorse, *Moxostoma congestum:* Uncommon. Perennial waterways (rivers) and spring-fed streams. Throughout the Edwards Plateau.

Family CHARACIDAE: Characins

Mexican Tetra, *Astyanax mexicanus*:* Common. Perennial waterways and spring-fed streams. Introduced (released bait); throughout.

Order SILURIFORMES: Siluriforms

Family ICTALURIDAE: Bullhead Catfishes

Black Bullhead, *Ameiurus melas:* Abundant. Perennial waterways, spring-fed streams, intermittent streams, and small impoundments. Native throughout but also widely stocked.

Yellow Bullhead, *Ameiurus natalis:* Common. Perennial waterways, spring-fed streams, intermittent streams, and small impoundments. Throughout.

Blue Catfish, *Ictalurus furcatus:* Common. Perennial waterways, spring-fed streams, and intermittent streams. Throughout.

Headwater Catfish, *Ictalurus lupus:* Historic; special concern throughout its modern range. Perennial waterways and spring-fed streams. Formerly found in the upper Colorado, Guadalupe, and San Antonio rivers but apparently extirpated from South Central Texas.

Channel Catfish, *Ictalurus punctatus:* Abundant. Perennial waterways, spring-fed streams, intermittent streams, and small impoundments. Throughout.

Tadpole Madtom, *Noturus gyrinus:* Rare. Perennial waterways and spring-fed streams. Throughout.

Freckled Madtom, *Noturus nocturnus:* Rare. Perennial waterways. Brazos River drainage.

Flathead Catfish, *Pylodictis olivaris:* Uncommon. Perennial waterways. Throughout.

Widemouth Blindcat, *Satan eurystomus:* Endangered. Caves within the Edwards Aquifer 300 to 600 meters underground. Known only from deep water wells in the San Antonio vicinity (Bexar County).

Toothless Blindcat, *Trogloglanis pattersoni:* Endangered. Caves within the Edwards Aquifer 300 to 600 meters underground. Known only from deep water wells in the San Antonio vicinity (Bexar County).

Family LORICARIIDAE: Suckermouth Catfishes

Armadillo Del Rio, *Hypostomus* sp.*: Uncommon or rare. Spring-fed streams. Introduced (released pets); restricted to the headwaters of the Comal and San Antonio Rivers (Comal and Bexar counties, respectively).

Order SALMONIFORMES: Salmoniforms

Family ESOCIDAE: Pikes

Grass Pickerel, *Esox americanus vermiculatus:* Uncommon. Perennial waterways. Brazos River drainage, primarily in the Gulf Coastal Plains.

Northern Pike, *Esox lucius*:* Rare or historic. Perennial waterways (large reservoirs). Introduced; stocking attempts in the area have not proven successful.

Family SALMONIDAE: Salmons

Coho Salmon, *Oncorhynchus kisutch*:* Historic. Perennial waterways (rivers). Introduced; stocking attempts failed.

Rainbow Trout, *Oncorhynchus mykiss*:* Rare or historic. Perennial waterways (rivers). Introduced; stocking attempts have not produced a self-sustaining population but do provide a "put-and-take" fishery in the Guadalupe River and elsewhere.

Family APHREDODERIDAE: Pirate Perch

Pirate Perch, *Aphredoderus sayanus:* Possible. Perennial waterways. If present in South Central Texas, restricted to the Brazos River drainage in the southeastern part of the area.

Order ATHERINIFORMES: Atheriniforms
Family BELONIDAE: Needlefishes

Atlantic Needlefish, *Strongylura marina:* Uncommon. Perennial waterways (rivers). Generally a marine species. Occurred in rivers throughout the Gulf Coastal Plains prior to dam construction. Now restricted to the southeastern part of the area.

Family CYPRINODONTIDAE: Killifishes

Diamond Killifish, *Adinia xenica:* Possible. Perennial waterways. Generally a marine species. If present in South Central Texas, restricted to the southeasternmost part of the area.

Red River Pupfish, *Cyprinodon rubrofluviatilis:* Possible. Perennial waterways. Native to the upper Brazos River and introduced in parts of the Colorado River drainage. If present in South Central Texas, probably restricted to the northwesternmost part of the area.

Sheepshead Minnow, *Cyprinodon variegatus:* Uncommon. Perennial waterways. Found in the lower reaches of most rivers of the Gulf Coastal Plains prior to dam construction and introduced at scattered localities in the San Antonio River drainage.

Golden Topminnow, *Fundulus chrysotus:* Possible. Perennial waterways. If present in South Central Texas, restricted to the southeastern part of the area as far south as the Lavaca River drainage.

Starhead Topminnow, *Fundulus dispar:* Possible. Perennial waterways. If present in South Central Texas, restricted to the southeasternmost part of the area as far south as the Brazos River drainage.

Gulf Killifish, *Fundulus grandis:* Uncommon to locally common. Perennial waterways. Generally a marine species. Native to lower reaches of rivers in the Gulf Coastal Plains, particularly the Brazos River drainage. Widely introduced inland, including the South Central Texas area.

Blackstripe Topminnow, *Fundulus notatus:* Uncommon to locally common. Perennial waterways. Throughout.

Bayou Killifish, *Fundulus pulvereus:* Possible. Perennial waterways. Generally a marine species. If present in South Central Texas, restricted to the southeasternmost part of the area.

Longnose Killifish, *Fundulus similis:* Possible. Perennial waterways. Generally a marine species. If present in South Central Texas, restricted to the southeasternmost part of the area.

Plains Killifish, *Fundulus zebrinus:* Rare or historic. Perennial waterways. A native population in the Colorado River at Austin (Travis County) was extirpated. Extant in South Central Texas, in the vicinity of Johnson City and Llano (Blanco and Llano counties, respectively).

Family POECILIIDAE: Livebearers

Western Mosquitofish, *Gambusia affinis:* Abundant. Virtually all aquatic habitats. Native throughout and widely stocked for mosquito control.

Largespring Gambusia, *Gambusia geiseri:* Locally common. Spring-fed streams. Headwaters of the Comal and San Marcos rivers (Comal and Hays counties, respectively).

San Marcos Gambusia, *Gambusia georgei:* Extinct. Perennial waterways (rivers). Formerly known from the San Marcos River in Hays County, but there are no recent records of this species.

Amazon Molly, *Poecilia formosa*:* Locally common. Perennial waterways and spring-fed streams. Introduced. Scattered localities in the San Antonio and San Marcos rivers. An all-female species that reproduces by gynogenesis.

Sailfin Molly, *Poecilia latipinna*:* Locally common. Spring-fed streams. Probably introduced (released pets). Scattered localities along the Balcones Escarpment and on the Edwards Plateau.

Guppy, *Poecilia reticulata*:* Locally common. Perennial waterways. Introduced (released pets) throughout but naturalized only in the San Antonio River in Bexar County.

Family ATHERINIDAE: Silversides

Inland Silverside, *Menidia beryllina*:* Abundant. Perennial waterways, particularly large reservoirs. Generally a marine species occurring naturally in Texas coastal waters and the lower reaches of coastal streams. Introduced. Throughout.

Tidewater Silverside, *Menidia peninsulae:* Possible. Perennial waterways (rivers). Generally a marine species. If present in South Central Texas, restricted to the southeasternmost part of the area.

Family SYNGNATHIDAE: Pipefishes

Chain Pipefish, *Syngnathus louisianae:* Possible. Perennial waterways (rivers). Generally a marine species. If present in South Central Texas, restricted to the southeastern part of the area.

Gulf Pipefish, *Syngnathus scovelli:* Possible. Perennial waterways (rivers). Generally a marine species. If present in South Central Texas, restricted to the southeastern part of the area.

Order PERCIFORMES: Perciforms

Family PERCICHTHYIDAE: Temperate Basses

White Bass, *Morone chrysops*:* Common. Perennial waterways, particularly large reservoirs. Introduced. Scattered localities throughout.

Striped Bass, *Morone saxatilis*:* Rare to uncommon. Perennial waterways (large reservoirs). Introduced. Scattered localities throughout, but few self-sustaining populations have resulted.

Family CENTRARCHIDAE: Sunfishes

Rock Bass, *Ambloplites rupestris*:* Uncommon to locally common. Perennial waterways (rivers) and spring-fed streams. Introduced. Comal, San Marcos, and upper Guadalupe rivers.

Banded Pygmy Sunfish, *Elassoma zonatum:* Uncommon to locally common. Perennial waterways (rivers). Lower Brazos River drainage.

Redbreast Sunfish, *Lepomis auritus*:* Uncommon to locally common. Perennial waterways. Introduced. Throughout.

Green Sunfish, *Lepomis cyanellus:* Common. Perennial waterways, spring-fed streams, intermittent streams, and small impoundments. Native throughout but also widely stocked.

Warmouth, *Lepomis gulosus:* Common to locally abundant. Perennial waterways, spring-fed streams, intermittent streams, and small impoundments. Throughout.

Orangespotted Sunfish, *Lepomis humilis:* Common. Perennial waterways, spring-fed streams, intermittent streams, and small impoundments. Native throughout the Brazos and Colorado River drainages but introduced elsewhere in the area.

Bluegill, *Lepomis macrochirus:* Common. Perennial waterways, spring-fed streams, intermittent streams, and small impoundments. Native throughout but also widely stocked.

Longear Sunfish, *Lepomis megalotis:* Abundant. Perennial waterways, spring-fed streams, intermittent streams, and small impoundments. Native throughout but also widely stocked.

Redear Sunfish, *Lepomis microlophus:* Abundant. Perennial waterways, spring-fed streams, intermittent streams, and small impoundments. Native throughout but also widely stocked.

Spotted Sunfish, *Lepomis punctatus:* Uncommon. Perennial waterways (rivers), spring-fed streams, and intermittent streams. Throughout.

Bantam Sunfish, *Lepomis symmetricus:* Possible. Perennial waterways (rivers) and intermittent streams. If present in South Central Texas, it is restricted to the southeastern part of the area.

Smallmouth Bass, *Micropterus dolomieu*:* Uncommon to locally common. Perennial waterways (particularly large reservoirs) and spring-fed streams. Introduced. Scattered localities throughout the area but primarily in the Edwards Plateau. Commonly hybridizes with Guadalupe Bass, *M. treculi.*

Spotted Bass, *Micropterus punctulatus:* Locally common. Perennial waterways. Throughout the Gulf Coastal Plains as far south as the Guadalupe River drainage.

Largemouth Bass, *Micropterus salmoides:* Abundant. Perennial waterways, spring-fed streams, intermittent streams, and small impoundments. Native throughout but also widely stocked, particularly in large reservoirs.

Guadalupe Bass, *Micropterus treculi:* Special concern. Perennial waterways and spring-fed streams. Throughout the Edwards Plateau and lower Colorado River. Threatened by hybridization with introduced Smallmouth Bass, *Micropterus dolomieu.* State fish of Texas.

White Crappie, *Pomoxis annularis:* Abundant. Perennial waterways, spring-fed streams, and small impoundments. Native throughout but also widely stocked, particularly in large reservoirs.

Black Crappie, *Pomoxis nigromaculatus:* Common to locally abundant. Perennial waterways, spring-fed streams, and small impoundments. Native throughout the Gulf Coastal Plains but also widely stocked.

Family PERCIDAE: Perches

Bluntnose Darter, *Etheostoma chlorosomum:* Locally common. Perennial waterways (rivers), spring-fed streams, and intermittent streams. Gulf Coastal Plains as far south as the Guadalupe River drainage.

Fountain Darter, *Etheostoma fonticola:* Endangered. Spring-fed streams. Restricted to the headwaters of the Comal and San Marcos rivers (Comal and Hays counties, respectively). The present population at Comal Springs was reintroduced in the early 1970's after the original population was extirpated in the mid-1950's, when Comal Springs ceased to flow for an extended period.

Slough Darter, *Etheostoma gracile:* Locally common. Perennial waterways (rivers), spring-fed streams, and intermittent streams. Throughout the Gulf Coastal Plains.

Greenthroat Darter, *Etheostoma lepidum:* Locally common. Perennial waterways (rivers) and spring-fed streams. Edwards Plateau as far north as the Colorado River drainage.

Orangethroat Darter, *Etheostoma spectabile:* Locally common. Perennial waterways (rivers) and spring-fed streams. Throughout the Edwards Plateau.

Texas Logperch, *Percina carbonaria:* Abundant. Perennial waterways and spring-fed streams. Throughout the Edwards Plateau.

Bigscale Logperch, *Percina macrolepida:* Locally common. Perennial waterways (rivers) and spring-fed streams. Throughout.

Dusky Darter, *Percina sciera:* Locally common. Perennial waterways (rivers) and spring-fed streams. Throughout as far south as the Guadalupe River drainage.

River Darter, *Percina shumardi:* Locally common. Perennial waterways (rivers). Guadalupe and San Antonio river drainages of the Gulf Coastal Plains.

Walleye, *Stizostedion vitreum*:* Locally common. Perennial waterways. Introduced. Large reservoirs throughout, but few self-sustaining populations have resulted.

Family SPARIDAE: Porgies

Pinfish, *Lagodon rhomboides*:* Historic. Perennial waterways. Generally a marine species. Inadvertently released with stocked gamefish. No self-sustaining population in South Central Texas.

Family SCIAENIDAE: Drums

Freshwater Drum, *Aplodinotus grunniens:* Common. Perennial waterways and spring-fed streams. Throughout.

Spotted Seatrout, *Cynoscion nebulosus*:* Historic. Perennial waterways. Generally a marine species. Inadvertently released with stocked gamefish. No self-sustaining population in South Central Texas.

Atlantic Croaker, *Micropogonias undulatus*:* Historic. Perennial wa-

terways. Generally a marine species. Inadvertently released with
stocked gamefish. No self-sustaining population in South Central
Texas.

Red Drum, *Sciaenops ocellatus*:* Rare or historic. Perennial waterways.
Generally a marine species. Both deliberate and inadvertent stock-
ing have failed to produce self-sustaining populations in South
Central Texas.

Family CICHLIDAE: Cichlids

Rio Grande Cichlid, *Cichlasoma cyanoguttatum*:* Abundant. Perennial waterways, spring-fed streams, and intermittent streams. Introduced. Throughout as far north as the San Gabriel River
(Brazos River drainage).
Blue Tilapia, *Tilapia aurea*:* Locally common. Perennial waterways,
particularly reservoirs where heated water is discharged (i.e., at
power stations and industrial sites). Introduced (aquacultural species). Guadalupe, San Antonio, and parts of the Colorado river
drainages; possibly other scattered localities. Further introductions banned by state regulations.
Mozambique Tilapia, *Tilapia mossambica*:* Locally common to abundant. Perennial waterways (rivers) and spring-fed streams. Introduced (aquacultural species). Guadalupe, San Marcos, and San Antonio river drainages along the Balcones Escarpment and vicinity.
Further introductions banned by state regulations.
Redbelly Tilapia, *Tilapia zilli*:* Locally common. Spring-fed streams.
Introduced (released pets); headwaters of the San Antonio River
(Bexar County). Further introductions banned by state regulations.

Family MUGILIDAE: Mullets

Mountain Mullet, *Agonostomus monticola:* Possible. Perennial waterways (rivers). Generally a marine species. If present in South Central Texas, restricted to the southeasternmost part of the area.
Striped Mullet, *Mugil cephalus:* Uncommon. Perennial waterways (rivers). Occurred in rivers throughout the Gulf Coastal Plains prior
to dam construction. Now restricted to the southeastern part of
the area.
White Mullet, *Mugil curema:* Uncommon. Perennial waterways (rivers).
Occurred in rivers throughout the Gulf Coastal Plains prior to
dam construction. Now restricted to the southeastern part of
the area.

Order PLEURONECTIFORMES: Pleuronectiforms

Family BOTHIDAE: Lefteye Flounders

Southern Flounder, *Paralichthys lethostigma*:* Historic. Perennial waterways. Generally a marine species. Inadvertently released with stocked gamefish. No self-sustaining population in South Central Texas.

Family CYNOGLOSSIDAE: Tonguefishes

Blackcheeked Tonguefish, *Symphurus plagiusa*:* Historic. Perennial waterways. Generally a marine species. Inadvertently released with stocked gamefish. No self-sustaining population in South Central Texas.

CHAPTER 7

Land Snails of Travis County

RAYMOND W. NECK

TRAVIS COUNTY has a varied group of land snails befitting its position between the wetter eastern lowland prairies and riparian woodlands and the drier western upland Edwards Plateau. Some species of land snails found in the county are restricted to only one of the above two areas, whereas other snails have widespread geographical ranges. Several snails and slugs have been introduced. These are indicated by an asterisk (*).

Human influence upon the land snail fauna is reflected not only in the number of introduced species but also in the destruction of rich habitats that resulted from urban sprawl and multiple damming of the Colorado River. Other human-induced effects include the creation of new, artificial habitats, such as cultivated and fallow fields, orchards, gardens, greenhouses, asphalt parking lots, landfills, drainage canals, and many other settings that afford unique conditions for land snail colonization.

The annotated list which follows represents all species of land snails and slugs known to have occurred in the county in the recent past. All literature records have been utilized. Contemporary populations are known for fifty-three of the fifty-six species included herein. Hopefully, further collections will reveal extant populations of the three species not documented. Most of the names used in this checklist are from *How to Know the Eastern Land Snails* by John B. Burch (1962), to which the reader is also referred for figures of the species. If, because of taxonomic revisions, a name differs from that found in Burch, the name used by Burch is given following the currently accepted name. Habitat descriptions and other relevant data as known at this point in the study are given. See Selected References for the complete list of sources.

Class GASTROPODA
Subclass PROSOBRANCHIATA
Order ARCHAEOSGASTROPODA

Family HELICINIDAE

Oligyra orbiculata (*Helicina orbiculata* in Burch): Shell 5–8 mm. Only operculate land snail in area. Throughout, in all terrestrial habitats. Urban tolerance moderate.

Subclass PULMONATA
Order BASOMMATOPHORA

Family CARYCHIIDAE

Carychium mexicanum: Shell whitish; less than 2 mm. Mesic floodplain woodlands. Related to aquatic pulmonates.

Order STYLOMMATOPHORA
Suborder ORTHURETHRA

Family PUPILLIDAE

Pupilla muscorum: Shell dark brown; 3–4 mm. Isolated record in Colorado River floodplain.
Pupoides albilabris: Shell brown; 4–5 mm. Throughout, in well-drained sites. Common in urban areas.
Gastrocopta cristata: Shell brownish; 2.5–3 mm. Western upland areas. Under rock in juniper brakes.
Gastrocopta pellucida hordeacella: Shell brownish; 2–2.5 mm. Throughout in woodlands, prairies, and urban areas.
Gastrocopta procera procera: Shell brownish; to 3 mm. Throughout, in woodlands, prairies, and urban areas.
Gastrocopta tappaniana: Shell whitish; 3–4 mm. Protected sites in canyon woodlands.
Gastrocopta contracta: Shell whitish; 2.5 mm. Throughout, in riparian woodlands.

Family STROBILOPSIDAE

Strobilops texasiana: Shell beehive-shaped; ribbed; 2 mm. Throughout, in riparian woodlands.

Suborder HETERURETHRA

Family SUCCINEIDAE

Succinea luteola: Shell white; large aperture; 12–15 mm. Throughout, in well-drained sites.

Succinea forsheyi: Shell transparent; horn-colored; 9–15 mm. Wet margins of streams and ponds, usually with shallow soil over calcareous bedrock.

Catinella vermeta (*C. avara* in Burch): Shell amber; 8–10 mm. Edges of streams and ponds; upland sites with cover.

Suborder SIGMURETHRA

Division AULACOPODA

Family ENDODONTIDAE

Anguispira strongylodes (*A. alternata* in Burch): Shell amber with chestnut spots; 15–18 mm. Riparian woodlands in eastern part of county.

Helicodiscus eigenmanni: Shell ribbed; open umbilicus; 4–5 mm. Rocky slopes above streambeds in western part of county.

Helicodiscus inermis: Shell white; 4 mm. Clay soils in protected microhabitats in canyon woodlands.

Helicodiscus nummus: Shell white; disc-shaped; 2 mm. Mesic woodlands in canyons in western part of county and creek woodlands in eastern part of county.

Helicodiscus singleyanus: Shell white; disc-shaped; 4–5 mm. Throughout county, including urban areas.

Punctum vitreum: Shell translucent; 1.5 mm. Protected canyon woodlands in western part of county.

Family LIMACIDAE

Limax flavus*: Mottled yellow-brown slug; 100 mm extended. Introduced from Europe. Urban areas. Common.

Limax valentianus* (*Lehmannia poirieri* in Burch): Pink slug; two dark lines; 60 mm. Introduced from Europe. Common pest in urban gardens.

Deroceras laeve: Small gray slug; 35 mm. Native. Generally uncommon but locally abundant in gardens.

Milax gagates*: Keeled gray slug; 40 mm. Introduced from Europe. Uncommon. In mesic areas.

Family ZONITIDAE

Glyphyalinia roemeri (Retinella roemeri in Burch): Shell flat; transparent; 4 mm. Caves and wet areas in western part of county.

Glyphyalinia umbilicata (Retinella indentata in Burch): Shell shiny with radiating lines; 5–7 mm. Throughout. Abundant in urban areas.

Mesomphix friabilis: Gray-black body; horn-colored shell; to 25 mm. Riparian woodlands in eastern part of county.

Hawaiia minuscula: Shell pale gray; 2–3 mm. Mesic canyon woodlands with deep leaf litter.

Euconulus trochulus (Euconulus chersinus in Burch): Shell beehive-shaped; no ribs; 13 mm. Riparian woodlands.

Zonitoides arboreus: Shell flat; 5–6 mm. Throughout; most common in mesic woodlands.

Striatura meridionalis: Horn-colored; 1.5–2 mm. Mesic soil pockets in protected canyon woodlands.

Division HOLOPODA

Family SPIRAXIDAE

Euglandina rosea*: Shell rose-brown; spindle-shaped; to 75 mm. Introduced into central Austin neighborhoods.

Euglandina singleyana: Shell spindle-shaped; to 50 mm. Largest native snail. Predaceous, feeding on snails and slugs. Cedar brakes in western part of county.

Family SUBULINIDAE

Rumina decollata*: Tip of shell almost always broken off except in young snails; 25–40 mm. Introduced from Mediterranean region. Most common in urban areas but does well in natural areas.

Lamellaxis mauritianus*: Shell glossy white; 11 mm. Introduced. Found in Austin. May be restricted to greenhouses.

Opeas pyrgula*: Body yellowish; 8 mm. Introduced from Mediterranean region. Known only from urban gardens.

Cecilioides acicula*: Shell white; 4 mm. Introduced from Europe. Found in residential gardens and moist stream banks in urban areas.

Family UROCOPTIDAE

Microceramus texanus (*M. pontificus* in Burch): Shell pupa-shaped;
8–12 mm. Talus slopes in western part of county.
Metastoma goldfussi (*Holospira goldfussi* in Burch): Shell pupa-shaped;
10–15 mm. Rocky hillsides in western part of county.
Metastoma roemeri roemeri (*Holospira roemeri* in Burch): Shell pupa-
shaped; 15–20 mm. Rocky slopes in western part of county.

Family BULIMULIDAE

Rabdotus dealbatus dealbatus (*Bulimulus dealbatus* [in part] in
Burch): Light-colored streaking on shell; 15–25 mm. Riparian
woodlands; hybridizes with *R. mooreanus.*
Rabdotus mooreanus (*Bulimulus dealbatus* [in part] in Burch): Shell
whitish; may have tan-colored base; 15–25 mm. Most abundant
in grassland areas; hybridizes with *R. dealbatus dealbatus.*

Family POLYGYRIDAE

Polygyra cereolus* (*Polygyra septemvolva* in Burch): Shell flattened;
many coils; 7–12 mm. Introduced from coastal Texas.
Polygyra auriformis: Shell shaped like ear; apertural teeth; 7–12 mm.
Riparian woodlands; most of habitat now flooded by reservoirs.
Polygyra gracilis: Shell brownish-white; 7–10 mm. Mesic woodlands in
canyons in western portion of county.
Polygyra mooreana: Shell slightly domed; 6–9 mm. Xeric upland wood-
lands in western part of county.
Polygyra texasiana texasiana: Shell flattened; few ribs; 7–12 mm.
Throughout, in woodland prairies.
Euchemotrema leai aliciae (*Stenotrema leai* in Burch): Long lamella
in front of aperture of shell; 7–9 mm. Mesic riparian woodlands;
most of habitat now flooded by reservoirs.
Praticolella berlandieriana: Shell white; may be banded; 9–13 mm.
Woodlands and mesic prairie areas.
Praticolella pachyloma (*Praticolella berlandieriana* [in part] in Burch):
Shell translucent; brown; 10–14 mm. Found in open habitats in
sandy soil terraces.
Mesodon thyroidus: Shell brown; 18–25 mm. Riparian woodlands in
eastern part of county.
Mesodon roemeri: Shell golden brown; 18–25 mm. Riparian woodlands
throughout county.
Mesodon leatherwoodi: Flattened shell; 15–18 mm. Moist talus slopes;

only known county record is from West Cave in western part of county.

Triodopsis cragini*: Shell reddish horn; semiglossy; 8–10 mm. Introduced into residential yards along urban creeks in Austin.

Family HELICIDAE

Helix aspersa*: Shell brown; to 40 mm. Introduced from Europe. Urban gardens.

Otala lactea*: Shell white; may be banded; to 35 mm. Introduced from Mediterranean region. Urban gardens.

Eobania vermiculata* (*Otala vermiculata* in Burch): Shell white and brown; to 35 mm. Introduced from Mediterranean region. Urban gardens.

CHAPTER 8

Butterflies

RAYMOND W. NECK AND EDWARD A. KUTAC

THE BUTTERFLIES of South Central Texas comprise 182 known species, all of which have a temperate and/or tropical distribution. Species of the order Lepidoptera that are referred to as butterflies belong to two superfamilies. The true butterflies, which include most of the familiar brightly colored species known to everyone, make up the superfamily Papilionoidea. This group is divided into several families as noted in the checklist below. Less known to the general public are the skippers of the superfamily Hesperioidea. Although there are several spectacular exceptions, most skippers are dark brown, orange, or patterned gray in appearance. Their flight patterns are usually jerky or skipping, hence the name *skippers*. Moths, another large group among the Lepidoptera, are not treated here. The list below includes all of the sixty-four skippers and 118 true butterflies known to inhabit the South Central Texas region.

The butterfly fauna of South Central Texas exhibits very definite seasonal patterns in terms of timing of adult occurrences. A moderate number of species may be observed on warm winter days. These species overwinter as adults, becoming active above particular threshold temperatures and may be seen flying in search of nectar or moisture sources. Spring is the season in which the greatest number of species occur as adults. Some of these spring butterflies are single-generation species that have caterpillars that are adapted to feeding on plants present only during the early spring. Other spring species may be found throughout the year until fall frosts kill the leaves of foodplants. Summertime is usually a season of fewer species of flying (adult) butterflies. The number of species active during the summer is dependent upon moisture levels. In dry summers, the number of active species is very low, but species abundance may be quite high during wet summers. Autumn brings another peak of activity. The return of moisture and cooler temperatures permits further generations of the year-round species. Additionally, species that are normally found only in far South Texas, or even farther south in northern Mexico, often move northward in the fall, possibly to take advantage of seasonally moist conditions. Hurricanes or other strong inland-moving rain systems may produce a massive infusion of these tropical species into Central Texas. Autumn is also the time of greatest migration of at least one temperate species, the monarch, which flies southward in great numbers to wintering areas in Mexico.

Zoogeographically, South Central Texas is located in a zone of complex range overlap, both along the east-west axis and the north-south axis. The Balcones Escarpment is a very significant barrier to certain species of butterflies as with other life forms. Obviously, the escarpment is not an absolute physical barrier as butterflies can readily fly through the area. Rather the barrier is ecological in nature; for example, there is the lack of a suitable foodplant on one side. Many species of butterflies are present on both sides of the escarpment zone; however, they often utilize different foodplant species on either side. The north-south blend is a function of the winter temperature tolerance of tropical species that normally occur farther south. During relatively warm periods with sufficient moisture, these tropical species move northward and may persist until temperatures drop too low for them to survive.

"Bumper years" of incredible butterfly diversity and abundance occur when moisture, temperature, and wind patterns allow the transport and survival of species usually not found in the area or that typically occur in only small numbers. Most of these species are tropical, normally found much farther south, or moisture-loving species that are normally confined to the Texas coastal region. Snout butterflies are resident species that are normally found in very low densities. However, heavy rainfall that causes extensive growth of hackberry branches may produce vast numbers of this butterfly, which then migrate northward. In drought years, however, species from the west, such as California sister, extend farther east than normal. These species may be observed in South Central Texas until the return of normal moisture levels limits their survival.

Human impact upon the native butterfly fauna of South Central Texas has been manifold. The most obvious impact involves the direct destruction of habitat through placement of concrete, asphalt, and structures on previously productive land. Additionally, most residential lawns are dominated by landscapes of low floral diversity, which limit the variety of butterfly and other faunas. Many cultivated plants are nonnative and contain natural phytochemicals that are toxic to our native butterflies. Exceptions are the sachem, *Atalopedes campestris*, which utilizes both St. Augustine and Bermuda grasses. Additionally, the cabbage white, *Pieris rapae*, is a native of Europe that has been introduced into North America and feeds largely on cultivated cabbage and other mustards.

The scientific and English names of butterflies and the order of the list below essentially follows conventional usage as demonstrated in *The Audubon Society Field Guide to North American Butterflies* by Robert Michael Pyle (1981). This popular field guide is readily accessible to the general public and illustrates most of the species listed here. The order of species is the phylogenetic sequence; that is, the most ancient forms at the beginning and the most recently evolved at the end. The list includes subspecies names when known.

The account below is based primarily on the only two published lists of butterflies for the South Central Texas area, namely, "The Butterfly Fauna of Barton Creek Canyon on the Balcones Fault Zone, Austin, Texas" (Christopher J. Durden, 1982) and "Butterflies of the Ottine Area" (H. B. Parks, 1956). All Gonzales County records are drawn from the latter reference. The abundance of Gonzales County records is not known. Records are from Travis County unless otherwise indicated. In those cases where a species or subspecies name found in one or both of these references differs from Pyle's terminology, that name is shown in parenthesis. See Selected References for additional sources.

Phylum ARTHROPODA: Jointed-leg invertebrates
Class INSECTA: Insects
Order LEPIDOPTERA: Moths and Butterflies
Superfamily HESPERIOIDEA: Skippers
Family HESPERIIDAE: True Skippers

Named for a characteristic strong, darting flight pattern. Most species are brown or orange in general coloration although a few tropical species have iridescent blue and red patches.

Silver-spotted Skipper, *Epargyreus clarus clarus* (*E. tityrus*): Abundant, permanent resident. Gonzales and Travis counties.

Silver-banded Skipper, *Chioides catillus albofasciatus* (*C. albofasciatus*): Uncommon, periodic.

Zilpa Longtail, *Chioides zilpa zilpa:* Scarce, periodic.

Long-tailed Skipper, *Urbanus proteus* (*Eudamus proteus*): Bastrop and Gonzales counties.

Lilac-banded Longtail, *Urbanus dorantes dorantes* (*U. d. rauterbergi*): Scarce, periodic.

Golden-banded Skipper, *Autochton cellus* (*Achalarus cellus*): Gonzales County.

Hoary Edge, *Achalarus lyciades:* Gonzales County.

Coyote Skipper, *Achalarus toxeus* (*A. coyote*).

Southern Cloudywhite, *Thorybes bathyllus:* Bastrop and Gonzales counties.

Northern Cloudywhite, *Thorybes pylades:* Uncommon, permanent resident.

Eastern Cloudywhite, *Thorybes confusis:* Bastrop and Travis counties.

Texas Acacia Skipper, *Cogia outis:* Uncommon resident.

Slythius Skipper, *Bolla clytius:* Rare, periodic.

Scalloped Sootywing, *Staphylus hayhurstii:* Uncommon, permanent resident.

Texas Powdered Skipper, *Systasea pulverulenta:* Abundant, permanent resident.

Arizona Powdered Skipper (Zampa), *Systasea zampa:* Gonzales County.

Sickle-wing Skipper, *Achlyodes thraso tamenund* (*A. mithridates tamenund*): Common, periodic.

False Dusty Wing, *Gesta gesta invisus* (*G. invisus llano*): Uncommon, resident. Bastrop, Llano, and Travis counties.

White Patch, *Chiomara asychis:* Very rare. Hays County (John Gee, personal communication).

Southwestern Oak Dusky Wing, *Erynnis brizo burgessi* (*E. burgessi*): Blanco County. Possibly locally extirpated.

Juvenal's Duskywing, *Erynnis juvenalis juvenalis:* Uncommon, permanent resident. Gonzales and Travis counties.

Southern Duskywing, *Erynnis meridianus:* Scarce, permanent resident.

Horace's Duskywing, *Erynnis horatius:* Abundant, permanent resident.

Mottled Duskywing, *Erynnis martialis:* Bastrop County.

Zarucco Duskywing, *Erynnis zarucco.*

Funereal Duskywing, *Erynnis funeralis* (*Thanaos funeralis*): Abundant, permanent resident. Gonzales and Travis counties.

Wild Indigo Duskywing, *Erynnis baptisiae.*

Common Checkered Skipper, *Pyrgus communis* (*Syrichtus* [*Tuttia*] *communis communis; S.* [*T.*] *c. albescens*): Abundant, periodic.

Tropical Checkered Skipper, *Pyrgus oileus* (*S.* [*T.*] *oileus; Hesperia montivaga*): Travis and Gonzales counties.

Desert Checkered Skipper, *Pyrgus philetas:* Uncommon, permanent resident.

Laviana (Tropical White Skipper), *Heliopetes laviana* (*H. lavianus*): Scarce, periodic.

Common Streaky Skipper, *Celotes nessus* (*Hesperia nessus*): Abundant, permanent resident. Gonzales and Travis counties.

Common Sootywing, *Pholisora catullus:* Abundant, permanent resident.

Mexican Sootywing, *Pholisora mejicana.*

Julia Skipper, *Nastra julia:* Abundant, permanent resident.

Clouded Skipper, *Lerema accius:* Abundant, permanent resident.

Least Skipperling, *Ancyloxypha numitor:* Lee and Travis counties.

Tropical Least Skipperling, *Ancyloxypha arene:* Llano County.

Orange Skipperling, *Copaeodes aurantiaca (C. aurantiacus)*: Abundant, permanent resident.

Southern Skipperling, *Copaeodes minima (C. minimus)*: Abundant, permanent resident.

Fiery Skipper, *Hylephila phyleus phyleus:* Abundant, permanent resident.

Apache Skipper, *Hesperia woodgatei.*

Cobweb Skipper, *Hesperia metea licinus (H. licinus)*: Bastrop County.

Dotted Skipper, *Hesperia attalus attalus.*

Green Skipper, *Hesperia viridis:* Uncommon, permanent resident.

Dixie Skipper, *Hesperia meskei meskei:* Bastrop County.

Tawny-edged Skipper, *Polites themistocles:* Bastrop County.

Whirlabout, *Polites vibex brettoides (Tymelicus brettus)*: Uncommon, permanent resident. Gonzales and Travis counties.

Broken Dash,*Wallengrenia otho otho:* Abundant, permanent resident.

Sachem, *Atalopedes campestris huron:* Abundant, permanent resident.

Beard-grass Skipper, *Atrytone arogos arogos, (A. a. iowa)*: Fayette and Travis counties.

Delaware Skipper, *Atrytone logan logan (A. delaware lagus)*: Uncommon, permanent resident.

Tropical Blackvein, *Atrytone mazai:* Rare, very periodic.

Broad-marsh Skipper, *Poanes viator zizaniae (P. v. viator)*: Lee County.

Dun Skipper, *Euphyes vestris metacomet (E. v. osyka; E. ruricola)*: Abundant, permanent resident.

Pepper-and-salt Skipper, *Amblyscirtes hegon (A. samoset)*: Gonzales County.

Mottled Roadside Skipper, *Amblyscirtes nysa:* Uncommon, permanent resident.

Dotted Roadside Skipper, *Amblyscirtes eos:* Uncommon, permanent resident.

Roadside Rambler, *Amblyscirtes celia:* Abundant, permanent resident.

Bronze Roadside Skipper (Bronzed Skipper), *Amblyscirtes aenus aenus (A. erna)*: Gonzales and Travis counties.

Blue-dusted Roadside Skipper, *Amblyscirtes alternata:* Bastrop and Lee counties.

Eufala Skipper, *Lerodea eufala:* Abundant, permanent resident.

Brazilian Skipper, *Calpodes ethlius:* Uncommon, periodic. Gonzales and Travis counties.

Long-winged Skipper, *Panoquina ocola:* Abundant, permanent resident.

Family MEGATHYMIDAE: Giant Skippers

Large, heavy-bodied, fast-flying skippers that utilize yuccas and agaves as larval food plants.

Colorado Giant Skipper, *Megathymus coloradensis kendalli* (*M. c. reinthali*): Uncommon, permanent resident. Caldwell, Gonzales, Lee, Travis, and Williamson counties.

Superfamily PAPILIONOIDEA: True Butterflies

Family PAPILIONIDAE: Swallowtails

Large, flashy, strong-flying butterflies that are easily recognized by the narrow extensions of the hindwings known as tails.

Pipevine Swallowtail (Blue Swallowtail), *Battus philenor philenor* (*Papilio philenor*): Abundant, permanent resident. Gonzales and Travis counties.

Polydamas Swallowtail (Gold Rim), *Battus polydamas polydamas:* Gonzales and Travis counties.

Eastern Black Swallowtail, *Papilio polyxenes asterias* (*P. p. curvifasci; P. asterias; P. rudkini*): Abundant, permanent resident. Gonzales and Travis counties.

Thoas Swallowtail, *Heraclides thoas autocles.*

Giant Swallowtail (Orange Dog), *Heraclides cresphontes* (*Papilio cresphontes*): Abundant, permanent resident. Gonzales and Travis counties.

Tiger Swallowtail, *Pterourus glaucus glaucus* (*Papilio turnus*): Uncommon, permanent resident. Gonzales and Travis counties.

Two-tailed Swallowtail, *Pterourus multicaudatus:* Uncommon, permanent resident.

Spicebush Swallowtail (Green-clouded Swallowtail), *Pterourus troilus troilus* (*Papilio troilus*): Gonzales and Travis counties.

Family PIERIDAE: Whites and Sulphurs

A large number of small- to moderate-sized butterflies that are generally yellow, orange, or white in color; black markings of various shapes may be present.

Florida White, *Appias drusilla poeyi:* Scarce, periodic.

Checkered White, *Pontia protodice* (*Pieris protodice*): Abundant, permanent resident. Gonzales and Travis counties.

Cabbage White, *Pieris rapae* (*Artogeia rapae rapae*): Abundant, periodic.

Falcate Orangetip, *Paramidea midea midea* (*Anthocharis midea an-*

nickae; Euchloe genutia): Abundant, permanent resident. Gonzales and Travis counties.

Southern White, *Ascia monuste monuste (Ascia phileta phileta)*.

Common Sulphur, *Colias philodice philodice:* Bastrop and Gonzales counties.

Orange Sulphur, *Colias eurytheme eurytheme:* Abundant, permanent resident. Gonzales and Travis counties.

Dogface Butterfly, *Zerene cesonia cesonia (Meganostoma caesonia)*: Abundant, permanent resident. Gonzales and Travis counties.

White Angled Sulphur, *Anteos chlorinde (A. c. oivifera)*: Rare, irregular visitor.

Yellow Angled Sulphur, *Anteos maerula lacordairei:* Gonzales and Travis counties.

Cloudless Giant Sulphur, *Phoebis sennae eubule (P. s. sennae; P. s. s. marcellina; Catopsilia eubale* [sic])*: Abundant, periodic. Gonzales and Travis counties.

Orange-barred Giant Sulphur, *Phoebis philea philea:* Scarce, periodic.

Orange Giant Sulphur, *Phoebis agarithe agarithe (P. a. maxima; Catopsilia agarithe)*: Abundant, periodic. Gonzales and Travis counties.

Statira, *Aphrissa statira jada (A. s. statira)*.

Lyside, *Kricogonia lyside lyside (K. l. terissa; K. l. fantasia)*: Abundant, periodic. Gonzales and Travis counties.

Fairy Yellow (Barred Sulphur), *Eurema daira daira.*

Mexican Yellow, *Eurema mexicanum (E. mexicana; Terias m.)*: Abundant, permanent resident. Gonzales and Travis counties.

Tailed Orange, *Eurema proterpia:* Abundant, periodic.

Little Yellow, *Eurema lisa lisa (Terias lisa)*: Abundant, permanent resident. Gonzales and Travis counties.

Mimosa Yellow, *Eurema nise nelphe:* Scarce, periodic.

Sleepy Orange, *Eurema nicippe nicippe (E. n. flava; Terias nicippe)*: Abundant, permanent resident. Gonzales and Travis counties.

Dwarf Yellow, *Nathalis iole:* Abundant, permanent resident. Gonzales and Travis counties.

Family LYCAENIDAE: Gossamer Wings

Generally small butterflies that are less obvious than many of the larger, more dramatically colored species. However, many of the species in this family have very thin tails and intricate eyespots on the hindwing.

Harvester, *Feniseca tarquinius tarquinius:* Scarce, permanent resident.

Great Purple Hairstreak (Great Blue Hairstreak), *Atlides halesus estesi*

(*Thecla halesus*): Abundant, permanent resident. Gonzales and Travis counties.

Red-banded Hairstreak, *Calycopis cecrops* (*Thecla cecrops*): Gonzales County.

Silver-blue Hairstreak, *Ministrymon clytie* (*Thecla clytie*): Gonzales County.

Succulent Hairstreak, *Xamia xami texami* (*Thecla belenina* [*sic*]): Gonzales County.

White M Hairstreak, *Parrhasius m-album* (*Panthiades m-album m-album; Thecla m-album*): Uncommon, permanent resident. Gonzales and Travis counties.

Henry's Elfin, *Incisalia henrici solata* (*Callophrys henrici turneri; C. solatus*): Abundant, permanent resident. Llano and Travis counties.

Olive Hairstreak, *Mitoura grynea grynea* (*M. gryneus gryneus; Callophrys gryneus gryneus; C. g. auburniana*): Abundant, permanent resident. Bastrop and Travis counties.

Central Texas Olive Hairstreak, *Mitoura grynea castalis* (*Callophrys sweadneri*).

Banded Hairstreak, *Satyrium calanus falacer* (*Thecla calanus*): Uncommon, permanent resident. Gonzales and Travis counties.

Soapberry Hairstreak, *Phaeostrymon alcestis alcestis* (*Thecla alcestis*): Gonzales, Travis, and Williamson counties.

Silver-banded Hairstreak, *Chlorostrymon simaethis sarita* (*Thecla smaethis*): Gonzales and Williamson counties.

Dusky Blue Hairstreak, *Calycopis isobeon:* Abundant, permanent resident.

Oak Hairstreak (Southern Hairstreak), *Fixsenia ontario autolycus* (*Thecla autolycus; T. favonius*): Abundant, resident. Gonzales and Travis counties.

Gray Hairstreak (Common Hairstreak), *Strymon melinus franki* (*S. m. melinus; Thecla metinus* [*sic*]): Abundant, permanent resident. Gonzales and Travis counties.

Alea Hairstreak, *Strymon alea:* Abundant, permanent resident.

Columella Hairstreak, *Strymon columella istapa:* Scarce, periodic.

Western Pygmy Blue, *Brephidium exilis exilis* (*B. exilis; Lycaena exilis; L. isophthalma*): Scarce, permanent resident. Gonzales and Travis counties.

Cassius Blue, *Leptotes cassius striatus* (*L. c. striata*): Scarce, periodic.

Marine Blue, *Leptotes marina* (*L. marinus*): Uncommon, periodic.

Cyna Blue, *Zizula cyna* (*Lycaena cyna*): Scarce, permanent resident. Gonzales and Travis counties.

Antillean Blue, *Hemiargus ceraunus zachaeina:* Uncommon, periodic.

Reakirt's Blue, *Hemiargus isola* (*Echinargus isola alce; Lycaena isole*):
Abundant, permanent resident. Gonzales and Travis counties.
Eastern Tailed Blue, *Everes comyntas comyntas* (*E. texana*): Uncommon, periodic.
Spring Azure, *Celastrina argiolus ladon* (*C. ladon*): Scarce, permanent
resident.

Family RIODINIDAE: Metalmarks

*Small butterflies that often seem somewhat drab until one notices the
large number of small silver flecks on the wings. Flight may be strong
or weak but is usually erratic.*

Little Metalmark (Virginia Metalmark), *Calephelis virginiensis* (*C. caenius:* Gonzales County.
Fatal Metalmark, *Calephelis nemesis australis* (*C. australis*): Abundant, permanent resident. Gonzales and Travis counties.
Lost Metalmark, *Calephelis perditalis:* Uncommon, permanent
resident.
Southwest Metalmark, *Calephelis rawsoni* (*C. guadeloupe; C. sinaloensis nuevoleon*): Abundant, permanent resident.
Red-bordered Metalmark (Schaus' Metalmark), *Caria ino melicerta*
(*Apodemia mulliplaga*): Gonzales County.
Mormon Metalmark, *Apodemia mormo mejicana* (*A. m. mejicanus*):
Bastrop and Travis counties.

Family LIBYTHEIDAE: Snout Butterflies

Readily recognized by the pair of enlarged palps that project from either side of the head. Rather drab in general appearance, these butterflies resemble dark leaves when at rest.

Snout Butterfly, *Libytheana bachmanii bachmanii* (*L. b. larvata; Libythea b.*): Abundant, permanent resident. Gonzales and Travis
counties.
Southern Snout, *Libytheana carinenta mexicana:* Scarce, periodic.

Family NYMPHALIDAE: Brush-footed Butterflies

*Named for their shortened forelegs, which are covered with hairs, thus
resembling brushes. Many of the South Central Texas butterflies belong to this family and vary in appearance from variable brown patterns to leaf mimics to brightly colored patterns.*

Gulf Fritillary, *Agraulis vanillae* (*Dione vanillae incarnata*): Abundant,
permanent resident. Gonzales and Travis counties.

Mexican Silverspot. *Dione moneta poeyi.*

Julia, *Dryas iulia moderata (Colaenis julia; C. delila)*: Abundant, periodic. Gonzales and Travis counties.

Zebra Longwing, *Heliconius charitonius vazquezae*: Abundant, periodic. Gonzales and Travis counties.

Isabella Tiger, *Eueides isabellae zorcaon:* Travis County (Single sight record).

Variegated Fritillary, *Euptoieta claudia claudia:* Abundant, permanent resident. Gonzales and Travis counties.

Mexican Fritillary, *Euptoieta hegesia hoffmanni:* Scarce, periodic.

Texan Crescentspot (Texas Eresia), *Anthanassa texana texana (Eresia texana)*: Abundant, permanent resident. Gonzales and Travis counties.

Vesta Crescentspot, *Phyciodes vesta:* Abundant, permanent resident. Gonzales and Travis counties.

Phaon Crescentspot, *Phyciodes phaon:* Abundant, permanent resident. Gonzales and Travis counties.

Pearly Crescentspot, *Phyciodes tharos distincta:* Abundant, permanent resident.

Gorgone Crescentspot, *Charidryas gorgone carlota:* Scarce, periodic.

Silver Crescentspot, *Charidryas nycteis:* Abundant, permanent resident.

Bordered Patch (Lacinia), *Chlosyne lacinia adjutrix (Syncholoe lacinia)*: Abundant, permanent resident. Gonzales and Travis counties.

Janais Patch (Crimson Patch), *Chlosyne janais (Syncholoe janais)*: Gonzales and Travis counties.

Theona Checkerspot (Thekla Checkerspot), *Thessalia theona bollii (Melitaea thekla)*: Burnet and Gonzales counties.

Dymas Checkerspot (Chara Checkerspot), *Dymasia dymas (Melitaea dymas; Melitaea chara)*: Gonzales County.

Beardtongue Checkerspot (Smaller Checkerspot), *Poladryas minuta minuta (Melitaea minuta)*: Gonzales County.

Elada Checkerspot (Ulric's Checker Spot), *Texola elada ulrica (Melitaea ulrica)*: Abundant, permanent resident. Gonzales and Travis counties.

Question Mark, *Polygonia interrogationis (Grapta interrogationis)*: Abundant, permanent resident. Gonzales and Travis counties.

Comma, *Polygonia comma (Grapta comma)*: Scarce, permanent resident. Gonzales and Travis counties.

Mourning Cloak, *Nymphalis antiopa lintnerii (Vanessa antiopa)*: Scarce, permanent resident. Gonzales and Travis counties.

American Painted Lady (Hunter's Butterfly; Virginia Lady), *Vanessa vir-*

giniensis (*Pyrameis huntera*): Abundant, permanent resident. Gonzales and Travis counties.

Painted Lady (Thistle Butterfly; Cosmopoliate), *Vanessa cardui* (*Pyrameis cardui*): Abundant, periodic. Gonzales and Travis counties.

Red Admiral (Alderman), *Vanessa atalanta rubria* (*Pyrameis atalanta*): Abundant, permanent resident. Gonzales and Travis counties.

Buckeye, *Junonia coenia coenia* (*Precis coenia*): Abundant, permanent resident. Gonzales and Travis counties.

Dark Buckeye (Lavinia), *Junonia genoveva zonalis* (*J. nigrosuffusa; J. lavinia auctorum; Precis nigrosuffusa; P. genoveva genoveva; P. g. zonales*): Uncommon, periodic. Gonzales and Travis counties.

White Peacock, *Anartia jatrophae jatrophae:* Scarce, periodic. Gonzales and Travis counties.

Malachite, *Siproeta stelenes biplagiata* (*Victoria stelenes*): Gonzales and Travis counties.

Red-spotted Purple, *Basilarchia arthemis astyanax* (*B. astyanax; Limenitis astyanax astyanax*): Uncommon, permanent resident. Gonzales and Travis counties.

Viceroy, *Basilarchia archippus archippus* (*Limenitis archippus watsoni; B. disippus*): Abundant, permanent resident. Gonzales and Travis counties.

California Sister, *Adelpha bredowii* (*Limenitis bredowii eulalia*): Abundant, periodic.

Dyonis Greenwing, *Dynamine dyonis:* Rare, extremely periodic.

Amymone, *Mestra amymone* (*Mestra hypermnestra amymone; Cystineura amymone*): Abundant, periodic. Gonzales and Travis counties.

Crimson-banded Black, *Biblis hyperia aganisa.*

Banded Daggerwing, *Marpesia chiron* (*Timetes chiron*): Scarce, periodic. Gonzales and Travis counties.

Goatweed Butterfly, *Anaea andria andria* (*Pyrrhanaea andria*): Abundant, permanent resident. Gonzales and Travis counties.

Tropical Leafwing, *Anaea aidea:* Abundant, periodic.

Hackberry Butterfly (Hackberry Emperor), *Asterocampa celtis celtis* (*A. c. alicia; Chlorippe celtis; C. alcia*): Abundant, permanent resident. Gonzales and Travis counties.

Empress Antonia, *Asterocampa celtis antonia* (*A. antonia antonia; Chlorippe antonia*): Abundant, permanent resident. Gonzales and Travis counties.

Empress Leilia, *Asterocampa leilia:* Abundant, periodic.

Tawny Emperor, *Asterocampa clyton clyton* (*A. c. texana*): Abundant, permanent resident. Burnet and Travis counties.

Empress Louisa, *Asterocampa clyton louisa* (*A. louisa*): Uncommon, permanent resident.

Family SATYRIDAE: Satyrs or Browns

Includes a few species of generally brown-colored butterflies that are small to moderate in size.

Pearly Eye, *Enodia portlandia missarkae* (*Debis portlandia*): Gonzales County.

Gemmed Satyr, *Cyllopsis gemma gemma* (*Neonympha gemma*): Gonzales and Lee counties.

Hermes Satyr, *Hermeuptychia hermes* (*Neonympha hermes; N. sosybius*): Gonzales and Travis counties.

Little Wood Satyr, *Megisto cymela cymela* (*Neonympha eurytus*): Abundant, permanent resident. Gonzales and Travis counties.

Red Satyr, *Megisto rubricata rubricata:* Abundant, permanent resident.

Large Wood Nymph (Blue-eyed Grayling; Texas Satyr), *Cercyonis pegala texana* (*Satyrus alope*): Abundant, permanent resident. Gonzales and Travis counties.

Family DANAIDAE: Milkweed Butterflies

Includes a very few generally well-known species whose caterpillars feed on milkweed plants.

Monarch, *Danaus plexippus plexippus:* Abundant, periodic. Gonzales and Travis counties.

Queen, *Danaus gilippus strigosus* (*D. berenice*): Abundant, permanent resident. Gonzales and Travis counties.

Tropic Queen, *Danaus eresimus montezuma:* Abundant, periodic.

Description of Terms

THE FOLLOWING is a brief definition of descriptive terms used in the species accounts. These terms reflect the habitat requirements and status of each species as it exists in the nineteen counties of South Central Texas covered by this book.

Status Terms

Abundant. The species is widespread in the area and represented by a large local population; individuals are often urban tolerant and are very frequently encountered.

Accidental. At best, only one record during one time period in ten years. Not expected.

Common. The species is represented by a large local population and/or individuals are conspicuous and thus regularly encountered. May be *abundant* in some sections of the area.

Endangered. The species is in possible imminent danger of extinction and requires protection and/or other assistance. This term is used only in relation to species formally recognized as endangered by the U.S. Fish and Wildlife Service and/or the Texas Parks and Wildlife Department.

Erratic. Occurs at irregular intervals, sometimes in numbers.

Extant. Living now.

Extinct. The species no longer survives either in the wild or in captive breeding programs.

Extirpated. The species is not currently represented by a local population, although individuals formerly occupied the area within historic times. Species survives elsewhere.

Formerly recorded. No record since 1970, more or less. Date of last record shown, if known.

Historic. Same as *extirpated.*

Hypothetical. Usually a single, unconfirmed sight record by one party, but believed reliable. The species needs confirming evidence such as a specimen, photo, or tape of voice to confirm status.

Introduced. The species is not indigenous to South Central Texas; that is, it was transplanted by humans. Denoted by an asterisk (*).

Occasional. In the case of birds, occurs less than five years out of ten, with often a single record. Should be reported as a Rare Bird Alert.

Possible. The species may occur within the area, although its status is unconfirmed by recorded observations.

Rare. The species is represented by a very small local population; individuals are secretive and are very infrequently encountered. In the case of birds, occurs at infrequent intervals, always a good find.

Special concern. The species has undergone a significant reduction in abundance and/or range that may cause it to be threatened.

Threatened. The species is threatened with extinction and may become endangered in the near future. This term is used only in relation to species formally recognized as threatened by the U.S. Fish and Wildlife Service and/or the Texas Parks and Wildlife Department.

Uncommon. The species is represented by a small, local population and/ or individuals are retiring and thus seldom encountered. May require a higher degree of competence by the observer than species described as *common.*

Habitats

Caves. Subterranean cavities with ground surface access.

Croplands. Cultivated acreage.

Cultural areas. Areas of urban and/or rural development. Towns, farmyards, or in proximity to human activity.

Fence rows. Grasses, brush, vines, tangles, or other growth along a fence.

Floodplain. That portion of a valley at and below the greatest recorded high-water level.

Intermittent streams. Inconstant-flowing water courses (such as creeks).

Invaded fields. Formerly cultivated acreage and/or pastures now overgrown with scrub vegetation (such as honey mesquite, Roosevelt weed, and paloverde).

Marshes. Submerged waterside areas overgrown with emergent aquatic vegetation (such as cattails, rushes, and arrowhead).

Perennial waterways. Constant-flowing streams and large, permanent reservoirs. These include the Highland Lakes, Lake Bastrop, Stillhouse Hollow Reservoir, Calaveras Lake, Braunig Lake, and the rivers of the area.

Range and pastures. Grazing lands normally overgrown with grasses, herbs, and occasional low shrubs.

Riparian baregrounds. Unvegetated waterside areas, generally within the floodplains of the bordering streams or reservoirs. Sandbars, rocks.

Riparian woodlands. Waterside areas overgrown with woody vegetation (such as black willow, boxelder, baldcypress, and eastern cottonwood) adapted to constantly wet soils.

Small impoundments. Reservoirs of very limited surface area. Farm ponds.

Spring-fed streams. Water courses that receive emergent groundwater.

Springs and seepage slopes. Areas of groundwater emergence.

Throughout. May be found in any habitat. Usually widespread.

Understory vegetation. Grasses, shrubs, and small trees below the tall tree canopy.

Upland Baregrounds. Unvegetated hillsides (generally with steep slopes).

Wastewater ponds. Artificial impoundments maintained for the purpose of purifying sanitation wastewater; water levels are inconstant. These include Hornsby Bend Ponds (Austin) and Mitchell Lake (San Antonio).

Wooded uplands. Tree-covered hillsides and areas that are higher in elevation than the floodplains of bordering streams and are overgrown with woody vegetation (such as oaks, elms, junipers, and sumacs).

Selected References

Chapter 1. Natural Features

Geology

Abbott, Patrick L., and C. M. Woodruff, Jr., eds. 1986. *The Balcones Escarpment: Geology, Hydrology, Ecology and Social Development in Central Texas.* Published for Geological Society of America Annual Meeting, San Antonio, November 1986.

American Association of Petroleum Geologists. 1973. *Geological Highway Map of Texas.* Tulsa.

Barnes, Virgil E., W. C. Bell, S. E. Clabaugh, P. E. Cloud, Jr., R. V. McGehee, P. U. Rodda, and Keith Young. 1972. *Geology of the Llano Region and Austin Area.* Field Excursion Guidebook no. 13. Austin: Bureau of Economic Geology, University of Texas.

Bureau of Economic Geology. 1974. *Geologic Atlas of Texas,* Austin Sheet. Austin: University of Texas.

——. 1979. *Geologic Atlas of Texas,* Seguin Sheet. Austin: University of Texas.

——. 1981. *Geologic Atlas of Texas,* Llano Sheet. Austin: University of Texas.

——. 1983. *Geologic Atlas of Texas,* San Antonio Sheet. Austin: University of Texas.

Ewing, T. E., and S. C. Caran. 1982. Late Cretaceous volcanism in South and Central Texas—stratigraphic, structural, and seismic models. *Gulf Coast Association of Geological Societies Transactions* 32: 137–145.

Ferguson, W. K. 1986. *The Geographic Provinces of Texas.* Austin: Texas Mosaics.

Kutac, Edward A., and S. Christopher Caran. 1976. *A Bird Finding and Naturalist's Guide for the Austin, Texas, Area.* Austin: Oasis Press.

Soil Conservation Service. 1974. *Soil Survey of Travis County, Texas.* Washington, D.C.: U.S. Government Printing Office.

Spearing, Darwin. 1991. *Roadside Geology of Texas.* Missoula, Mont.: Mountain Press Pub. Co.

Texas Highway Department. n.d. *Texas, Land of Contrast.* Austin.

Trippet, A. R., and L. E. Garner. 1976. *Guide to Points of Geologic Interest in Austin.* Guidebook no. 16. Austin: Bureau of Economic Geology, University of Texas.

U.S. Fish and Wildlife Service. 1979. *Unique Wildlife Ecosystems of Texas.* Washington, D.C.

U.S. Fish and Wildlife Service. 1991. *Proposed Balcones Canyonlands National Wildlife Refuge.* Albuquerque.

Plants

References below are included for information, even though plants are not included in this work except in a general manner. Plant scientific names follow Correll and Johnston. If name is changed in Hatch et al., the new name is shown in parentheses. English names are from various sources.

Ajilvsgi, Geyata. 1979. *Wild Flowers of the Big Thicket, East Texas, and Western Louisiana.* College Station: Texas A&M University Press.

Burlage, Henry M. 1973. *The Wild Flowering Plants of Highland Lakes Country of Texas.* Henry M. Burlage.

Correll, Donovan S., and Marshall C. Johnston. 1970. *Manual of the Vascular Plants of Texas.* Renner, Tex.: Texas Research Foundation.

Enquist, Marshall. 1987. *Wildflowers of the Texas Hill Country.* Austin: Lone Star Botanical.

Gould, Frank W. 1975. *The Grasses of Texas.* College Station: Texas A&M University Press.

Hatch, Stephen L., Kancheepuram N. Gandhi, and Larry E. Brown. 1990. *Checklist of the Vascular Plants of Texas.* College Station: Texas Agricultural Experiment Station.

Irwin, Howard S., and Mary Motz Wells. 1961. *Roadside Flowers of Texas.* Austin: University of Texas Press.

Johnston, M. C. 1990. *The Vascular Plants of Texas, A List, Up-dating the* Manual of the Vascular Plant of Texas, *Second Edition.* Austin.

McMahan, C. A., R. G. Frye, and K. L. Brown. 1984. *The Vegetation Types of Texas, Including Cropland.* Austin: Texas Parks and Wildlife Department.

Rickett, Harold William. 1970. *Wildflowers of the United States.* Vol. 3, parts 1 and 2 (Texas). New York: McGraw-Hill.

Texas Forest Service. 1972. *How to Know the Trees of Texas.* College Station.

Vines, Robert A. 1960. *Trees, Shrubs, and Woody Vines of the Southwest.* Austin: University of Texas Press.

Weniger, Del. Undated. *Cacti of the Southwest.* Austin: University of Texas Press.

Whitehouse, Eula. 1967. *Texas Flowers in Natural Colors.* Dallas: Dallas County Audubon Society.

Chapter 3. Birds

American Ornithologists' Union. 1983. *Check-list of North American Birds.* 6th ed. (including amendments through the 38th supplement, 1991). Washington, D.C.

Arnold, Keith A., et al. 1984. *Checklist of the Birds of Texas.* Austin: Texas Ornithological Society.

Bryan, Kelly, Tony Gallucci, Greg Lasley, and David H. Riskind. 1991. *A Checklist of Texas Birds.* Technical Series no. 32. Austin: Texas Parks and Wildlife Department.

Bull, John, and John Farrand, Jr. 1977. *The Audubon Society Field Guide to North American Birds.* Eastern Region edition. New York: Alfred A. Knopf.

Farrand, John, Jr., ed. 1983. *The Audubon Society Master Guide to Birding.* 3 vols. New York: Alfred A. Knopf.

National Geographic Society. 1987. *Field Guide to Birds of North America.* 2d ed. Washington, D.C.

Oberholser, Harry C., and Edgar B. Kincaid, Jr. 1974. *The Bird Life of Texas.* Austin: University of Texas Press.

Peterson, Roger Tory. 1963. *A Field Guide to the Birds of Texas and Adjacent States.* Boston: Houghton Mifflin.

Robbins, Chandler S., et al. 1983. *A Guide to Field Identification: Birds of North America.* Rev. ed. New York: Golden Press.

Simmons, George Finlay. 1925. *Birds of the Austin Region.* Austin: University of Texas Press.

Chapter 4. Mammals

Block, S. B. and E. G. Zimmerman. 1991. Allozymic variation and systematics of plains pocket gophers (*Geomys*) of south-central Texas. *The Southwestern Naturalist* 36(1):29–36.

Davis, W. B. 1974. *The Mammals of Texas.* Bulletin 41. Austin: Texas Parks and Wildlife Department.

Jones, J. K., Jr., C. Jones, and D. J. Schmidly. 1988. *Annotated Checklist of Recent Land Mammals of Texas.* Occasional Papers of the Museum, no. 119:1–25. Lubbock: Texas Tech University Museum.

Jones, J. K., Jr., R. S. Hoffman, D. W. Rice, Clyde Jones, R. J. Baker, and M. D. Engstrom. 1992. *Revised Checklist of North American Mammals North of Mexico, 1991.* Occasional Papers of the Museum, no. 146:23. Lubbock: Texas Tech University Museum.

Lee, T. E., Jr. 1987. Distributional record of *Lasiurus seminolus* (Chiroptera: Vespertilionidae). *Texas Journal of Science* 39(2):193.

Manning, R. W., J. K. Jones, Jr., R. R. Hollander, and C. Jones. 1987. Notes on the distribution and natural history of some bats on the Edwards Plateau and in adjacent areas of Texas. *Texas Journal of Science* 39(3):279–285.

Nowak, R. M. 1979. *North American Quaternary Canis.* Monograph of the Museum of Natural History, University of Kansas, no. 6:1–154. Lawrence.

Peterson, R. L. 1946. Recent and Pleistocene mammalian fauna of Brazos County, Texas. *Journal of Mammalogy* 27:162–169.

Schmidly, D. J. 1983. *Texas Mammals East of the Balcones Fault Zone.* College Station: Texas A&M University Press.

———. 1991. *The Bats of Texas.* College Station: Texas A&M University Press.

Texas Organization for Endangered Species. 1988. *Endangered, Threatened, and Watch List of Vertebrates.* Publication no. 6. Austin.

Chapter 5. Amphibians and Reptiles

Blair, W. Frank (Professor, Zoology Department; Director, Brackenridge Field Laboratory, University of Texas at Austin). 1974–1975. Personal communication, January 1974 and February 1975.

Chippendale, Paul T., Andrew H. Price, and David M. Hillis. 1993. A new species of Perennibranchiate salamander (*Eurycea*: Plethodontidae) from Austin, Texas. *Herpetologica* 49(2): 248–259.

Collins, Joseph T. 1990. *Standard Common and Current Scientific Names for North American Amphibians and Reptiles.* 3d ed. Herpetological Circular no. 19. Lawrence, Kan.: Society for the Study of Amphibians and Reptiles.

Conant, Roger, and Joseph T. Collins. 1991. *Reptiles and Amphibians: Eastern/Central North America.* 3d ed. The Peterson Field Guide Series, no. 12. Boston: Houghton Mifflin.

Dixon, James R. 1987. *Amphibians and Reptiles of Texas.* W. L. Moody, Jr., Natural History Series, no. 8. College Station: Texas A&M University Press.

Garrett, Judith M., and David G. Barker. 1987. *A Field Guide to Reptiles and Amphibians of Texas.* Texas Monthly Field Guide Series. Austin: Texas Monthly Press.

Hampton, Nan. 1975. Annotated checklist of the amphibians and reptiles of Travis County, Texas. Natural History Survey of Central Texas, Occasional Paper, no. 3. In *A Bird Finding and Naturalist's Guide for the Austin, Texas, Area,* by Edward A. Kutac and S. Christopher Caran. Austin: Oasis Press.

Resource Protection Division. 1991. *Endangered Resources Annual Status Report* (E.R.A.S.R.) Austin: Texas Parks and Wildlife Department.

Ryan, Michael (Professor, Zoology Department, University of Texas at Austin). 1991. Personal communication, July 1991.

Sweet, Samuel A. 1984. Secondary contact and hybridization in the Texas cave salamanders *Eurycea neotenes* and *E. tridentifera. Copeia* 1984(2):428–441.

Tennant, Alan. 1984. *The Snakes of Texas.* Austin: Texas Monthly Press.

Texas Natural Heritage Program. 1991. *Special Animal List.* Austin: Texas Parks and Wildlife Department.

Texas Natural Heritage Program. 1991. *Watch List of Animals.* Austin: Texas Parks and Wildlife Department.

Vermersch, Thomas G., and Robert E. Kuntz. 1986. *Snakes of South-Central Texas.* Austin: Eakin Press.

Chapter 6. Fishes

Caran, S. C. 1976. Annotated checklist of the fishes of Travis County, Texas. In *A Bird Fishing and Naturalist's Guide for the Austin, Texas, Area,* by Edward A. Kutac and S. Christopher Caran, 71–83. Austin: Oasis Press.

Conner, J. V. 1977. Zoogeography of freshwater fishes in western Gulf slope drainages between the Mississippi and the Rio Grande. Ph.D. dissertation, Tulane University, New Orleans.

Edwards, R. J., G. Longley, R. Moss, J. Ward, R. Mathews, and B. Stewart. 1989. A classification of Texas aquatic communities with special consideration toward the conservation of endangered and threatened taxa. *Texas Journal of Science* 41:231–240.

Hubbs, C., R. J. Edwards, and G. P. Garrett. 1991. An annotated checklist of the freshwater fishes of Texas, with keys to identification of species. *Texas Journal of Science* 43 (Supplement).

Knapp, F. T. 1953. Fishes found in the freshwaters of Texas. Brunswick, Ga.: Ragland Studio and Litho Printing Co.

Robins, C. R., R. M. Bailey, C. E. Bond, J. R. Brooker, E. A. Lachner, R. N. Lea, and W. B. Scott. 1991. *Common and Scientific Names of*

Fishes from the United States and Canada. American Fisheries Society Special Publication, no. 20. Washington, D.C.

Tilton, J. E. 1961. Ichthyological survey of the Colorado River of Texas. Master's thesis. University of Texas at Austin.

Williams, J. E., J. E. Johnson, D. A. Hendrickson, S. Contreras-Balderas, J. D. Williams, M. Navarro-Mendoza, D. E. McAllister, and J. E. Deacon. 1989. Fishes of North America—endangered, threatened, or of special concern. *Fisheries* 14:2–20.

Chapter 7. Land Snails of Travis County

Burch, John B. 1962. *How to Know the Eastern Land Snails.* Dubuque, Iowa: William C. Brown.

Hubricht, Leslie. 1985. The distributions of the native land mollusks of the eastern United States. *Fieldiana (Zoology)* n.s. (no. 24):1–191.

Neck, R. W. 1976a. *Cecilioides acicula* (Muller): Living colonies established in Texas. *Sterkiana* (no. 61): 19–20.

———. 1976b. Preliminary checklist of land snails of Travis County. In *A Bird Finding and Naturalists' Guide for the Austin, Texas, Area,* by Edward A. Kutac and S. Christopher Caran, 124–129. Austin: Oasis Press.

———. 1977. New county records of land snails in Texas. *Sterkiana* (no. 65–66):5–6.

———. 1981. Noteworthy gastropod records from Texas. *Texas Conchologist* 17:69–72.

———. 1984. Occurrence of *Euglandiana rosea* in central Texas. *Texas Conchologist* 20:64–66.

———. 1989. Additional terrestrial gastropods of Travis County, Texas. *Malacology Data Net* 2:135–143.

Pilsbry, Henry A. 1939–1948. *Land Mollusca of North America (North of Mexico).* Academy of Natural Science of Philadelphia. Monograph no. 3. 2 vols. Philadelphia.

Chapter 8. Butterflies

Brues, C. T. 1905. The occurrence of a tropical butterfly in the United States. *Entomology News* 16:11–12.

Doyle, J. F. III. 1979. Temporary range extension and larval foodplant of *Dynamine dionis* (Nymphalidae) in Texas. *Journal of the Lepidoptera Society* 33:20.

Durden, Christopher J. 1982. The butterfly fauna of Barton Creek Canyon on the Balcones Fault Zone, Austin, Texas, and a regional list. *Journal of the Lepidoptera Society* 36(1):1–17.

Engelhardt, G. P. 1934. Tornados and butterfly migrations in Texas. *Bulletin of the Brooklyn Entomological Society* 29:16.

Masters, J. H. 1970. Distributional notes on the genus *Mestra*. (Nymphalidae) in North America. *Journal of the Lepidoptera Society* 24:203–208.

Neck, R. W. 1977. Effects of 1933 hurricanes on butterflies on central and southern Texas. *Journal of the Lepidoptera Society* 31:67–68.

———. 1978. Climatic regimes resulting in unusual occurrences of Rhopalocera in central Texas in 1968. *Journal of the Lepidoptera Society* 32:111–115.

———. 1983. Additional comments of the butterflies of the Austin, Texas, region. *Journal of the Lepidoptera Society* 37:320–321.

Parks, H. B. 1956. Butterflies of the Ottine area. In *Palmetto State Park, Ottine, Texas*, by G. K. Shearer, 23–25. Austin: Texas State Parks Board.

Pyle, Robert Michael. 1981. *The Audubon Society Field Guide to North American Butterflies*. New York: Alfred A. Knopf.

Index of Natural Features and Locations by Counties

(Page numbers for locations and features mentioned in Chapters 1 and 2 and in the introductions to Chapters 3–8, inclusive)

Index of Animals
and Plants